EUROPE
WITHOUT
AMERICA?

EUROPE WITHOUT AMERICA?

The Crisis in Atlantic Relations

JOHN PALMER

Oxford   New York

OXFORD UNIVERSITY PRESS

1987

Oxford University Press, Walton Street, Oxford OX2 6DP

Oxford New York Toronto
Delhi Bombay Calcutta Madras Karachi
Petaling Jaya Singapore Hong Kong Tokyo
Nairobi Dar es Salaam Cape Town
Melbourne Auckland
and associated companies in
Beirut Berlin Ibadan Nicosia

Oxford is a trade mark of Oxford University Press

British Library Cataloguing in Publication Data
Palmer, John
Europe without America? : the crisis in
Atlantic relations. 1. Europe — Foreign relations — United
States 2. United States — Foreign
relations — Europe
I. Title
327.7304 D1065.U5
ISBN 0–19–215894–5

Library of Congress Cataloging in Publication Data
Palmer, John, 1930–
Europe without America? : the crisis in
Atlantic relations/John Palmer.
p. cm.
Includes Index.
1. Europe—Politics and government—1945– . 2. North
Atlantic Treaty Organization. 3. Europe—Foreign
relations—United States. 4. United States—
Foreign relations—Europe. I. Title.
D1058.P338 1987
327.4073—dc19 87–16498
ISBN 0–19–215894–5

Printed in Great Britain
at the University Press, Oxford
by David Stanford
Printer to the University

To my Mother and in memory of Dad

Preface

Books have a fearfully long gestation period. For most of the past twelve years I have been writing about European affairs, as the European Editor of the *Guardian*, based in Brussels. It struck me repeatedly during this time that a fundamental change was taking place in the European–American relationship which would have profound implications for the future of Europe. I was also struck by the low level of the debate about what kind of future that should be. Changes in anything as deep-rooted in our history as the Atlantic relationship proceed slowly. So it never seemed quite the right moment to stand back and examine the implications of what appeared to be the irreversible break-up of the Atlantic partnership and the wider Atlanticist economic, political, and security system.

A period of temporary secondment from the *Guardian* back to London provided both the time and the vantage point to try and make sense of what was happening. The disturbing impact of the Reagan administration and its policies provided the stimulus. Oxford University Press provided the opportunity to put pen (or more accurately word processor) to paper. I am very grateful to them all.

Many friends and colleagues have contributed to this book, some of them without realizing it. I am indebted to Ben Lowe, who was most generous in sharing with me the benefit of the research he has done into NATO's history; to Mary Kaldor, of the European Nuclear Disarmament journal editorial collective; to Roger Morgan, of the London School of Economics; and to William Wallace, deputy Director of the Royal Institute for International Affairs, who read my manuscript and corrected my grosser errors of fact and interpretation.

I want to express a special word of appreciation for the help I received from Jeremy Beale of Sussex University and Nicholas Richmond, with research material. Thanks also to Mike Cooley, John Lambert, and the colleagues of Agenor in

Brussels, Jan Kavan, Robert Taylor of European Research Associates in Brussels, John Williams, and so many others from whose conversation and views I have learned so much over the years. Heartfelt thanks also to my wife, Claude, for her indispensable help in preparing my text.

It goes without saying that none of the above share the slightest responsibility for the conclusions I have drawn or the options for the future which I have canvassed. Many of these are controversial but at a time when the whole tempo of events in both East–West relations and European–American relations have moved into a new gear, I hope that they form part of a long overdue debate about what kind of Europe we want to build as part of a wider international society.

Over the years I have read many testimonies by writers to the patience and loving support of wives and families during the trials and tribulations of book writing. They have never been more deserved than in the case of my wife and my three children, Marie-France, Liam, and Roisin. My love to them all.

20 April 1987   JOHN PALMER

Contents

Abbreviations   xi

1 Outlines of a Crisis   1

2 The American Empire   30

3 Atlantic Strife   59

4 Britain—The Reluctant European   82

5 Dawn in the East   107

6 European Disunion   132

7 After Atlanticism—Agenda for a New Europe   156

   Notes   193

   Index   211

Abbreviations

ABM	Anti-Ballistic Missile
ANZUS	Australia, New Zealand, United States Area Alliance
AWACS	Airborne Early Warning Radar System
CAP	Common Agricultural Policy
CENTO	Central Treaty Organization
CIA	Central Intelligence Agency
COCOM	NATO Co-Committee to monitor trade with the Eastern bloc
COMECON	Council for Economic Co-operation
ECSC	European Coal and Steel Community
EEC	European Economic Community
EFTA	European Free Trade Association
EMS	European Monetary System
ESPRIT	European Strategic Programme in Research and Development in Information Technology
EUREKA	European Research Co-ordination Agency
FBI	Federation of British Industries
GATT	General Agreement on Tariffs and Trade
IMF	International Monetary Fund
IISS	International Institute for Strategic Studies
NATO	North Atlantic Treaty Organization
NICs	Newly Industrialized Countries
NIMROD	British-designed airborne radar system
OECD	Organization for Economic Co-operation and Development
OEEC	Organization for European Economic Co-operation
OPEC	Organization of Petroleum Exporting Countries
PASOK	The Pan-Hellenic Peoples Socialist Party
PCI	Partito Comunista Italiano
RDF	Rapid Deployment Force
SDI	Strategic Defence Initiative
SEATO	South-East Asia Treaty Organization
SPD	Sozialdemokratische Partei Deutschlands
WEU	Western European Union

·1 | Outlines of a Crisis

The economic, military, and political world of the Atlantic Alliance, in which two generations of Americans and Europeans have grown to adulthood since 1945, is visibly crumbling. Since the early 1980s the media on both sides of the Atlantic have regularly reported new developments in an increasingly conflict-prone relationship between the United States and its Western European allies in the North Atlantic Treaty Organization.

What, it might be argued, is so new about that? It is true that transatlantic friction is in itself nothing new. And there have been several earlier periods—notably in the early 1970s—when those frictions looked as though they might get out of hand and even threaten the fundamentals of the Atlantic relationship. They did not do so.

The situation today is different both in terms of the scale and complexity of those differences and in the way in which economic, political, and security policy differences interact with each other and are profoundly altering the overall character of the Alliance. Even the most sober of observers now openly discuss the crisis in the Atlantic partnership and how long it can survive in anything like its present form.

It is clear that the crisis in American–European relations is no passing phase but a central feature of a systemic crisis of the Western economic and political order. As a result of deepening conflicts over world markets, control of the international financial system and capital flows, diverging geopolitical interests and new political pressures, the world system is evolving into a series of increasingly protectionist global regions.

As far as Europe is concerned these developments present enormous dangers but also exciting new opportunities: foremost among them is the possible re-emergence of a European unity, embracing not only Western Europe but Europe east of the Iron Curtain. However, Europe's divisions by the Cold War imperialisms of West and East and its ever-present tendency to revert to a political Balkanization pose major challenges to European political parties across the spectrum. The politicians of the right and centre and the established left have failed this challenge to date. The purpose of this book is to examine the roots of this failure and outline the economic and political choices which will have to be made between now and the end of the century in what is likely to be an increasingly post-Atlantic Europe.

This emerging geopolitical conjuncture has coincided with a thorough-going crisis in European social democracy, which in turn has facilitated the ascendancy of a monetarist and militarist new Conservatism in Western Europe, particularly since the late 1970s. But in reaction a new, radical socialism is now taking shape, drawing inspiration from sources as diverse as the ecological and green movements, from feminism and community activism, from new strategies for industrial democracy and socially useful production emerging from the trade union movement, and which has been inspired by the resolute internationalism of activists for peace and non-alignment in Western Europe. If answers are not found from within the existing political establishment—to the arms race, to structural unemployment, to poverty and deprivation, and above all to the Cold War divisions of Europe—this new, anti-capitalist, anti-Stalinist left could become the authentic voice of a reassertive Europe in the 1990s.

*   *   *

There is no doubt but that the issues which pit the United States and much of Western Europe against each other are proliferating. On the one side there is a significant section of Western European public opinion which no longer trusts its security in the hands of an American administration and which would welcome the withdrawal not only of American nuclear missiles and bases but also of those US troops stationed on this side of the Atlantic.

On the other hand, a different section of European public opinion, including a number of key Western European governments, openly distrust the current direction of US strategy on securing nuclear and other arms-control agreements with the Soviet Union. They fear that the United States may be about to retreat into a political and defence laager, putting its trust in an untried system of strategic defence, the so-called Star Wars project, and looking to disentangle itself from its present commitment to the defence of its European allies.

Some Europeans dislike the bellicosity and unpredictability of American foreign policy in sensitive regions of the world, such as the Middle East and Latin America. Others suspect that their security interests are being disregarded in the superpower arms-reduction negotiations between the United States and the Soviet Union.

In the United States there is resentment at what many policy makers see as the disloyal attitude of the Western Europeans and a tendency to disregard the obligations of their alliance with the United States. There is resentment at what many Americans see as the reluctance of the Europeans to shoulder a proper share of the burdens of providing for their own defence. Neither all Europeans nor all Americans agree with each other or with their respective governments in the angry debate across the Atlantic, but few of them question that the Alliance is in poorer shape now than at any time since the end of the Second World War.

More is at stake than just foreign and defence policy. The global economic background against which these differences have emerged is also gloomier than at any time in recent decades. There has been, for example, a gradual but unmistakable drift by Western Europe and the United States towards a trade war with each other and with Japan.[1]

Western European governments have long since ceased to disguise their profound disquiet over the way in which successive American administrations have managed the US economy, particularly their seeming inability to control the now astronomic financial deficits in both the Federal Budget and the external balance of trade. The result is a world currency and trading system which, many Europeans fear, is now dangerously vulnerable to disaster.

The combination of economic, military, and political conflicts and divergences of view have inevitably raised the question in Western Europe of what might happen if the Atlanticist consen-

sus collapsed. During the early months of 1987 intensive discussions got under way within the revived Western European
Union about possible alternative European security strategies in
the event of a progressive withdrawal of the American 'nuclear'
guarantee to Western Europe. But little if any thought has been
given to the wider economic and political consequences of the
prospective demise of Atlanticism. Yet the impact on all aspects
of European society could be enormous.

Even America's closest allies among Western European
governments are uncertain how to react to the developing crisis
across the Atlantic. They are deeply critical of aspects of US
policy but they know that criticism may, as General Rogers, the
former American commander of NATO forces in Europe, has
warned, only hasten the day of United States disengagement
from Europe.[2] And they are fearful that a breach with the
United States might encourage those in Western Europe who
would like to see both parts of the divided Continent withdraw
from the forty-year-old military alliances of the Cold War, and
the political map of Europe laid down at Yalta redrawn.

These are not just the over-excited preoccupations of some
remote coterie of politicians, military strategists, bankers, and
journalists. The crisis of confidence in Europe's relationship
with Ronald Reagan's America is permeating European public
opinion to an unprecedented extent.

In a remarkable opinion poll carried out in April 1986 for
British Independent Television News, the Harris Organisation
found that no less than 49 per cent of those interviewed
believed Britain's so-called 'special relationship' with the
United States was 'harmful'. A remarkably modest 39 per cent,
by comparison, felt it was 'helpful'.

It is true that the poll was carried out in the aftermath of President Reagan's controversial bombing raid from US bases in
Britain against President Qadaffi's Libya, whose government
had been charged by Washington with supporting Middle East
terrorism. In the eyes of most Europeans, the bombing symbolized a characteristically irresponsible, brutal, and politically
counter-productive use of American military power.

Polls taken in other European countries also trace a sharp
decline in American popular standing.[3] There is a growing view
that American and European interests and attitudes towards

key international issues are diverging and that Europe should pursue increasingly independent policies, even if these conflict with American leadership of the Alliance.

Among even those European leaders most sympathetic to the United States, some have concluded that the US establishment does not understand the dangerous complexities of a rapidly changing modern world, that it has an increasingly isolationist and egocentric view of its own interests, and that its overly ideological approach to the Soviet Union and the East–West strategic relation jeopardizes European security.[4] The radical European left and the peace movement now urge a break with the United States, the removal of American nuclear and other military forces, and the development of foreign and security policies based on European non-alignment between the superpowers.

On the other side of the Atlantic the geopolitical shift of internal US economic power from the economically declining, traditionally Atlantic-oriented north-east to the economically ascendant, Pacific-oriented west and south-west seems linked to the rise of ideological Reaganism.

Certainly some hard-line Reaganites do not disguise their contempt for European allies they regard as unreliable, disloyal freeloaders who are content, however, to shelter behind the US 'nuclear shield', while opposing America's economic and political interests elsewhere. Something of this attitude was revealed by the former US Assistant Secretary for Defence, Richard Perle, who, when asked about critical European reactions to President Reagan's Star Wars initiative, replied in terms seen as insultingly dismissive by some Europeans.[5]

This degree of European disenchantment with the US alliance is comparatively recent. With the partial exceptions of France, notably under President de Gaulle, and for different reasons of Greece and Spain, Western European public opinion has been overwhelmingly 'pro-American' for the greater part of the period since the end of the Second World War.

Atlanticism provided the ideological bedrock of the foreign as well as the international economic and financial policies of virtually all the major West European political parties. European Conservative, Christian Democratic, Liberal, and Social Democratic governments all loyally made the alliance with the United States an overarching commitment in government.

Until recent years there was overwhelming support for the proposition that Europe's economic prosperity, its Parliamentary democratic institutions, and, above all, its freedom from either Soviet conquest or political domination, were assured almost exclusively by the Atlantic Alliance. In the immediate post-war period there was some 'anti-Americanism' on the Right. This was fed by resentment at the way the United States used wartime Lend Lease to prise open European control of their dwindling colonial markets, particularly through the attempted destruction of Britain's system of 'Imperial Preference'. US policy makers also offended those European colonialists affected by American replacement of the British and other colonial powers in key and traditional 'spheres of interest' and export markets.[6]

In his masterful account of the links between US anti-colonialism, global economic liberalism, and the pro-Atlanticist section of American big business Kees van der Pijl[7] recounts the reluctant agreement of the US leaders to an episodically uneasy alliance with the Western European colonial powers. This alliance was fully entrenched only in the period immediately prior to the outbreak of full-scale Cold War with the Soviet Union.

The British and other Western European colonial powers had by the end of the Second World War reluctantly concluded that they no longer had the economic or military power to hold on to their colonial possessions, except with American backing. The overriding objective of the European powers was therefore to secure American support for the recovery of 'their' colonies. Some of these had been liberated from the Japanese by national movements determined to resist a return to colonialism.

The anti-Americanism of the Right reached a climax when the Eisenhower administration scuppered the Anglo-French conspiracy with Israel to seize the Suez Canal in 1956. Since then it has not been a significant political force outside the ranks of the marginal right-wing politicians such as Enoch Powell, who still believes that, once it relied on the United States for its 'own' nuclear deterrent, 'Britain became conceptually and morally a satellite of the United States'.[8]

During the late 1940s and early 1950s there was opposition to US foreign and military policy on the European Left, notably in the period prior to West German rearmament. It was organized principally by the large European Communist Parties and benefited from the fact that, despite the emerging horrors of Stalinism, there was still a degree of popular sympathy for the Soviet Union as a former wartime ally.

The situation today for the European Left is quite different. The influence of the Communist Parties, outside Italy where the PCI is actually pro-NATO, is negligible. The role of Stalinism and the Soviet Union in the crushing of the Hungarian revolution, during the Prague 'spring', and in the repression of Polish 'Solidarnosc', as well as in the testimony of victims of the Soviet Gulags, has left the contemporary European Left hostile to both superpowers. But the United States is still seen as the greater immediate threat to peace in Europe.[9]

Some historians trace the origins of the change in European perceptions of the United States to the period after the assassination of President Kennedy, and most obviously to the Vietnam War. This war, and the continued nuclear arms build-up in the 1960s, triggered revulsion and a new radicalism among the young, the effects of which are still to be felt today. The image of the United States as protector of democracy gave way, in the eyes of many young Europeans, to that of the blundering and bullying superpower.

This reassessment of the role of the United States in world affairs is by no means restricted to the Left or to the radical peace movement. Criticism of important aspects of current US policy, ranging from the Strategic Defence Initiative (SDI) to Nicaragua, from US budgetary policy to the rights of the Palestinians, is commonplace among the European parties of the political centre and even among some conservatives. The bombing of Libya and the US use of bases in Britain for the operation was, according to opinion polls, disapproved of by British voters across the political spectrum.[10]

While members of Western European centre and right-wing parties now question US leadership of the 'free world' and want major changes in the Alliance, attitudes have radicalized significantly further in the mainstream European social democratic parties. The British Labour Party and the West German SPD, for example, have adopted foreign and defence policies, including demands for the withdrawal of US nuclear missiles, which are sharply at variance with the views of the US administration and place a question-mark over the future of NATO.[11] The problem facing the Centre-Right in Europe is that they do not know how to come to terms with the reality of America's progressive loss of economic and political hegemony over Western Europe. They alternate, unpredictably, from angry criticism of US self-interest to appeals for a renewal of American leadership.

It is not, however, just a matter of foreign and defence policy. There are also profound commercial and economic tensions building up between the allies. They were, for example, at the heart of the controversy in Mrs Thatcher's cabinet during the spring of 1986 over the rival American and European takeover bids for the ailing British company Westland, the helicopter manufacturer. The resulting row split the cabinet and led to the politically damaging resignation of the Defence Minister, Mr Michael Heseltine. He and his supporters waged a fierce struggle against what they deplored as the supine lack of British resistance to increasing US penetration and control of key British industries, particularly in the technologically advanced defence-related sectors. Some of Heseltine's supporters regarded US big business as operating a policy of 'commercial imperialism' which, if unchallenged, would condemn Britain and its European partners to an industrially disastrous and politically unacceptable subordination to US interests.[12] In the case of Westland and other controversial attempted takeover bids for British companies, notably in the motor industry, they have urged government intervention to block the US companies and to facilitate alternative mergers with other European interests.

The story is not dissimilar in other countries in the European Community where there is growing alarm at Europe's technological backwardness and commercial vulnerability to US—and Japanese—capital. Indeed, the European Economic Community (EEC) Commission and member states see the reorganization of European big business as essential in order to reduce its technological dependence on the Americans and the Japanese. They have risked US anger by employing direct and indirect subsidies in projects to encourage independent 'European' high-technology research and development.[13]

In the escalating transatlantic trade disputes there is no monopoly of virtue on either side. The Americans justifiably accuse the Europeans of employing nakedly protectionist policies in agriculture, of gradually moving in the direction of a commercial and economic 'Fortress Europe', and of progressively abandoning the free-trade philosophy which has underpinned the Atlantic Alliance for the past three decades.

For their part the Europeans accuse the United States of giving way to domestic protectionist lobbies in a growing number of industries, such as steel, and of using federal budgetary powers to prop up American farm output. Certainly other trading nations believe that both the EEC and the United States are more or less equally responsible for the crisis of overproduction on world food markets.[14]

European governments tend to see the overall conduct of US economic, monetary, and trade policy as ultimately motivated by American determination that its economic partners will pay the price for the crisis in the American economy. They believe that America has managed its economic affairs with decreasing regard for its partners since at least the mid-1960s. Then, under the pressures of rising military spending, and President Lyndon Johnson's 'Great Society' programme of higher social spending, the US deficits began to escalate. These deficits, seen by the Europeans as 'benign' in the conditions of post-war capital scarcity, have in recent years been regarded as increasingly malign and dangerously destabilizing to the world economy.[15]

Given the Reagan administration's refusal to raise taxes, these deficits have been funded increasingly by the United States drawing in scarce capital from abroad, a state of affairs encouraged by the privileged status of the dollar in the world monetary system.. In effect American living standards, US Federal government expenditure, and investment by US multinational companies are being indirectly funded (and subsidized) by non-Americans.

It was this abuse, as the Europeans saw it, by America of its control of the dollar-based world financial system which, in the late 1960s and early 1970s, generated a runaway monetary growth, that is, one not backed by a commensurate increase in real productive wealth, first in the United States and then internationally. This, in turn, laid the basis for the international inflation of the 1970s. That inflation was made chronic by the inability of Western governments to counter rising production costs either by boosting productivity to the extent required or by driving down the prevailing level of real wages. The result was that the rate of profit began to decline throughout the industrialized economies.

Another consequence was a marked deterioration in the terms of trade between all the industrialized economies and the raw-material- and commodity-exporting nations of the developing Third World. This created the pressure for the Organization of Petroleum Exporting Countries (OPEC) oil producers to exploit the opportunity created by the 1973 Middle East War to use their cartel power to impose a fourfold increase in oil prices on the consuming states.

The subsequent story of successive recessions, growing unemployment, and the structural decline of whole sectors of the older Western economies is well known. Not all the blame should be put on American shoulders. But European finance ministers resent the persistently high real international interest rates which they blame on the US deficits and the way they are being financed. The outcome, they fear, will be to deepen the long-term trend towards the 'stagflation' of the world capitalist economies.

Even the government in West Germany has been driven to ill-concealed fury at what the former Federal Chancellor, Mr Helmut Schmidt, has described as the 'misuse of the dollar as an instrument of US foreign policy'. The Nixon, Ford, Carter, and Reagan administrations have all been blamed in Europe for dereliction of the wider international economic responsibilities of the United States. After more than fifteen years of episodic crises, slower economic growth, sectoral industrial decline, and semi-permanent mass unemployment, there is little European trust any more in official US expressions of commitment to economic or monetary 'internationalism'.

What the Europeans have been slower to see is that the international monetary chaos, the stagflation and all that follows from it, is not just a consequence of American 'egocentrism', as the French describe it, but a crisis of a world-wide economic system of which they are an intrinsic part.

European Community alarm at the misuse of the dollar's privileged position in the world currency system encouraged the EEC states to distance themselves in monetary policy from the United States in the late 1970s. Persistent pressure by Chancellor Schmidt and his close ally, President Valéry Giscard d'Estaing of France, led—despite British opposition—to the creation by the EEC in 1979 of the European Monetary System (EMS).

The Europeans took that first step towards greater monetary cohesion and partial autonomy from the United States because of what they saw as the irresponsible and increasing 'unilateralism' of the Americans in financial matters. Although the development of the EMS has not been matched, thus far, by a parallel integration of taxation, public spending, or domestic monetary policy, the Western European ambition to construct a regional currency bloc independent of the United States did mark a radical change in direction. This is also reflected in the efforts to restructure European industry and reduce its vulnerability to technological or commercial 'subordination' by outside—primarily US or Japanese—interests.

The break-up of the dollar-dominated monetary system also marked the end of the earlier Atlantic consensus enshrined in the Bretton Woods Agreement of 1944. Until the 1980s that consensus on the management of the world economy has restrained episodic differences from escalating into an open breach between Western Europe and the United States.

Post-war US economic hegemony was, of course, a reflection of the realities of power. War-devastated Europe was dependent on the United States—first through Lend-Lease, then through the Marshall Plan—for the reconstruction of its economies. To many Europeans the only alternatives appeared to be domination by the United States or conquest by a totalitarian Russia.

In the two decades which followed, the US position in Western Europe was consolidated through a wave of investment by American multinationals both in mass production and in high-technology-based industries. But these were the years of the long boom, when it seemed that there would never be any shortage of markets to satisfy both the giant US economy and its increasingly assertive European partners. Not surprisingly, any transatlantic conflicts had a very marginal impact.

The United States had a more or less free hand in determining the rules and operating policies of the various international institutions established in the post-war period to help regulate the global system. US leadership of the International Monetary Fund, the World Bank, the General Agreement on Tariffs and Trade, and (later) the Organization for Economic Co-operation and Development, was unchallenged until the end of the 1960s. However, the domination of the United Nations by America and its major allies was effectively broken by the early 1960s with the arrival of large numbers of newly independent African and Asian former colonies.

Although in the final analysis these Third World regimes remained, through the operating dynamic of the world economic system, in an economically subordinate position to the advanced industrialized powers, some did support the non-aligned movement after the Bandung Conference in 1955. Although it has kept its all-important position on the UN Security Council, the last time America was really able to use the United Nations as an instrument for implementing its security policy objectives was at the start of the Korean War.

The challenge to American leadership within NATO is very much more recent. It is the paradoxical result of two contradictory trends within Western Europe as well as of the shift in the priority accorded to its Atlantic commitments within the US ruling establishment.

On the one hand, there has been an undoubted loss of European confidence in US policy. America is widely seen as primarily responsible for the escalating nuclear arms race and the fragility of *détente*. On the other hand, European governments suspect that Western Europe may no longer necessarily be able to rely on America to commit nuclear suicide in Europe's defence, a view very much encouraged by US statesmen such as Henry Kissinger.[16] This has meant that America has simultaneously been condemned on this side of the Atlantic for imperilling Europe by brandishing its 'nuclear shield', and also, by some allied governments, for imperilling Europe by threatening to withdraw it.

The tenor of transatlantic economic relations began to change significantly during the mid-1960s when Western Europe, whose core states had already formed the European Economic Community, began first to draw level with and then to overtake the United States as the leading world trading power. The partial eclipse of the United States by the EEC countries and the more recent and dynamic challenge from Japan and the so-called Newly Industrialized Countries (NICs) of the Pacific Rim make the restoration of a single international economic consensus more problematic since there is no single power able to impose its will on the wider 'Western' community. While the EEC is still the largest single international trading bloc, the European Community has not developed the integrated productive potential of the United States. Although highly internationalized in certain sectors, European industry is held back by Europe's still relatively Balkanized economy.[17] Europe's political muscle has also not developed in tandem with its commercial weight in international affairs. Efforts to encourage full European economic and political union have been blocked by a powerful residual nationalism. The result is that the EEC, and more widely, Western Europe, still lack a coherent and united voice in world politics. Its underdeveloped common foreign and defence policies, in turn, deny Europe status and influence comparable to those of the United States or the Soviet Union. More than that, Europe's political weakness ultimately threatens its economic power.

During the past decade transatlantic monetary, economic, and trade disputes have become more intractable. Since 1978 both sides have had to set up special bilateral 'crisis management' diplomatic machinery to prevent the conflicts getting out of control. However, the relentless rise in mass unemployment on both sides of the Atlantic is continuing to feed directly into lobbies and pressure groups agitating for overtly protectionist policies. Although the Reagan administration has resisted some of these pressures, the Democratic Party, which now controls Congress, is committed to extensive protectionism, a stand its next Presidential candidate may have to endorse.

There has at the same time been a collective loss of industrial and technological competitiveness by both the United States and Western Europe to Japan and the Pacific Rim NICs. The immediate threat of trade war may arise either from the United States and the EEC being unable to deal with their farm surpluses, or as a result of Japanese goods, denied access to America, being diverted to Europe.

The Atlantic relationship has suffered from the intertwining of politics in trade disputes. America has tried, sometimes successfully, to browbeat its European partners into ineffective trade boycotts and economic sanctions against their better judgement. American pressure for sanctions—against the Soviet Union in 1980 after the invasion of Afghanistan and in 1981 after the declaration of martial law in Poland, and in both 1983 and 1986 against Libya for its alleged involvement in Middle East terrorism—was resented in Europe. The Europeans have usually opposed such measures, or at the very least sought to minimize their impact. In the European view, sanctions rarely succeed in their stated object. In some cases they have been directed against the wrong target, as when the United States attacked Libya for backing terrorist actions which, if they enjoyed official backing from anywhere, were to be linked to some sections of the Syrian state rather than the Qaddafi regime. Professional European diplomats do not disguise their contempt for the poor political intelligence and lack of overall political grasp of the complex politics of the Middle East displayed over many years by successive US administrations.

The explosive potential of these part-commercial, part-political disputes was manifest when the Americans tried to use the COCOM organization, set up by the NATO states to monitor trade with the Soviet Union involving technologies which have a potential defence significance, to restrict European imports. The United States, for example, sought to prevent European exports of equipment for the Soviet natural gas pipeline between Siberia and Western Europe in 1982. The Americans defended their actions by saying that the Soviet Union was using commercial links to acquire technologies which would enable them to catch up with the United States in the defence field. On the other hand, some European experts argue that the way America has used COCOM has done more harm to the Western European economies, reinforcing their dependence on the United States, than to the Soviet Union.[18] American intelligence reports that the Soviet authorities have used the false

cover of commercial deals to acquire sensitive military technology are regarded somewhat cynically by European industrialists.

All of these problems may intensify if the Western capitalist
economies cannot find their way out of the 'stagflation' crisis of
shorter cycles of inflationary expansion and longer cycles of
recession. Protracted unemployment, de-industrialization, and
intensified struggles for export markets threaten what is left of
Atlanticist economic consensus.

There are signs, indeed, that the world economic system,
under the impact of the continuing economic and trade crisis, is
coagulating into a new global regional pattern. A number of new
'global regions' are emerging, each with its own sphere of
influence and all caught up in a struggle for global industrial and
technological pre-eminence. It is a trend which, if it continues,
will throw the pattern of world politics back into the melting-pot.

What are these emerging global regions? The United States
clearly remains at the heart of a powerful region dominating
much of Central and South America and (resentfully) Canada
as well. Financially it is structured around the dollar and the
giant US market but it is vulnerable to potential mass debt
defaults as a result of the chronic indebtedness to American
banks of some of its biggest Latin American 'client' economies.

Then there is a Western European bloc, with the EEC as its
core, but also including the countries of the European Free
Trade Association (EFTA), whose economies increasingly arti-
culate with those of the EEC. Although, like the United States,
it is formally committed to global free trade, the EEC is protected by a common external trade tariff and has its own
embryo international currency, the European Currency Unit, a
product of the EMS.

The Soviet Union effects economic and political control over
its Eastern European client states (as well as Mongolia and,
more problematically, Cuba) primarily through the Council for
Economic Co-operation (Comecon) and the Warsaw Pact. That
control does come under episodic challenge both from 'dissident' Eastern European oppositions and indirectly from some
of Russia's satellite bureaucracies seeking greater national
autonomy from Moscow.

The cautious assertion of their desire for greater national

autonomy is reflected in the overtures made by the Hungarian and Polish governments, following the example set by Yugoslavia and Romania, for privileged bilateral trade agreements with the European Community. In the past the Soviet Union has refused to recognize the EEC and has insisted that bilateral trade agreements should be concluded only between Comecon and the EEC. Interestingly, the Soviet Union has now effectively conceded recognition and no longer impedes bilateral deals between the EEC and individual Eastern European states.

There are also some signs of an increasing East German challenge to the Soviet Union as the dominant industrial power within Comecon. The extent and complexity of the commercial links between the two halves of Germany are far greater than is widely appreciated. One bizarre side-product of farm trade between the two Germanies is that East German foodstuffs can, indirectly, be sold into official EEC reserves in the West, thus adding to the EEC food surpluses.[19]

These trends do pose the question, which will be examined later, whether and to what extent there can be any political coming together of divided Europe. Profound obstacles remain, but the growing integration of the Eastern European economies into the wider European and international market is already a reality. On the other hand, the crisis in the Western economic world is reawakening a traditional Western European, and specifically a West German, interest both in the markets and in the investment opportunities of Eastern Europe. This economic fact is one important constituent element in the strength and durability of Ostpolitik under different governments in Bonn. It might form the economic cement for an eventual political re-alignment in central Europe.

There are also some precedents for believing that steps taken towards disengagement from the United States in Western Europe could have a repercussive effect in Eastern Europe. President de Gaulle's decision to take France out of the NATO military command in the late 1960s was followed by a mirror-image series of measures taken by the Ceauşescu regime in Romania which secured for itself greater autonomy within both Comecon and the Warsaw Pact. Few academics outside the more extreme Cold-War-oriented institutions now seriously question the desire of most Eastern European regimes to reduce their present dependence on the Soviet Union. On the other hand, the ruling Eastern European bureaucracies will be loath to move faster than Moscow is willing to tolerate. And they will not take initiatives involving mass political upheavals lest these threaten the bureaucratic ruling class and the entire system, as so nearly happened in Hungary, Poland, and Czechoslovakia.

There is an emerging consensus between new left and militant Green political tendencies in Western Europe and the Eastern European dissident and 'independent' peace groups. Both are mapping out alternatives to the alliance of their countries with the United States and the Soviet Union. These ideas are now beginning to influence some of the mainstream West European social democratic parties.

However, any radical breakthrough towards European unification is unlikely to be achieved without drastic changes within the Soviet Union, or uncontainable, quasi-revolutionary pressures in Eastern Europe, or an equally dramatic severing of Western Europe's military links with the United States—or all three. The Soviet Union is extremely nervous at talk of German reunification but it might be willing to sacrifice some degree of control over East Germany if West Germany decided to move out of the military and political orbit of the United States.

The emergence in the Soviet Union of a new leadership around Mr Mikhail Gorbachev resulted in many of these possible developments being the subject of active discussion towards the end of 1986. Mr Gorbachev's policies of Glasnost (openness) and his economic reforms have meant that, at least temporarily, the impetus for a better relationship with Western Europe was provided by Moscow rather than the Eastern European governments as such.

It is uncertain how secure the reform strategy and the position of Mr Gorbachev himself are within the Soviet hierarchy and power structure. But his radical proposals for reductions in the nuclear and conventional arsenals of the superpowers, made in the early months of 1987, restimulated debate about a possible new political settlement in central Europe which might even involve some countries on both sides of the Iron Curtain distancing themselves from their respective military alliances.

If Western Europe does move away from America it does not necessarily follow that the way will be clear for closer relations with Eastern Europe. If, for instance, Western Europe moved to become an independent nuclear power in its own right, with direct participation by West Germany, the net result might actually be to destabilize East–West relations, undermine arms control prospects, drive the eastern bloc states back to the Soviet Union, and drive the Soviet leadership back towards a Cold War stance. But, as I shall argue, a Western Europe which was ready to disengage from the United States and actively seek a new political, overall European settlement to replace the 'Europe of the blocs', set up as a result of the Yalta Agreement and the Cold War, in which the European states were denuclearized and non-aligned, could make a major contribution to reducing the threat to world peace.

Japan also lies at the heart of another incipient global region which could eventually embrace large areas of the Pacific Rim, including such industrially dynamic nations as South Korea and the countries of the Association of South-East Asian Nations. But while Japan may be the 'natural' economic leader of such a regional bloc, its leadership of such an economically and politically diverse region is quite another issue.

America is, ironically, anxious for Japan to take over a far larger political and military role in Eastern Asia as they seek to make savings in their massive overseas military budget (in part to help fund the planned Star Wars initiative). There are also those in the United States and elsewhere who calculate that if the Japanese were persuaded to undertake commitments which involved a major defence burden, this might act as a 'brake' on Japan's explosive commercial success and its economic competitiveness.[20] But simultaneously curbing Japan's exports and encouraging militarism might prove lethal. The opposition of a large proportion of the Japanese people to a deliberate strategy to build up its armed strength and thus encourage the nationalist right wing, is formidable. It will grow if Japan is pressed to deploy nuclear weapons. Memories of Hiroshima and Nagasaki are still politically potent, in spite of the undoubted revival of right-wing, quasi-militarist political tendencies in recent years. Furthermore, the peoples of East and South-East Asia, with bitter memories of wartime Japanese occupation, have no desire to see Japanese forces replace Americans on their soil. The prospect has frequently led to anti-Japanese demonstrations on occasions when Japanese leaders have canvassed closer political links with some of their regional neighbours.

It is a matter of speculation whether, in a different economic and political system, Japan and the countries of the Pacific might not find a more co-operative and complementary relationship. The same is equally true of the Sino-Japanese relation—which is, for the present, likely to be the most important in giving an overall shape to the geo-politics of the region.

A major question-mark must, however, hang over the ability of other leading Asian nations, notably China and India, to form the core of power of new global regions. As recent upheavals in China demonstrate, it may not be possible for China to sustain economic 'take-off' without taking what, for its political élite, would be unacceptable political and social risks. Equally, despite OPEC's temporary emergence as a major force in the world economy, the subsequent collapse of the oil price has weakened the aspirations of the Arab Middle East to the status of global power. However, the Arab Gulf states are attempting to develop a regional currency of their own on the European model.

It is against this radically changing international environment that the decline and potential disintegration of Atlanticism is taking place. It is no longer fanciful, therefore, to speak of the prospect of 'Europe without America'. However, events are moving faster than the ability of European leaders to react with coherent policy alternatives.

A crucial question is whether any American disengagement from Europe takes place by mutual consent over a significant period of time and is negotiated in an atmosphere of relative accord, or whether it is the product of a major crisis in the entire Atlantic system. Although governments on both sides of the Atlantic are determined to manage carefully any possible future run-down of America's military presence in Europe and to contain any economic tensions, this may prove extremely difficult in practice.

In Western Europe the mainstream political parties have barely begun to think through the consequences of a break with the United States or even a radical reconstruction of the

Alliance and a 'post-Atlanticist' economy. The obvious question to be answered, therefore, is 'If Atlanticism is crumbling, what is to take its place?' With few exceptions, the political parties in Europe are in no position to give a credible response. Indeed, since the early 1970s, and particularly since the calls for US troop reductions in Europe, more thought has been given to this contingency in America than in Europe.

One obvious response would be to accelerate progress towards full European economic, industrial, and political union—including steps to draw European countries in EFTA, and maybe even those in Comecon, much closer to the member states of the European Community. In a post-Atlantic world the whole question of an independent and self-reliant European security and defence policy would be a priority.

A more detailed look at what would be involved will be taken later, but the obstacles are considerable. In spite of repeated efforts by the European Commission and some member states in the EEC Council of Ministers, the Community is still a long way from even being a full 'common market'. There is still powerful opposition from national states, reflecting undoubtedly influential domestic lobbies and sections of public opinion, to any radical steps beyond the achievement of a genuine internal market, towards economic, let alone political, union. There is still deep reluctance in the national states to surrender sovereignty to the degree necessary if effective decision-making is to be transferred to the European level. On the other hand, new political forces in Europe with a strong base in the regions and local communities are more ready to see the national state cede at least some of its power to European institutions. They have been exercising increasing political influence in Britain and West Germany in recent years but they have greater popular support in some other countries, notably Italy and Spain. A new breed of progressive regional and local authorities has even struck up an alliance of convenience with the European Community in an effort to secure greater resources for the more economically deprived regions. They share an interest in seeing some weakening of the institutions of the national state and greater powers for both regional- and European-level institutions.

Neither the Right nor the Left in European politics has yet

seriously conceptualized European strategies beyond the completion of the Common Market. Certainly little thought has been given to the way in which the existing institutions should be either reformed or replaced in order better to confront the economic and social problems facing modern Europeans. It has even proved painfully difficult to move the current twelve EEC member states towards more decision-making by majority vote in the Council of Ministers, although almost everyone sees the necessity of this if effective action is to be taken by the Community to implement existing objectives and common policies. Some hope that the endorsement by all twelve member states of the Single European Act agreed in principle at Luxembourg in 1985 may mean a greater willingness to transcend the narrow nationalism of the 1960s and 1970s.

Britain, however, together with Greece, Portugal, and Spain, still stands outside the operation of the EMS system of fixed currency exchange rates. Little has been achieved even in concerting basic monetary and fiscal policies to tackle unemployment and technological decline. Despite initiatives by the French socialist government and modest Commission proposals for a concerted reflation of the EEC economies, the attitude of the larger member states, such as Britain and West Germany, remains suspicious.

This could change with an electoral swing from what are predominantly conservative free-market governments in the core EEC states over the next few years. Significantly the economic debate in the Labour and trade union movement in Western Europe gives increasing priority to a variety of co-ordinated European strategies for recovery.[21]

Much debate has taken place in recent years about a common European industry and technology development policy to confront the serious decline in Europe's international competitive position. There has been general agreement in industrial circles that without urgent steps to boost European technological innovation, and the deliberate encouragement of powerful European multinationals, what is left of European industry will eventually fall in thrall to American and Japanese big business. Some important programmes such as ESPRIT and EUREKA have been introduced both by the EEC and, in the case of EUREKA, on a wider Western European basis, to help address these problems. But European firms are notoriously reluctant to pursue common, long-term strategic goals or to form partnerships to counter US and Japanese commercial penetration, preferring instead short-term commercial gain to longer-term technological autonomy.

Political and macro-economic logic may demand greater interdependence and co-operation on technology and investment between big European companies. Commercial logic for individual companies, however, more often than not points to closer collaboration with American or Japanese rather than European companies. Market pressures often force European companies to agree to arrangements with US and Japanese corporations which condemn the Europeans to being mere assemblers of other people's technologies and designs—precisely because the non-European firms are already dominant in global markets.[22]

In spite of the increased emphasis on European Political Co-operation by the EEC governments in the late 1970s (which has also involved, informally, some non-EEC countries in EFTA), the Community does not yet operate a fully 'common' foreign policy. But the steps which have been taken to concert and co-ordinate foreign policy are very much a response to growing differences with the United States. These pressures on EEC governments have pushed them to define a more independent foreign policy. It was European disagreement with the approach of both the Carter and the Reagan administrations to the Arab–Israeli problem, and to the national rights of the Palestinians in particular, that led to the launch of the European Community's own Middle East initiative after its Venice summit in 1979. Since then the EEC has evolved an increasingly distinctive European foreign-policy line on other international issues, including problems in Latin America, which the US has always seen as its unchallenged regional 'sphere of interest'.[23]

The right-wing government majority in the EEC Council of Ministers has done its best to minimize friction with the United States and rather to use its collective strength to try to influence US policy-making. There is little evidence, however, that the EEC has had any real success in this regard, at any rate under the Reagan administration.

The most sensitive area in the event of any break between the

United States and Western Europe would obviously be defence and security policy. With the partial exceptions of Britain and France, where a strongly (and in the French case dominant) 'national' element has always been present, European security has been something almost exclusively conceived within the framework of NATO. However, in 1982 dissatisfaction with NATO as a necessarily American-dominated forum for discussing specifically European defence interests led seven important NATO states to revive the Western European Union (WEU), which had originally been set up in 1954 by those governments which had signed the Brussels Treaty of 1948 establishing NATO. It was conceived as a 'European only' forum to enable European governments to hammer out distinctively European stands on defence co-ordination, disarmament strategy, and collective security, without US participation. Although the relaunch of the WEU met with ill-disguised American irritation and warnings that it could 'undermine NATO solidarity', it has so far achieved little of significance. Indeed, under pressure from the Americans, the WEU initially agreed not to discuss, let alone decide, a separate policy to the Americans on arms reduction negotiations.[24]

However, as the pace of arms-reduction talks between the United States and the Soviet Union accelerated early in 1987, the British and French governments redoubled their efforts to give the WEU the primary role for shaping Western European security policy. On this occasion it became clear that the Europeans would not accept any unilateral restrictions on the role of the WEU sought by Washington. At the same time it was made clear that the seven existing member states—all of whom, apart from Luxembourg, had nuclear weapons on their soil—would not welcome approaches to join from other Western European states such as Denmark, Greece, or Spain whose governments were critical of any aspect of NATO's nuclear strategy.

America's European partners are at present driven in two conflicting directions at the same time. On the one hand, they increasingly distrust the overall thrust of US security policy and suspect a long-term American intent to 'wind down' its commitment to Western Europe. On the other hand, they are not really prepared for the implications of providing for their own defence, particularly if this had to take place outside the American 'nuclear umbrella'.

Defence ministers in the predominantly right-wing European NATO states fear that if they publicly conceded that an American withdrawal was inevitable they could be opening a Pandora's Box which might release the 'genie' of European neutralism and hostility to any nuclear-based security strategies. The result has been a 'private' debate among strategists about the crisis in European security policy, conducted so far with minimal participation by the wider European public.

There is growing distrust of the Reagan administration's defence 'instincts' among even right-wing European allies. This surfaced in the almost universal European rejection of President Reagan's SDI (better known as Star Wars) when it became public in 1985. Most European strategists doubt its scientific feasibility and fear its destabilizing impact on the precarious Soviet–American nuclear balance.[25] European nuclear strategists saw it as a disavowal of the doctrine of nuclear deterrence, on which Atlantic defence strategy had always been based. They believe that the very notion of a 100 per cent effective defence against hostile missiles is a chimera. European confidence was not increased when the United States advanced a Mark 2 version of SDI, promising only a partial defence of existing US intercontinental nuclear missile silos. Indeed, the current American SDI policy seems a bizarre mixture both of elements of deterrence and of a Star Wars astrodome 'defence'.

America's NATO partners are very concerned that research into SDI could, by breaching the ABM Treaty, trigger a new escalation of the arms race. They were, however, unable to mount a coherent response to SDI, partly because of their desire not to be excluded from the potentially lucrative research contracts which the Pentagon was offering European companies and scientific establishments.[26] But the European NATO states were also unwilling to open up a public breach with the Reagan administration during a critical period for negotiations between the superpowers on nuclear arms reductions and while Reagan and Gorbachev were seeking a new relationship. Even after the failure of the 1986 Reykjavik summit, the Europeans were still hoping to persuade Washington to keep SDI research within the terms of the ABM Treaty.[27]

The European NATO governments are going to have to decide whether the progressive 'uncoupling' of the United States from Western Europe is something which can or should be reversed or whether they should learn to live in a Europe without the United States—until now an unthinkable option. This refusal to face a world without the US nuclear 'guarantee' explains in part why leading European NATO governments, spurred on by the warnings of the former US Secretary of State, Dr Henry Kissinger, about American unwillingness to put itself at risk in the event of a limited war in Europe, backed the NATO 'Twin Track' decision of 1979. This offered nuclear arms negotiations to the Soviet Union but also led directly to the deployment of cruise and Pershing intermediate-range missiles in Belgium, Holland, Italy, the United Kingdom, and West Germany—ostensibly to match the steady increase in the number of Soviet SS20 missiles as well as other intermediate-range missiles, some of which had been deployed years earlier. The decision, born of American anxiety to recover its potency as 'the' world military power, proved one of the most contentious in NATO's history and aroused bitter opposition from the Western European peace movement. Ironically there were also doubts among some hardliners in the United States, who feared that this additional lever in the US–European security coupling could lock America too deeply into European commitments and thus impede its freedom to pursue its own wider global interests and security.[28]

Two European NATO states—Britain and France—also possess nuclear weapons of their own, although the operational independence of the British Polaris nuclear force—and its planned replacement, the US Trident system—is limited by dependence on the United States for supplies and satellite targeting back-up. The relationship of both weapons systems to wider NATO strategy will be examined later, but some believe they might be combined in some way to provide the core of a purely European 'minimum' nuclear deterrent.[29] It is difficult to see the British or French governments winning a decisive popular mandate for such a policy, although in the aftermath of a withdrawal of US troops from Europe it might be taken up by other pro-NATO political parties. But the proposal has already been criticized as further complicating and destabilizing the so-called East–West nuclear balance.

What, for example, would be the relationship of West Germany and other European NATO states to the control and development of such a European nuclear force? High-level and confidential discussions have reportedly already taken place between Paris and Bonn, in the context of wider, Franco–German conventional defence co-operation, about the possible extension and deployment of France's Hades nuclear missiles to 'cover' the Federal Republic, particularly if cruise/Pershing is abandoned. What if there were ever to be a German finger on a European nuclear weapons system? It is conceivable that the European NATO states might agree to fill any gap in NATO's conventional forces created by the withdrawal of American troops or even to replace the US nuclear umbrella with a purely European nuclear force. But would European NATO governments win votes for new nuclear weapons of their own or for diverting public spending to defence to replace part or all of the $165 billion spent annually by the United States on 'the defence of Europe'? Much would depend on whether, in the aftermath of a US decision to wind down its commitment to Western Europe, there was any fundamental reappraisal of the alleged military and political 'threat' from the Soviet Union. NATO orthodoxy insists that there is such a threat and that it demands a continuing Western military response on the present scale. European public opinion is sceptical, however, and is likely to become more so in the future.

Meanwhile, apart from the radical changes to NATO strategy which have been proposed by the British and West German Labour parties, even right-wing NATO states are already 'unilaterally' redefining their commitments to NATO's present strategy. The centre-right coalition government in Denmark, for instance, has opted to withdraw some troops pledged to NATO command in West Germany as part of their national emphasis on 'defensive' defence. The Christian Democrat–Liberal coalitions in Belgium and Holland have unilaterally reduced the scale of the minor 'nuclear tasks' accorded to their forces by NATO. The Dutch have indicated that following the unsatisfactory outcome to the Reykjavik summit of 1986 they might not after all agree to the siting of those cruise missiles allocated to the Netherlands. Norway and Spain have also made it clear that they will not accept nuclear weapons on their soil, while the Canadian Liberal opposition party is committed to banning US testing of cruise missiles over its territory, which it wishes to make into a 'nuclear-free zone'.

What then are the prospects for a decisive rupture in relations between the Atlantic partners? Whether there is gradual, amicable reform of the existing alliance or a fully fledged crisis that would take Western Europe decisively out of the American sphere of influence probably depends on three main factors.

The first would be a swing in the European political pendulum resulting in the election of left or left-of-centre governments committed to some far-reaching economic, political, and defence policy changes. After the British and West German elections of 1987 this is not an immediate likelihood. But the future election of the West German Social Democrats (particularly if they had to form a coalition with the strongly anti-nuclear and anti-NATO non-alignment Green Party) as well as the election of the British Labour Party with its current defence policies could trigger just such a crisis. The West German SPD remains committed to seeking the withdrawal of all the cruise missiles already deployed and to halting any further deployment, as well as to making further overtures towards the Soviet Union. The British Labour Party is committed not only to scrapping its own nuclear forces, but to the removal of all US nuclear bases from the United Kingdom, and to radical changes in NATO's own nuclear strategy including a clear commitment to 'no first use' of nuclear weapons.

Elsewhere, the Belgian, Danish, Dutch, and Norwegian Labour Parties are moving away from the limited commitment of their countries to NATO's nuclear strategy while the Greek PASOK government is still formally committed to winding down American bases on its soil. Enthusiasm for the NATO commitment is restricted, among left-of-centre parties, to the Italian and Spanish Socialists and the Italian Communists, although the French Socialists and Communists ardently support a purely national nuclear force.

The second factor which will determine the future of the Atlantic relationship will be the outcome of the nuclear and other arms reductions negotiations between the United States and the Soviet Union, and the general climate of East–West relations. Any failure, especially if attributed to intransigence or lack of imagination on the part of the United States, could itself precipitate a major crisis of confidence within the Atlantic Alliance.

In the months after the abortive Reykjavik summit, considered later, the Western Europeans did not disguise their unease at the drift of US policy. In essence they feared that the United States was planning to retreat behind its SDI shield and allow the 'security' of Western Europe to be progressively uncoupled from that of the United States. The subsequent progress on a so-called 'zero/zero' agreement on the long-range intermediate nuclear forces (cruise and Pershing 2) deployed in 1979 as a response to the Soviet SS20 missiles and the talk of a possibly similar abolition of some categories of short-range intermediate missiles accentuated these fears. The British and French governments made pointed appeals to the Americans not to agree to the total 'denuclearization' of Western Europe, even though this had been held out to the peace movement as a common objective shared with Western European governments during the protest campaigns against cruise and Pershing.

These tensions were if anything added to as a result of hints from Moscow that the Soviet leadership might be willing to consider far-reaching reductions in the conventional nuclear forces deployed by the Warsaw Pact in central Europe. It began in the spring of 1987 to seem that the Western European governments in NATO would be placed in the invidious position of restraining the United States from a radical arms-reduction agreement where earlier the European complaint had tended to be that the Americans were dragging their feet on arms reductions.

In essence there were now two sharply divided European reactions, one desperately clinging to the remnants of the American nuclear guarantee to Europe and (in the case of the British and French) seeking to construct a possible 'European deterrent', and the other, around the European peace movement, urging their governments to take the Soviet offers seriously and press as far as possible down the road of disarmament and disengagement from the Cold War structures. In either case the European view conflicted with that of the United States.

The third factor will be the evolution of the broader economic and political relationship. A new world economic recession leading to escalating protectionism and trade war as well as further strains and possible breakdown in the international banking and monetary system, would threaten the entire basis of Atlanticism.

While the election of a liberal Democratic President in 1988 might alleviate some of the transatlantic foreign and defence policy tensions, some Democrats have been leading the demand for a withdrawal of US troops from Europe. Since the Democrats are more responsive to pressure for measures to save American jobs than the more ideologically oriented Free Trade Republicans, a Democratic administration might be quicker to unleash the dogs of a trade war.

Of course any alliance that has lasted as long as the Atlantic Alliance will have sunk some deep political roots. While determined to secure a bigger voice in NATO decisions, European governments know what could be at stake if the interrelated complex of economic, political, and defence tensions ran out of control. As we shall see, the Atlanticist-minded political parties deploy considerable political and financial resources. They are certain to mount an all-out attempt to persuade the electorate in countries such as Britain and West Germany not to return parties to office which might precipitate a crisis with the Americans. But time is running out and the odds in favour of avoiding such a crisis are steadily diminishing. Popular opinion is increasingly critical of the United States. The cultural bonds which have traditionally bound the allies on either side of the Atlantic seem to be weakening, with the EEC authorities now proposing, for instance, to limit the extent to which American news and entertainment should be allowed to dominate European television.[30]

The question now is less what can be done to preserve the Atlantic Alliance than what kind of alternative economic, political, and security arrangements are right for the people of Europe. But for Europeans to determine their own futures, in an era of growing world instability, it is vital that they understand the forces which shaped modern Europe. It is only through coming to terms with those forces that they will be able to make coherent choices between the very different futures now on offer.

2 | The American Empire

History, it is said, is written by the victors and historical orthodoxy is shaped by the values and perspectives of the powerful. The history of America's relationship with Western Europe since the 1940s has, for the most part, been written within an ideological framework determined by the academic and political advocates of 'Pax Americana'.

The European experience of that 'Pax Americana' has invariably been interpreted through the perspective of a Cold War ideology manufactured in outline, if not in detail, by the United States rather than by Europe. Generations of Europeans have, for example, been taught to believe that America's enormous military presence in Europe has been primarily for Europe's good, not America's, and that without it Western Europe's democratic system and possibly its very political existence would be in jeopardy. America's involvement in Western Europe tends to be presented as a commitment of selflessness and generosity unparalleled in modern history. The political consensus, which embraces all the major Western European political parties, insists that there can be no acceptable future for Europe outside of an Atlantic Alliance in which Western Europe is a loyal, if occasionally anxious, junior partner of the United States.

It is as well, therefore, to recall that even before the end of the Second World War some US policy-makers were urging acceptance of the objective of 'military and economic supremacy for the United States within the non-German world'.[1] Another adviser was stressing in 1942 the near certainty that 'the British empire as it existed in the past, will never reappear and . . . the United States will have to take its place'.[2]

At that time, US policy advisers were divided between those advocating that America institute a global economic and political order, reflecting broadly the needs of its giant manufacturing companies for world markets, and those urging a more isolationist perspective where America would dominate its traditional 'sphere of interest'. This was, incidentally, interpreted to mean Canada and Central and South America, but also to take in the British Empire's Caribbean colonies.[3]

Before the end of the hostilities some advisers were already warning that any expansion of American power and influence would have to confront the Soviet Union. In November 1944 the 'Post Hostilities Planning Staff' predicted this confrontation and urged the formation of a sympathetic (to the Americans) 'West European security grouping'. Others, such as the Secretary of State Cordell Hull, firmly believed that the Soviet Union might be willingly absorbed into a dynamic, US-led, new world capitalist order.

The truth is that there was, during this period, a shortage of people in the senior echelons of the US administration, with any real expertise on Russia or the problems of Eastern Europe. The one exception was that of Poland, thanks to the very significant and continuing immigration of Poles to North America.

At the same time the US government was advised to promote its foreign policy objectives in the language of 'ordinary people'. In an early example of modern political public relations hype, the government was advised to find ways of expressing its goals through an 'idealistic' language, stressing America's commitment to democracy internationally, rather than directly emphasizing its narrow interests.[4]

From the outset, therefore, America's global ambitions tended to be expressed in the language of Woodrow Wilsonian political liberalism and a free-market international economic order. It marked the post-war ascendancy within the United States of what Kees van der Pijl has characterized as 'corporate liberalism'. This had emerged after the New Deal and now sought an international restructuring of the capitalist system, in partnership with sections of the leaderships of organized labour and social reformers within the State.[5]

Thus, in the domestic debate in the United States during and after the Bretton Woods conference, it was stressed how an open world-trade system was in the interests of America's international banks and companies. But this drive towards a liberal world economic order also provided the ideological underpinning for the American campaign, begun during the war years when the Lend Lease agreement was being negotiated, for the abolition of Britain's protectionist system of 'imperial preference'.

There continued to be two American approaches to the postwar world, but the faction upholding US interests in terms of a global free-trade and liberal political order was dominant at least until the dollar crisis and the new economic policy of the Nixon administration in the early 1970s. As American economic and political power has declined in recent years, elements of the old globalism and the new nationalism have been recombined in ways that have brought it into increasing conflict with the Western Europeans.

Quite apart from its key role in creating the IMF and the World Bank, America exercised the decisive influence in the establishment and operations, for at least its first two decades, of the United Nations. But behind the rhetoric of the new internationalism, Washington exercised a calculating eye for America's own interests. This was vital in overcoming powerful internal opposition to the United States adopting world-wide responsibilities.

Even the former Republican isolationist, Senator Vandenberg, agreed to lead the US delegation to the United Nations. He commented in his diary: 'The striking thing about [the UN] is that it is so conservative from a nationalist standpoint . . . . This is anything but a wild-eyed internationalist dream of a world state . . . . I am deeply impressed and surprised to find Hull so faithfully guarding our American veto in his scheme of things.'[6]

Of course America did not depend on the United Nations alone to secure its global interests. In 1945 it signed the Act of Chapultepec with its Latin American economic client states, which established the principle of military support in the event of a perceived 'threat'. This was used in the region to justify US military intervention against so-called internal subversion by purely indigenous revolutionary forces of what were frequently dictatorial regimes.

The story of the carve-up of Europe by the Allied leaders at Yalta is well enough known. In effect Roosevelt and Churchill gave Stalin a more or less clear hand in Eastern and much of Central Europe, on the understanding that Moscow would not foment trouble for their allies in the rest of Europe and above all in newly liberated and still socially and politically volatile France, Greece, and Italy. There were misunderstandings in Greece until Stalin made it clear that the majority left-wing forces opposed to the British-backed restoration of the power of the monarchist (and even pro-Nazi) right wing would not have his support. But at the end of the first phase of the Greek Civil War, in 1947, the British decided, because of inadequate military (and ultimately economic) resources, to hand over responsibility to the Americans.

Although the American establishment and the bulk of big business were united behind the 'globalist' financial and economic strategy pursued by Washington in the immediate post-war period, they were not happy about any major economic or military commitment to America's bankrupt allies in Western Europe. The case for Marshall Aid and for direct involvement in Western European security was not an easy one to carry before a sceptical American congress and public opinion. There was opposition to bailing out the discredited European (above all British) empires. It took the exploitation of rapidly moving events in post-war Europe to win public support for the momentous series of commitments now undertaken by the United States.

At their heart was the rapid deterioration in relations between America and the Soviet Union. There was the crisis in Greece, confrontation with the Soviet Union over its occupation of breakaway Kurdish and Azerbaijani regions in northern Iran (which quickly led to a Soviet withdrawal), and Anglo-American objections to the Russians' wholesale dismantling of German heavy industry and its transfer without proper accounting to the Soviet Union. But the Soviet Union's proposed redrawing of Poland's post-war boundaries had already created a climate of tension between the United States and the Soviet Union. American policy-makers were quite convinced of a looming Soviet threat to Western interests in Greece, Turkey, and Iran and through those states the Middle East. This led directly to the evolution of a doctrine of 'containment' of the Soviet Union, first enunciated by the diplomat George Kennan in a memorandum, the major thesis of which he later disavowed. It was used at the time by those advocating what today

would be described as a 'hawkish' policy towards Soviet Communism.[7] The new American President, Harry Truman, and his
Under-Secretary of State, Dean Acheson, lost no time in stepping up the pressure on their European allies with warnings
about the 'Soviet threat'. Already in February 1946 Churchill,
now out of office, had made his famous Fulton, Missouri speech
referring to the 'Iron Curtain' dividing Europe. He was in
America to plead for urgent economic aid for Britain and, more
widely, for an Anglo-American international alliance which he
saw as the sole means of assuring the future of the British
Empire.

Britain got Marshall Aid support just as its post-war economic crisis was assuming unmanageable proportions. The deal
was favourable in that the British did not have to abandon
their privileged colonial arrangements as some Americans
had wanted. They were even allowed to maintain the system
of sterling area controls, while being expected to do away
with them in due course. The new Labour government was
quick to signal its willingness to act in close concert with
America's international strategy. As early as March 1946
Prime Minister Clement Attlee reflected: 'It may be that we
shall have to consider the British Isles as an Eastern extension of a strategic area the centre of which is the American
continent.'[8]

By March 1947 the US administration was ready to unveil the
Truman Doctrine in which the President asserted that there had
to be a choice between 'two ways of life' and promised that
America would assist 'free peoples to work out their own destin-
ies'. The President placed a more strident emphasis on the 'containment' of Soviet power and the use of American military
power to achieve that goal. From that point on, American
leaders invariably interpreted unrest in terms of 'Communist
subversion', instigated and orchestrated by the Kremlin. Ironically, Soviet policy from 1945 to late 1948 was firmly opposed to
pro-Moscow Communists supporting, let alone leading, revolutionary anti-capitalist movements which challenged the established order in Western Europe or in the colonies. The
emerging national independence movements—many of them
later to form the 'non-aligned movement'—were in no way
creatures of the Soviet regime. Indeed, in power, many of them

repressed the local Communist parties with little concern for what Moscow might think.

In Moscow the Truman speech was read as a declaration of ideological war against the Soviet Union. Events then followed each other at bewildering speed. The US Congress, fearful about European economic collapse, the consequent loss of vital export markets, and the risk of political turmoil which might lead to left-wing governments coming to power, approved Marshall Aid. As Acheson put it in May 1947: 'We are going to have to concentrate our emergency assistance where it will be most effective in building political stability . . . and fostering liberal trading policies.'[9] The US administration also committed itself to the idea of a supranational Western Europe, partly as an aid for the Economic Recovery Programme, but primarily as the vehicle for the restructuring of the European economies in terms of the new global economic order. Again Acheson expressed America's 'European dilemma' in that it really needed an integrated Western European economy (or even better an all-European free-market system) to effect its global economic strategy, but this was impeded by Europe's own political history. 'The basic disparity in Western Europe today is the fact that the particular size of the unit necessary for its successful existence in the context of the world economy is larger than the actual size of the existing political units.'[10]

America disingenuously offered Marshall Aid to the Soviet Union and the occupied states of Eastern Europe, but on condition that it was given access to each recipient country's most sensitive economic intelligence and a commitment to free trade. American leaders well understood by 1947 that neither condition would be met by the Stalinist regime in the Soviet Union nor by its increasingly hand-picked puppets in Russian-occupied Eastern Europe.

Alongside Marshall Aid and the systematic stepping-up of a Cold War rhetoric, the Americans mounted an increasingly bold covert and semi-covert strategy to counter the influence of the Left and in particular the Communist parties in Western Europe. The objective of this CIA-orchestrated campaign has been described as designed 'to assist the emergence of a stable Europe . . . at best compliant to American wishes in a military alliance'.[11] Partly this campaign was to work for the division of the Western European labour movement along Cold War lines. Splits in the trade union movement in France and a number of other countries were encouraged, as were pro-US breakaways from a number of Western European Socialist parties, notably in Italy. In this the right-wing American Federation of Labour worked closely with organs of the US government, including the CIA and right-wing social democratic politicians and intellectuals in Western Europe.[12]

The US administration had concluded that in building an alliance of client states in Western Europe it would be obliged to give support to the European states in retaining their empires. This had been a firm condition laid down by the British, Belgian, French, and Dutch leaders who faced growing demands in their colonies for national independence which they knew they could not contain without the backing of the Americans. Given America's still lively anti-colonialist traditions, an inheritance from its own revolutionary past, this temporizing with colonialism was somewhat distasteful. But the Labour Foreign Secretary, Ernest Bevin, spoke for his fellow European colonialists when, after a disagreement between the United States and Holland over the future of Dutch Indonesia, he warned of 'a general reaction [by the US] that might happen upon any of us in similar circumstances when the United States might be moved by an emotional wave'.[13]

Although the British abandoned the Indian sub-continent and (after a vicious war against Chinese Communist guerrillas) Malaya, the bulk of the European colonial empires remained intact by the end of the 1940s. The Truman administration defended the role of the British in Malaya and elsewhere, and of the French in Indo-China, by referring to what he insisted was now a global confrontation with 'Communism' and the Soviet Union. But the Americans used their influence to push for liberal reform policies in the European colonies. They were, as a result, able to win support among a section of the developing nationalist middle class in the emerging post-liberation regimes, which enhanced the objective of replacing Western Europe as the hegemonic Western power in large areas of Asia and Africa.

This sense of global confrontation was immeasurably heightened as a result of the triumph of the Communists over the pro-American forces of Chiang Kai-shek in 1949. The 'loss of China' figured prominently in the attitudes of American politicians for years after and together with the loss of a nuclear monopoly to the Soviet Union and the outbreak of war in Korea, helped create a political climate of almost paranoid 'anti-Communism' which, in turn, encouraged the emergence of extremists such as Senator Joe McCarthy.

The swing of US support behind the European colonial powers' approach did not silence all US critics. One Congressman denounced the Economic Recovery Programme and noted: 'In helping Britain, France, Belgium, and the Netherlands hold on to their empires, Wall Street and Washington aim to keep these far-flung colonial empires, as well as their rulers, as allies against Communist aggression and, incidentally, safe for American profits.'[14] Over the years Washington's support for the European colonial states gradually resulted in America assuming imperial responsibilities for a large number of Third World client states.

The division of Europe into Cold War blocs was reinforced by the extension of Marshall Aid to West Germany. Equally fatefully, the Soviet Union moved to absorb the *cordon sanitaire* of buffer states created by Soviet occupation against what Moscow increasingly saw as the threat from the United States allied with a revived German militarism under US sponsorship. The brutal Czech *coup d'état* in 1948, the destruction of any remaining genuinely independent non-Stalinist elements in the governments of the Eastern European states, and their complete subordination to Moscow then followed. Industry was centralized and agriculture in most countries collectivized. Such political liberty as had survived was extinguished. A full-scale political terror was unleashed throughout the Eastern European states to eliminate any actual, potential, or imaginary local Titoites who might try to emulate Yugoslavia's successful nationalist defiance of Moscow. Meanwhile, the Western Communist parties swung from support for 'bourgeois' coalitions to an ill-fated and superficial campaign of industrial militancy. The political atmosphere in Europe turned icy.

By the late 1940s the Czech *coup* and the clumsy Soviet attempt to force the Western allies out of Berlin completed the polarization of Europe into two Cold War encampments.

Atlanticism emerged as the dominant ideology in all the major Western European political parties. The voice of 'neither Moscow nor Washington', Third Camp Socialism, was all but extinguished.

In March 1948 the North Atlantic Treaty was signed between Britain, France, Holland, Belgium, and Luxembourg, laying the basis for the NATO alliance. There were sensitive discussions about the precise circumstances in which the United States might intervene militarily in an allied state. The original US draft Article 4 of the Treaty spoke of 'indirect' as well as direct aggression against an ally and this was at first defined as 'an internal *coup d'état* or political change favourable to an aggressor'.[15] It was not clear whether 'political change' might embrace circumstances in which a Communist election victory was possible. European governments were sensitive to the likely public reaction and were uneasy at the prospect of US military intervention in such circumstances and forced a change in the US draft. So Article 4 finally referred to consultation with allies when they were faced with a threat to their 'territorial integrity, political independence or security'.

For more than two decades afterwards NATO itself had a contingency plan for possible US military intervention in the event of a Communist election victory. It was only in the late 1970s that Washington accepted that the 'Euro-Communist' parties in Western Europe could be regarded as 'legitimate' after the breach between the PCI and Moscow and the PCI's espousal of support for NATO itself.

In any event, the final stages of the Treaty negotiations were overshadowed by the crisis over Berlin. This followed Stalin's decision to impose a partial blockade in reaction to Western attempts to lay down a new political structure for West Germany. Stalin claimed that such a state would unleash 'revanchist' forces which would ultimately seek to overturn the Yalta Agreement. (Earlier the Soviet government had suggested the idea of a united but neutral Germany, but this had been rejected out of hand by the West.) The Russians failed to break the West's nerve with the Berlin blockade; but it created an atmosphere of near panic which helped European politicians win public support for the founding of NATO and the return of American soldiers to Europe. Some Western statesmen were quick to indulge in some essentially verbal brinkmanship with Moscow. Churchill hinted at a nuclear threat against the Soviet Union should it not withdraw from Berlin, while the US military commander in Germany also hinted he might call on nuclear weapons if needed to blast a way out of West Berlin. The subsequent climb-down by the Soviet Union in 1949 did not prevent the allies exploiting the apparent 'Soviet military threat' to Western Europe. In the tense international political atmosphere the British agreed to sanction new American military bases along with the despatch to the United Kingdom of B29 US bombers which had a nuclear-carrying capacity.

Tremendous political pressure was put on the other Western European states to fall into line and join the new alliance. Semifascist Portugal did join, as did Denmark, Italy, and Norway, but Sweden and Ireland refused in view of their commitment to non-alignment. The treaty setting up NATO was finally signed in April 1949 with overwhelming US Congressional approval.

For a period the United States had a total monopoly of nuclear weapons. This power gave the American leaders, above all Truman, immense self-confidence in dealing with the Russians. Given the widespread European revulsion against Stalinist tyranny in the Eastern bloc states, this meant that America and its allies were never really under any compulsion to pay serious attention to alternative ideas for assuring post-war European security. Proposals to give a key role to the newly founded United Nations or to agree to steps to neutralize Central Europe were never pursued.

In spite of the support the British had given US strategy leading up to the formation of NATO, the Americans did not have unbounded confidence in their ally. Although British scientists had played an essential part in developing atomic weapons during the 1940s, the United States refused the British access to US nuclear research secrets. However, following a secret decision taken by a handful of civil servants and Labour ministers in 1947, Britain launched a nuclear programme of its own.[16]

The subsequent story of the relationship between what rapidly became two armed, and ultimately nuclear-armed, superpower-dominated blocs is divisible into a number of different phases. Although there are problems with his restriction of the term 'Cold War' to only the most acute and tense phases of the East–West relationship of permanent rivalry and hostility, Fred Halliday has described more clearly than most these succeeding phases and related them to developments within and between the superpowers.[17]

Halliday identifies four main phases since 1945. He describes the 'First Cold War' as lasting from 1946 to 1953, followed by Phase 2, one of 'Oscillatory Antagonism', from 1953 to 1969. The third Phase, 'Détente', lasted just ten years (roughly from the Nixon to the Carter administrations)—1969 to 1979. The fourth and current phase, which he describes as the 'Second Cold War', began under Carter but was consolidated after the radical changes in foreign and security policy introduced by Reagan.

There are obvious differences as well as similarities between the two 'Cold War' phases. Both have been characterized by an escalation in the international arms race and a very frigid overall diplomatic and political relationship between Moscow and Washington. Furthermore, in both periods there was a strongly ideological tone to the way US policy interpreted global tensions and rivalries with the Soviet Union.

On the other hand, the Second Cold War has not seriously interrupted the steady increase in the depth and diversity of economic and commercial relations between the so-called 'Communist' and capitalist blocs. And while, in America, Reaganism has been associated with the revival of radical right-wing and even militarist political currents, there has been nothing to rival the McCarthyite repression of internal dissent and protest. Equally there has so far been no generalized purge and repression of actual or supposed 'deviationists' within the Soviet and Eastern European ruling bureaucracies comparable to the dreadful purges of alleged Titoites in the aftermath of Yugoslavia's defiance of Moscow in the 1940s. While the full force of the repressive state machine has been deployed against dissident opposition movements, notably Solidarity in Poland and the Charter 77 in Czechoslovakia, Moscow has encouraged a cautious 'liberalism' and even tolerated a degree of nationalist autonomy by some other Comecon governments, such as Hungary.

The other striking difference between the two periods of intense Cold War tensions has been the degree of unity within the NATO alliance. Whatever the unofficial or 'behind closed doors' tensions between America and its allies, US leadership of NATO was unquestioned and unquestionable during the First Cold War. The contrast with today is startling. Not only has America's economic and political power waned in relation to that of its European allies, but US leadership is questioned and widely mistrusted. Although the overall European attitude to the alliance with America remains incoherent, there has been a popular distancing by Europeans from identification with American cultural and even political values which would have been almost unthinkable back in 1948.

Some other contrasts with the situation today are rather more uncomfortably ambiguous. Thirty years ago the United States repeatedly denied that there was any real danger of war. In the spring of 1949, for instance, John Foster Dulles, who from 1953 was to be America's hawkish Secretary of State, told Senate hearings on NATO: 'I do not know of any high official, military or civilian . . . who believes that the Soviet [Union] now plans conquest by open military aggression.'[18] His attitude was to change radically after Korea. At the same time America developed contingency war plans of a most bellicose character. In 1949 US war-planning associated with the introduction of the nuclear-capable B29 bombers stipulated the following war objectives: 'to reduce or eliminate Soviet or "Bolshevik" control inside and outside the Soviet Union.'[19] It was a throw-back to an older Western policy objective: to 'roll back' Communism to a point prior to the 1917 Revolution. The implied threat did not go unnoticed in Moscow where it fed Stalinist paranoia.

In recent years the Reagan administration has adopted an echo of the language of post-war 'roll back' in speeches about the 'Evil Empire' and the Messianic commitment of America to 'anti-Communist' forces internationally. Even more alarming has been talk about the possibility of victory in a nuclear war 'limited' to European soil. Thus Richard Perle said in 1981: 'I am always worried less about what would happen in an actual nuclear exchange than the effect that the nuclear balance has on our willingness to take risks in local situations . . . . I worry about an American President feeling he cannot afford to take action in a crisis because Soviet nuclear forces are such that, if escalation took place, they are better poised than we are to move up the escalation ladder.'[20] Others have urged that the United States should regain unquestioned 'nuclear superiority' over the Soviet Union. Two writers who later became government officials wrote in 1980: 'The United States should plan to defeat the Soviet Union and to do so at a cost that would not prohibit US recovery. Washington should identify war aims that in the last resort would contemplate the destruction of Soviet political authority and the emergence of a post-war world order compatible with Western values . . . . Judicious US targeting and weapon procurement policies might be able to deny the USSR assurance of political survival.'[21]

While some Europeans were disquieted by US bellicosity in the 1940s, they never doubted American power to match words with actions. Today the remarkable ebbing of American power—and the seemingly systemic disarray of most contemporary US administrations, as evidenced by the covert US arms supplies to Iran in 1986—leads many Europeans to question whether a weaker and more internally divided Washington administration may not be more, not less, prone to disastrous miscalculation in a crisis with the Soviet Union.

During the First Cold War the US élite swallowed any distaste it might have felt in downplaying anti-colonialism and the espousal of universal democracy, the better to secure the alliance with the European colonial states. On the other hand, then, as now, the US attitude to consultation with its allies tended to be somewhat peremptory—if not cavalier—reflecting the American view that Europe is just one region in the global interests of the United States. This led Signor Manlio Brosio, an early Secretary General of NATO, to make some highly critical retrospective judgements about consultation in NATO. It was, he said, a way for the United States and on occasions Britain and France 'to legitimize and reinforce their foreign policy initiatives'. Worse still, America has been accused of declaring full-scale nuclear alerts without proper consultation and deploying nuclear weapons in nineteen situations of international tension.[22]

There has been particular European dissatisfaction with US influence on the operations of COCOM, the NATO-operated agency controlling the export to the Soviet Union by the allies of high-technology goods which might have a potential defence application. Long before the bitter dispute over European sales of equipment for the Soviet Siberian gas and oil pipeline in the 1970s, the Europeans accused the United States of using COCOM to gain and maintain a technological domination over European rivals.[23]

The Korean War, which broke out in 1950, marked a qualitatively new stage in Soviet–American superpower confrontation, moving from an almost exclusively European theatre to a world-wide basis. The 1950s saw the European colonial powers forced (by economic weakness and inability to counter the growing popular-based national liberation movements in the colonies) to concede independence. In many former colonies the United States now took over as the hegemonic power.

The manner in which independence was ceded, or alternatively forced from the colonialists, differed considerably from country to country. In the British case the relatively drawn-out and barely perceptible transformation from Empire to 'Commonwealth' served to lull the British ruling-class into a complacent disregard of the radical changes needed to arrest Britain's underlying chronic economic and political decline. On the other hand, the sudden and dramatic loss of Indo-China and North Africa to revolutionary nationalism impelled France to a sweeping modernization strategy on the return to power of General de Gaulle as President of the Fifth Republic in 1958. The lack of a British 'modernization strategy' explains in large measure the subsequent dramatic decline in the power of the United Kingdom compared with its Western European allies. At any event, European decolonization in the years after the Korean War accelerated the replacement by America of its European allies as the dominant Western power in important regions of Asia, Africa, and the Middle East. In Indo-China it was drawn ever deeper, after the French withdrawal in 1956, into what proved to be a disastrous attempt to halt the movement for national independence and unification.

The process by which the United States became the West's international anti-Communist *gendarme* was critical in 'overstretching' the resources of even the mighty American economy from the 1960s onwards. Indeed, by the time of *détente*, in the late 1960s, the European powers were for the most part well on the way to economic recovery and anxious to rebuild economic and commercial links with their former colonies or traditional 'spheres of interest'—notably in the oil-rich states of the Middle East. The seeds were thus sown for later transatlantic rivalries and conflicts.

In the aftermath of the Korean War, the Paris Agreements of 1954 codified the American strategy of 'militarizing' NATO. This included new 'force' goals for NATO's non-nuclear forces and the maintenance of ten divisions of American forces in Germany as well as more limited British, French, Belgian, and Dutch forces. The United States also cemented a series of other bilateral military alliances, including CENTO in the Middle East and SEATO in the Far East, effectively encircling the Soviet Union.

Stalin had died, and East–West relations had entered a new phase marked by alternating attempts at negotiated understanding and episodic confrontation. American power, enhanced by being first with the H-bomb and intercontinental missiles, was approaching its post-war apogee. The Korean War had concluded on relatively favourable terms for the West, and America could now begin to assert itself in areas hitherto dominated by the Europeans.

Although this was a period of controlled antagonism between East and West, it was punctuated by a series of crises: Suez and Hungary in 1956, the Berlin Wall in 1960, and Cuba in 1962, which cast a shadow of potential disaster. These were the years when the United States waged a bloody but fruitless war against the Vietnamese, and when the Warsaw Pact in 1968 put an end to the 'Prague summer' and Czech attempts to reform Stalinist rule and ease Russian control.   .

The years between 1954 and 1970 also witnessed a massive expansion in the scale and number of nuclear and other weapons of mass destruction. The introduction of H-bomb-carrying long-range bombers was followed by successive and ever more sophisticated generations of both strategic and short-range nuclear weapons. The evolution of more powerful conventional arms systems, notably for the European theatre, was accompanied by 'battlefield' nuclear weapons.

Since the 1960s both sides have possessed sufficient nuclear arsenals to destroy each other—and virtually all other life forms on the planet—many times over. Although both superpowers have contributed to the escalation in the arms race, America has persistently sought first to create and subsequently to maintain military superiority over the Soviet Union. Episodic US claims that it had lost that lead in destructive potential have invariably proved to be without foundation.

As far as the global balance of forces is concerned, there can be no question but that the West is massively more powerful and better armed than the East. The Stockholm Peace Research Institute, for instance, calculated in 1980 that total military spending by America and its allies was more than twice that of the Soviet Union and its allies. Moreover, given its relative economic weakness, arms-spending imposes a bigger relative burden on the Soviet bloc. As far as the balance of armed forces in Europe is concerned, the Warsaw Pact has more than six million soldiers to NATO's just over five million.[24] But this figure leaves out the army of Spain (now a NATO member), which together with that of France, whose forces co-ordinate closely with those of West Germany, totals nearly one million. The United States has a massive lead in the numbers and firepower of its strategic nuclear arsenal which will grow massively when they deploy the new MX and Trident D long-range missiles by the mid-1990s. NATO currently deploys fewer intermediate-range weapons in Europe than the number of medium-range Soviet SS20 missiles, but it has more bombers.

Senior American officers in NATO claim that in the event of a total surprise all-out attack by the Warsaw Pact, NATO forces might not be able to resist for as much as a week without having recourse to nuclear weapons. The question is rarely asked what conceivable motive the Soviet Union might have for such unprovoked aggression. There are no reasons for thinking that anyone in the Kremlin has at any time imagined that it could be in their interests to unleash such an attack. No serious Western strategist has ever attempted to make out the case for assuming an unprovoked Soviet attack as a rational possibility. Even NATO's military commander, General Rogers, says that the most likely 'hostility scenario' would be one in which the Soviet Union attempted to pressurize a militarily weaker Western Europe.

Although Soviet military technology has improved significantly in recent years, notably in the fields of missile accuracy and so-called 'counter force' weapons, there are very few areas where Soviet 'know-how' is superior to American. And it is only in the balance of conventional forces in Europe that there is any real question of whether there is a 'local' Warsaw Pact superiority over NATO. Even here, American and NATO propagandists have exaggerated this imbalance. Some US sources have claimed an imbalance of as much as eight to one in favour of the Warsaw Pact, although in 1986 the Institute for Strategic Studies in London calculated that neither side had sufficient force advantage to assure victory in a conventional war.[25] Even orthodox military experts in NATO concede that to have any chance of success in an unprovoked all-out attack, the Warsaw Pact would need to count on a minimum advantage of more than three to one in the balance of forces. No reputable independent body believes that the Warsaw Pact has any such advantage. The ISS noted that the West tended to 'exaggerate' Warsaw Pact superiority. It is clear that there is a rough balance in numbers of fighting units when account is duly taken of Spain and France.

Few Western strategists ever really allow for the fact that many Warsaw Pact soldiers are conscripts, briefly trained 'raw' recruits, many of whom are from Eastern European satellite states whose loyalty to the Soviet Union, and hence reliability in a crisis, is at least open to question. Moreover, although the Warsaw Pact has many more tanks than NATO, the latter has a far superior arsenal of sophisticated anti-tank weapons.[26]

Typical of this probing of US propaganda is a study in the journal of the Royal Services Institute for Defence Studies in London. It concludes that 'a detailed study of GSFG [Group of Soviet Forces in Germany] reveals many surprises: that the balance of conventional forces in Germany has been getting worse for the Russians for the last 30 years; that it is NATO, not the Warsaw Pact, that has set the tactical and technological pace in Europe; that GSFG has about 40,000 fewer men than it did in 1957; and that its readiness is lower than is often claimed.'[27]

Of course the balance of power between East and West in Europe was directly influenced by global developments which pitted the two systems one against the other. Thus the rise of Third World nationalist, anti-imperialist movements from the late 1940s– notably in the Middle East and the Far East—weakened Western influence. Indeed, the fall of the pro-Western monarchy in Iraq in the late 1950s led to the break-up of CENTO. And the revolutionary independence movement in Indo-China contributed to the demise of SEATO, even before America's military defeat in Vietnam.

Conversely, the success of the Nixon administration in forging an essentially anti-Soviet alliance with China in the 1970s, together with defeats for pro-Soviet forces in the Horn of Africa and Egypt, were important set-backs for the Soviet bloc.

The defeat of the United States in Vietnam and the monetary and economic crises that followed the partial unseating of the dollar as the linchpin of the world monetary system in the early 1970s, encouraged the phase of *détente* in East–West relations which began after 1969. The recognition of China and summit talks with Moscow led to the first Strategic Arms Limitation Treaty and Anti-Ballistic Missile Agreement in 1972. This period was to some extent characterized by an attempt by both superpowers to stabilize, legitimize, and above all secure their respective spheres of interest, particularly after the Test Ban Treaty. Faced with growing domestic unrest, the threat of revolution in Latin America, loss of influence in Asia following the Vietnam defeat, and embroilment in the flash-points of the Middle East conflict following the Arab–Israeli War of 1967, US strategists urged a pause and a rethink of American international policy. *Détente* was welcomed by the Western Europeans who had been pressing for a more systematic attempt to secure an understanding with the Soviet Union. But *détente* from the beginning meant significantly different things on either side of the Atlantic. Whereas for the Americans it meant legitimizing the superpower status quo, for the Europeans, and in particular the West Germans, it involved exploring to what extent a new relationship might be possible across the Iron Curtain.

It was against this background that the West German government made its first tentative moves towards 'Ostpolitik' with Moscow. Whereas the Western Europeans had no intention of challenging the internal status quo in the Soviet bloc, or in any way challenging the primacy of the United States in the Atlantic

Alliance, they were keen to see some basic changes in the relations between the two parts of Europe.

Even at the height of *détente*, any suggestion of a 'Europe–
Europe' dialogue was viewed with apprehension in Washington. Quite apart from ill-concealed fears that West Germany
might be 'drawn to the East', the renewed interest in better
relations with the Eastern bloc states also had a competitive
commercial aspect. American multinationals began to realize
the potential importance of the new market openings in the
East, and some feared that their European (specifically West
German) rivals might take advantage of the new political climate to get in first.

During the Nixon era there were open expressions of American resentment at what was perceived as increasing European
'disloyalty' towards the United States. Some Americans were
infuriated with the refusal of many Europeans to support the
United States not only in the Vietnam War but also in the many
other non-European theatres of confrontation with what Washington saw as the Communist threat. And it was during this
period that America first began to pressurize its European allies
to accept a bigger share of NATO support costs.

In Europe the late 1960s and early 1970s witnessed an
upsurge of popular movements opposed to US international
policy, particularly growing out of hostility to the US war in
Vietnam. One of the first post-war peace movements had been
the Campaign for Nuclear Disarmament founded in Britain in
1958. But it was only in its revival in the 1970s that the anti-
nuclear peace movement began to assume a truly mass and
more obviously 'European' character. Despite charges made
against it of 'anti-Americanism', the European peace movement has always valued its links with the small but significant
peace movement in the United States.

The *détente* years also exposed what appeared to some Europeans as the declining quality of US leadership. Nixon's fall from
office in the wake of the Watergate scandal was followed by the
brief and ineffective administration of Gerald Ford. In European eyes the Carter administration vacillated between support
for *détente* and a renewed emphasis on anti-Communism and
counter-insurgency.

The Carter administration's inability to secure the endorsement of Congress for the SALT 2 agreement with the Soviet Union symbolized the drift of the US political establishment away from *détente* and back to Cold War belligerency. Although originally opposed to the use of NATO forces for intervention operations outside the NATO area, it was the Carter administration which pushed the idea of a NATO Rapid Deployment Force (RDF) for possible use in the Gulf area of the Middle East from 1977.[28]

Some European NATO governments were attracted by the notion of such a force and the British, French, and Belgians had all in previous years mounted military actions in actual or former colonies, which on occasion involved the use of forces committed to the NATO command. But the majority of European NATO states remain reluctant to earmark NATO facilities in Europe to back up a US-led RDF. This seems to reflect doubts about the reliability of US judgements in an 'out-of-area' crisis. These doubts were reinforced after Washington had so disastrously misread and misunderstood the nature of the Iranian revolution. This lack of political grasp of the sources and goals of the Islamic revival and an episodic and uncertain proneness to adventurism was nowhere more pathetically illustrated than in the fiasco over the attempted rescue of the American hostages held by Iran in 1981.

All in all the claim by Carter's Security Adviser, Zbigniew Brzezinski, that it was the Carter administration which had shifted US policy towards the new 'hard line' vis à vis the Soviet Union well before Reagan, appears justified. Certainly the Carter administration's alarmist talk about a new Soviet military threat prefigured the style and approach of the Reagan Presidency and thus helped create the international climate for what Fred Halliday has called the 'Second Cold War'.[29]

The Middle East was emerging as a cockpit of conflicting American and European interests even before the OPEC oil-price increases of 1973. Whereas both the Americans and the West Europeans were anxious to defeat radical Arab nationalism and counter the challenge of the Palestinian movement, American intervention was exercised increasingly via its ally-client Israel, as well as the Shah's Iran. For their part the European governments stressed the need for a longer-term strategy to solve the Palestinian problem in ways which would strengthen and stabilize the conservative, pro-Western Arab regimes. The West German government was horrified when the United States used German bases, without its knowledge, to airlift arms to Israel.

The NATO doctrine of 'flexible response' designed in the 1960s to graduate the scale of Western response to meet the perceived Soviet threat was also used to justify the further escalation in US arms-spending under President Reagan. The doctrine emphasized 'regional nuclear options' and by instituting a new concept under which NATO might respond to aggression with limited 'European theatre'-based 'intermediate' nuclear forces, led to the call for the modernization of theatre nuclear forces in Europe in 1975. Significantly, this was some time before the actual arrival in European Russia of Soviet SS20 missiles, subsequently cited to justify NATO's decision in 1979 to station new intermediate-range cruise and Pershing medium-range missiles in Western Europe.[30]

The Americans certainly did not impose cruise and Pershing missiles on totally unwilling allies. A key group of European leaders, notably Chancellor Helmut Schmidt of West Germany, had become concerned at the developing crisis in Atlantic relations through the 1970s and at what seemed to be an incipient 'decoupling' of European security from the US 'nuclear umbrella'. Schmidt and the British Labour Defence Minister, Fred Mulley, waged a campaign to persuade the Carter Administration that the threat of Soviet SS20 missiles demanded new US missiles in Europe. Mulley, a weak politician much influenced by senior Defence Ministry officials, actually wrote to the US Defence Minister, Harold Brown, in 1977 to try and overcome last-minute American doubts about the political wisdom of the move to site cruise missiles in Europe.[31]

The cruise missile campaign was important, however, in helping the Americans reassert their authority within NATO. This had earlier come under challenge from the French, who left the integrated military command in 1966, from the Germans over the use of NATO bases to supply Israel, and from the Greeks over the refusal to work with the Turks in NATO's joint East Mediterranean command. The Europeans had also been recalcitrant in observing COCOM restrictions on trade with the Soviet Union. The Americans had been angered by the Europeans' lack of support for the proposed deployment in 1978 of the Enhanced Radiation Weapon, or 'neutron bomb', which would destroy human life but leave property intact. Even those Western European governments most sympathetic to the American desire to reassert NATO's potency were alarmed and dismayed at what they saw as confusion and inconsistency in the implementation of these strategies, particularly under the Carter administraton.

The Carter administration did try to improve consultation with the Europeans on broad alliance strategy, notably through the NATO High Level Group. But the wider attempt to build a 'Trilateral' global leadership with the Europeans and the Japanese foundered on their inability to hammer out a common strategy to tackle the major issues of the international economic crisis.

On the other hand, the 1970s did see the proliferation of international summits designed better to co-ordinate the strategies of the seven major 'Western' non-Communist powers (the United States, West Germany, Japan, France, Britain, Italy, and Canada) from 1974. The less frequent meetings of the United States, West Germany, France, and Britain were, however, vital in concerting key policy decisions, such as the modernization of NATO's intermediate nuclear forces (INF) at Guadeloupe in 1979.

The domestic background to the 'Reagan phenomenon' was one of complex and deep-seated changes in the US economic, political, and social situation, which had been maturing since at least the end of the Vietnam War. One element was the reaction of many Americans to the novel experience of protracted decline of the United States as a world power. The defeat in Indo-China, humiliation in Iran, the rise of Japanese and European economic rivals, the ceaseless propaganda about the Soviet threat and the loss of military superiority, the revival of Christian fundamentalism, the shift of power from the industrially declining Atlantic seaboard to the expanding South and West, the virtual collapse of the liberal coalition within the Democratic Party, the serious weakening of the American labour movement due to de-industrialization and mass unemployment, and the blunting of the black and radical challenge of the 1960s—these were just some of the factors which produced the Reagan phenomenon.[32]

At the heart of the Reaganite view of the world is a simple conspiracy theory of Soviet 'Communism' which sees Moscow as the centre of a spider's web of subversion, revolution, and potential aggression against the 'free world'. To many Europeans—Christian Democrats and Liberals as well as the left—a political philosophy which could embrace Pinochet's Chile, the Turkish military regime, authoritarian South Korea, or Duvalier's Haiti as even partial allies in defence of the 'free world' is deeply suspect. Even right-of-centre European governments do not believe that movements for radical change in the developing world are either best understood or best dealt with through a perspective which sees Moscow's hand at every turn. The rhetoric and values which were most revealingly expressed in the President's denunciation of the Soviet 'Evil Empire' betray a view of the world which almost all Europeans find difficult to relate to.[33]

When it comes to the alarmist assessments by the Reagan administration of the global arms balance between the United States and the Soviet Union, West European responses are more ambivalent. Although the governments of Western Europe in the 1980s have been overwhelmingly conservative, Atlanticist, and pro-NATO, they have been frankly sceptical about the need for the scale of American rearmament. Between 1980 and 1985 the US administration increased US military spending by no less than 51 per cent, after allowing for inflation, to $296 billion, a quarter being earmarked for 'modernization' and especially the new B1 bomber, the MX missile, and the Trident submarine. This build-up is planned to continue at a slower rate to the end of the century.[34] Although Henry Kissinger, among others, believes that any attempt by the Russians to try and match this kind of military spending would break the Soviet economy,[35] the Western Europeans are far from sure. They have given no explicit backing to the MX missile programme and have not disguised their serious reservations about the centrepiece of Reagan's rearmament programme, SDI.

The commitment to build an astrodome capable of protecting US nuclear missile sites—if not the population at large—combined with the deployment of the MX, Trident D–5 missiles, and top secret 'stealth bombers' over the next ten years, has refuelled European fears about the attractions to the Americans of a pre-emptive nuclear first strike. They note remarks such as that made by the former US Chief of Naval Operations, Admiral James Watkins, urging the case for 'advance battle groups' with the 'over goal . . . to shoot down the archer before he releases his arrows'.[36] Even the Conservative British Foreign Secretary, Sir Geoffrey Howe, had to be reprimanded by US administration officials for his initially sceptical response when Washington unveiled its Star Wars scenario in 1983.[37] There was even more alarm in Europe after the breakdown of the Reykjavik summit when it became clear that America was willing to break the terms of the ABM agreement limits on the testing of space weapons to push ahead with the development of SDI as well as breaking the SALT 2 Treaty limit on the permitted number of long-range ballistic missiles and bombers.[38] Taken together with worries about the continuing US programme of underground nuclear tests, differences over the emphasis on out-of-theatre-area military operations, and fears for the future of *détente*, the Reagan rearmament programme has added to the strains within NATO. Indeed, the direction of American policy since Reykjavik does seem to call into question the very basis of the NATO Alliance consensus. The response of the right-wing European NATO governments has been constrained by three major considerations.

The first is concern that to go public on their doubts about US ideas on the strategic balance of forces, and SDI in particular, might have the unintended effect of legitimizing the opposition of the Left and the peace movement to American and NATO nuclear strategy as a whole. Secondly, the European governments have been under pressure from their own military/industrial establishments to collaborate with SDI in the hope of US contracts for European firms.[39] Third, and most important, European NATO governments began to worry that the US strategic force build-up and SDI might lead to a progressive decoupling of US and European defence. Those apprehensions were enormously increased as a result of Reykjavik when it emerged that, for a moment, the US administration was willing to negotiate not only the removal of all intermediate-range nuclear missiles from Western Europe but also the complete elimination of strategic nuclear weapons over a ten-year period. The deal fell through because of Reagan's unwillingness to have his hands tied on the parallel testing and development of SDI and Gorbachev's insistence on linking the issue of SDI to a 'zero–zero' deal on Euro-missiles. But to the right-wing European governments, the US approach also suggested that the Americans might be ready to ignore their allies' views on issues such as the dangers of a virtual denuclearization of Europe despite what they saw as the imbalance in conventional forces between NATO and the Warsaw Pact, in order to facilitate a global deal with the Soviet Union. The British Conservative government was particularly alarmed at the possibility of America failing to supply Trident missiles to replace the ageing Polaris force if all strategic missiles were eliminated in an agreement with the Soviet government. This led to the extraordinary sight of European NATO governments, in the aftermath of Reykjavik, lobbying Washington to backtrack from its arms-reduction proposals, as far as they applied to European-theatre nuclear forces.

At the meeting of NATO foreign ministers in December 1986, the US administration backtracked in so far as it said that in future its immediate negotiating objectives in talks with the Soviet Union would be more modest than in Reykjavik. It would only agree to the withdrawal of all intermediate-range nuclear missiles capable of being sited in Europe on strict conditions. Furthermore, it would initially seek only a 50 per cent cut in US and Soviet strategic forces—thus seemingly guaranteeing the availability of the Trident missile as Britain's replacement for its Polaris nuclear force when it is phased out in the 1990s. The US Secretary of State, George Shultz, at the same time reaffirmed that a 'zero–zero' intermediate-range missile agreement, if not the total elimination of strategic nuclear weapons, would remain US policy. The European gamble therefore rested, in the early months of 1987, on the assumption that US–Soviet negotiations would not for the foreseeable future return to the more ambitious agenda items discussed at Reykjavik.

Even the more limited goals of the nuclear negotiations are now linked to two wider issues: the limits on American development of SDI (on the Russian side) and far-reaching reductions in Warsaw Pact conventional forces in Europe (on the NATO side). Meanwhile, the Soviet Union has warned that it might abandon its unilateral embargo on nuclear tests if America persists with its nuclear tests and defiance of the SALT 2 and ABM treaties.[40]

Given the depth of the disagreements between Washington and Moscow on some of these issues it is not surprising that by the end of 1986 earlier optimism about a breakthrough in the superpower negotiations about strategic, as opposed to intermediate, nuclear forces, had all but disappeared. The dogmatic adherence of the European NATO governments to the Soviet threat hypothesis, to the belief in a massive imbalance in forces in central Europe, and, in the case of the British, commitment to an 'independent' deterrent, all combined to deny European NATO a constructive role in assuring a superpower agreement.

However, the very development which the European NATO governments most fear—a decoupling of US and Western European security—may still come about as a result of the progressive 'de-nuclearizing' of NATO's arsenal, specifically the possible elimination of both long-range intermediate nuclear missiles and those with a shorter range (500 to 1,000 kilometres). That would offend against established NATO dogma which insists that the Americans cannot ever be relied on to commit their vast strategic nuclear forces in the event of a 'limited' war in Europe.

At the same time there are potential political developments in Europe to weaken American ties to NATO. In Washington it has been the possible return to power of the British Labour Party which in the recent past caused most concern. There are other signs of NATO doctrine fraying at the edges. Apart from the withdrawal of some of its NATO forces by the Danish right-wing government, the right-of-centre Belgian and Dutch coalitions have signalled their intent to reduce the number of their NATO 'nuclear tasks'. The Greek and Spanish governments now insist on changes in military agreements covering US bases. The Scandinavians, of course, refuse to accept any nuclear weapons on their soil. Despite the Christian Democrats' narrow victory in January 1987, the West German SPD and the Greens have moved closer to a common position which rejects US missiles and, by implication, NATO's basic nuclear strategy. The West German SPD and the British Labour Party's continuing commitment to 'no first use' of nuclear weapons and to tactics which could involve NATO in deep penetration attacks on Warsaw Pact territory in a war situation particularly alarms the United

States, despite the election defeats sustained by both parties in 1987. Cruise and Pershing missiles would also be removed by both parties. But it is the British Labour Party's determination to remove all US nuclear bases from Britain which has caused most anger in the United States. Senior American administration leaders have warned that there could be a chain reaction within NATO if European countries opt out of more and more aspects of NATO's nuclear strategy. This, it is said, would lead to the 'collapse' of NATO, precipitate the withdrawal of US forces in Europe, and put Western Europe at the mercy of the Warsaw Pact.

The leaders of the British Labour Party and, even more, the West German SPD are profoundly committed to NATO and the alliance with the United States. The British Labour leader, Neil Kinnock, went to America in December 1986 and again in March 1987 to try to reassure US leaders of his loyalty to the alliance. In a major speech in Boston he underlined Labour's commitment to NATO and to using the savings from cancelling Trident and Polaris to increase Britain's conventional defence spending.[41] This did not impress US politicians who, with an eye to the general election expected in the United Kingdom in 1987, redoubled their warnings about the crisis facing NATO. However, sensing the likelihood of Labour's defeat at the forthcoming British general election, the US administration did not disguise its bitter opposition to Labour's defence policy. The consequential humiliation of the Labour leader was an important factor in Labour's decline in the opinion polls and possibly in its subsequent election defeat.

Public opinion in Europe was not reassured by the revelations towards the end of 1986 about the involvement of the Reagan administration in illegal arms shipments to Iran and the transfer of funds to right-wing anti-government terrorists in Nicaragua. Neither was it clear whether attempts to frighten European voters with talk about the withdrawal of US troops would succeed or rebound. Certainly the case for British withdrawal from NATO and cynicism about the idea, canvassed by Labour leaders, that NATO could be readily re-formed from within, was received with more sympathy within the Labour Party, in part as a result of the intemperate US reaction to Labour's defence proposals.[42]

Whatever the outcome of future elections, European opinion

is likely to become even more sharply polarized for and against the Atlantic Alliance in the longer term. If the cohesion of NATO is as fragile as opponents of British 'unilateralism' suggest, it seems only a matter of time before some European NATO state takes an initiative which triggers an open crisis in the alliance.

The second force working towards the progressive decoupling of the US and its Western European allies is economic realities. At the start of 1987 a politically weakened US administration faced an astronomic government budget deficit and a weakening economy. In this inauspicious political climate the European NATO governments are coming under massive pressure from the United States to shoulder a much bigger share of NATO's costs, in spite of European claims that their true contributions to NATO's force goals at least are underestimated by the Americans. At present the European members of NATO spend an average of 3.8 per cent of their GDP on defence, and the British spend 5.5 per cent, compared with 6.4 per cent in the United States.[43] There is little sign that the Europeans will readily convince the United States that they cannot pay more. As a result the threat to withdraw at least some US troops over the next few years remains potent. However, few if any governments in Western Europe are in such a strong economic or political situation that they can pledge themselves to higher defence spending to take up any slack created by an American run-down in Europe.

One increasingly likely outcome of this transatlantic confrontation could be a progressive running-down of the 350,000 US troops in Europe, a refusal of the Europeans to make up the deficiency, and some *de facto* alteration of NATO military doctrine to take account of the new realities. Indeed, early in 1987, for a mixture of budgetary and other reasons, leading US Democrats, including Zbigniew Brzezinski, were reportedly considering an initial reduction of 100,000 US troops in Europe. Brzezinski suggested transferring some of them to the highly sensitive Persian Gulf area.

The question which cannot be answered at present is whether these changes will take place with at least a minimum of agreement between the Europeans and the Americans or as a result of a political rupture. The latter would raise the spectre of possible US sanctions against recalcitrant governments such as those imposed on New Zealand when in 1985 it banned visits by

US warships carrying nuclear weapons. New Zealand was denied access to US military intelligence and expelled from the ANZUS Pact.

On the other hand, countries such as Britain and West Germany have countersanctions of their own available. There are still many non-nuclear US bases and other facilities in Europe, deemed vital by the American military for the defence of the United States, which Washington could be denied if the going got really rough.[44] However, such a confrontation could all too quickly escalate beyond the carefully defined limits of the changes in the European–American relationship which the leaders of the European Social Democratic parties, including the British Labour Party, want to see.

Very little thinking has yet been done in Europe about the new foreign and security policy options which would be created in circumstances leading to American withdrawal. But already a debate is beginning between advocates of a more purely 'European' nuclear-based security system and advocates of radical alternatives based on European reunification and non-alignment. The outcome of this argument will rest in large measure on popular European acceptance of whether there really is a credible Soviet military threat to Western Europe. This in turn must be affected by developments in Eastern Europe, where moves towards reform and liberty will influence wider perceptions of the intentions and capacity of the Soviet Union as an allegedly 'expansionist' power.

To judge by the state of public opinion at present, most Europeans would be quite happy to see a run-down of the American presence in Europe, not least because they see Washington's foreign policy record in Central America and elsewhere as at least as aggressive as that of the Soviet Union in Afghanistan. But public opinion remains much more fluid as to whether Western Europe, and Britain and France in the first instance, should abandon their own nuclear weapons. Certainly in both these countries nuclear nationalism is stronger than support for the US nuclear presence.

It is for this reason that the debate on Europe's future defence and foreign policy is inextricably linked to the wider debate about what kind of society Europeans want to build for themselves during what remains of the twentieth century.

3 | Atlantic Strife

'It is not right, proper or wise for the United States to make decisions about keeping troops in Europe on the basis of whether the Common Market treats soyabeans fairly. But there is no way to prevent [this]. The political, military and economic issues in Atlantic relations are linked by reality, not by choice, nor for the tactical purpose of trading one off against the other.' Thus Henry Kissinger on 23 April 1973.[1]

There is no universal agreement as to when the Atlantic relationship between the United States and Western Europe turned sour. Some believe that conflict and contradiction between American and European interests were built into the Atlantic Alliance virtually from its inception. Others argue that the Atlantic partnership was essentially harmonious until the arrival in the White House of Ronald Reagan. According to this view, the new Reaganite political establishment has fundamentally different global economic, political, and strategic interests to those of Western Europe. Its ascendancy, it is argued, marks a sharp break with the traditional 'Atlanticism' of the American ruling élite. This may, in part, reflect a shift in the economic and political centre of gravity of US capital, from the traditionally Europe-oriented, but declining, North and East to the Pacific-oriented, and prosperous, South and West. The latter certainly provided a major element in Reagan's political constituency even before his election.

The truth may be more nuanced, but few deny the scale of the change which has overtaken the transatlantic relationship. André Gunder Frank has traced the rise of the economic divergences and conflicts within the Alliance over the past decade and concludes: 'It appears that the natural course of world capitalist development and its renewed structural crisis are undermining the economic basis of and generating ever sharper political conflict within the Atlantic Alliance.'[2] A British academic study of the Alliance has concluded in equally gloomy terms: 'Quite simply it [has] often appeared that Western European and American views of their obligations . . . were at odds and that this reflected fundamental tensions in the alliance; was NATO a concert of free nations or a protectorate; a coalition with a common purpose or a façade for a sphere of influence dominated by an increasingly feeble and capricious super-power?'[3]

Most experts now trace the watershed date in the American–European relationship to the Nixon era in the early 1970s. At first sight this seems surprising, since President Nixon and his powerful Secretary of State, Henry Kissinger, made the restoration of the Atlantic Alliance a major policy goal and even designated 1973 the 'Year of Europe'. In fact 1973 represented a watershed in United States attitudes to Europe, reflecting a new and harsher emphasis on shaping Alliance policies in more explicit reflection of American interests.

However, 1973 was also the year when Washington served notice that America would in future pursue its own 'national' economic and strategic interests, with far less regard to the impact on their European allies. Nixon's new economic policy was introduced in the aftermath of the recession which began in 1969. It also came in the wake of a succession of dollar crises, marking a radical change of direction for the United States. The abolition of the dollar–gold convertibility opened the way for an uninhibited drive to halt and reverse America's declining share of world markets.[4] Writing a few years later, senior American academic experts were in no doubt about the significance of the change in US strategy. Benjamin J. Cohen was particularly struck by the long-term consequences of the new American economic nationalism: 'The New Economic Policy has made economic warfare respectable again—for the first time since the "beggar my neighbour" days of the 1930s. Each side has adopted an arsenal of weapons at its disposal which is certainly more than adequate for the purpose. A process of disintegration in the Western world could easily be set in motion.'[5]

But the seeds of the Atlantic conflict had first been sown even earlier. The twenty years prior to 1970 had seen a remarkable decline in US economic power, relative to the other advanced industrialized capitalist economies and to the European Community in particular. Between 1950 and 1970 the US share of World Gross Domestic Product went down from 40 to 30 per cent while that of the EEC countries had risen from 11 to 15 per cent.[6] The economic decline was not across the board at this stage, but centred on a number of industrial sectors important in international trade. In the decade prior to 1973 the major continental European economies were also growing at nearly 6 per cent annually, or almost twice as fast as the US economy. The disparity in the growth of productivity—or output per worker—was even more striking. But by the early 1970s it was also clear that Japan's productivity was outstripping Europe and the United States.

However, the long-run decline in American global economic power was not, by itself, the cause of the deterioration in the transatlantic economic and commercial relationship. Rather, this had its origins in America's increasing resort to inflationary means of financing its domestic and international policies, and to what its trading partners saw as its abuse of the privileged and dominant position of the US dollar in the world monetary system. Some sectors of American business did well out of the lurch to inflationary policies, particularly those relatively insulated from foreign competition or directly linked to the arms race, but, overall, American industry's international competitiveness suffered.[7]

The alarm bells about US budgetary, fiscal, and monetary policy first began ringing at the height of the Vietnam War during the Presidency of Lyndon Johnson. The costs of the war coincided with the impact of the intercontinental missile programme begun by his predecessor, President Kennedy. Johnson had also sanctioned a big increase in 'Great Society' welfare expenditure in the 1960s—a strategy designed to counter the threat of social revolt against decades of discrimination and poverty by black and other minorities in the big-city ghettoes. The net result in the succeeding decades was a scale of Federal domestic budget deficit and, increasingly, balance-of-payments deficit without precedent in US history. At first, however, the deficits and consequential outflow of dollars into the world economy had been regarded as benign rather than malign, since Europe was still suffering the effects of the post-war dollar shortage. The deficits initially helped finance the mutual economic recovery of America's allied (and client) economies. But as the outflow of dollars turned into a mighty flood, American control over foreign banks grew by leaps and bounds. Between 1970 and 1975 the assets of overseas branches of US banks grew from $47 billion to $166 billion. The over-valued US dollar came to be seen as the means by which European industry was being acquired cheaply by US interests.[8] This was the period in which French writers in particular, such as Jean-Jacques Servan-Schreiber, developed a critique linking the use of US financial power to the dominating role of American multinational capital in Europe.

Since Bretton Woods in 1944 the dollar price of gold had been fixed and was thought to be as immutable as American hegemony over the international capitalist system. For as long as America's productive economy was equal to the task of financing its worldwide operations, the dollar system seemed to assure stability. All of this had changed radically by the mid-1960s, leading to President de Gaulle's famous aphorism 'The Americans only used the atom device twice on Asia . . . but they use the dollar on Europe every day.'[9]

The twenty years to the mid-1960s had proved a remarkable period of sustained economic growth throughout virtually all the advanced Western economies. The impetus for much of the growth, technological innovation, and employment expansion was generated directly and indirectly by the American armaments programme.[10] But sooner or later the costs of sustaining such massive spending on the 'non-productive' sector of the economy were bound to hamper America's overall competitiveness, given that its most potent trade rivals were not so burdened by arms-spending. Moreover, by the mid-1960s the penetration of the European economies by American multinational corporations had ceased to be so welcome in Europe. Fears were expressed that Western Europe was being turned into a fiefdom of the US multinationals, particularly through US domination in the new science-based industries.[11] By the late 1960s the gap between the US dollar's internal purchasing power and its international value had widened alarmingly. The Europeans were faced with the choice of either accepting these depreciating dollars (and thus, in effect, subsidizing the American economy and worldwide military and political commitments) or exploiting America's Bretton Woods commitment to swap dollars for gold at the fixed price.[12]

Led by President de Gaulle, America's economic partners

decided to swap externally held dollars for gold. Apart from concern about the takeover of European industry, European governments were also angered that the growing pool of dollars held—mainly by Americans—overseas was making it increasingly difficult for them to maintain firm control on monetary expansion and thus of domestic inflation.[13] Vast though the reserves of US gold held in Fort Knox and elsewhere appeared, they were, none the less, limited. Despite changes in the exchange rate between gold and the dollar, those reserves had begun to leak away at a frightening rate by the end of the 1960s. The situation was further exacerbated by the international recession which began in 1969 and hit America's exports more than those of its rivals, thus increasing pressure on the gold–dollar link. In the late 1960s the United States applied arm-twisting pressure to persuade the Western Europeans to support the dollar. Indeed, this pressure on the West Germans carried the implicit threat of political sanctions—such as the withdrawal of American troops—and even contributed to the downfall of the Erhard government.

President Nixon finally took the dollar off gold in August 1971, thus effectively devaluing it against the currencies of America's leading European and Japanese trade competitors. This was accompanied by a major US export drive, by pressure on America's allies to help restore its trade balance by stepping up purchases of US arms, and by a more aggressive use of US commercial resources, including the extension of export credit terms. In addition, an Export Administration Act removed many existing obstacles to American trade with the Soviet Union and Eastern bloc economies. This was very much the hard commercial core at the heart of Nixon's strategy of *détente* with the Soviet Union. It was in this more relaxed relationship between the nuclear superpowers that Nixon was able to extricate the United States from the humiliating fiasco of defeat in Vietnam and that the first Strategic Arms Limitation Agreement was signed between the United States and the Soviet Union in 1972.

As it emerged, America's new strategy was simultaneously aimed at seeking greater accommodation with the Soviet Union and at reasserting its dominance over its troublesome Western European allies. This found diplomatic expression in

Kissinger's ill-fated 'Year of Europe' initiative in 1973, which was intended to put American–European relations on a new and 'more realistic' footing. The new Nixon policy did result at least in a temporary improvement in the US economy, and the deficit in US foreign trade began to dwindle. America's *détente* overtures first to the Soviet Union and then to China did yield concrete diplomatic results, above all the Strategic Arms Limitation Treaty and an improvement in political relations with Moscow. *Détente* also held the promise that America would be better placed than its rivals to exploit new commercial openings for trade and possibly investment in the Soviet bloc economies and in China.

On the other hand, the US attempt to bring the Europeans into line and reassert US hegemony over the Atlantic Alliance was badly received by the allies. The Western Europeans rejected the mixture of patronizing assurances and crude warnings that American policy would in future be shaped more by its narrow security and commercial interests. Rather it generated a critical European backlash even in hitherto unquestionably loyal West Germany.[14] As one American study carried out at the time put it: 'Never before has the interdependence of economic, trade and monetary issues and . . . security and political problems become more clearly visible than in connection with America's attitude to Europe.' Beneath the surface of NATO and Atlanticist protestations of loyalty there was growing concern, even in Bonn and London, that some fundamental American and European interests were diverging.[15]

It was about this time that enthusiasm among American strategists for European economic and political integration began to wane. As one leading US diplomat put it: 'The US today faces a double challenge. The first lies in a growing tendency of the European states to separate themselves from American hegemony within the Atlantic system. The second lies in the gradual disintegration of the American "informal empire" over the Third World . . . '[16] Concern among policy-makers at the continuing loss of US power and influence coincided with a distinctly more hawkish evolution of US attitudes towards the Soviet Union. There was a renewed harping on the 'threat' of a new Soviet arms build-up, while some US policy advisers also recommended a tougher stand towards Europe. 'Only if the

United States in fact sees itself as a European power and acts accordingly, will [the Atlantic relationship] avoid a collapse. And only if the democratic élites in Western Europe orient their foreign and domestic activity towards the reality that there is no substitute for the US will they find productive answers to the manifold burdens facing the alliance in the future.'[17]

The international economic environment changed dramatically in the aftermath of the 1973 Middle East War. The combination of the war and the background of high levels of international inflation made it both possible and—in the eyes of the OPEC states—justified to push up the real value of producer earnings by quadrupling oil prices. The oil-price shock and the inflation and recession of the 1970s exacerbated the underlying transatlantic tensions. The Western Europeans objected to the United States exploiting the power of the big American oil companies to charge domestic US industrial and other consumers less than Europe had to pay for its oil. Certainly the US 'oil majors' did very well out of the crisis and America was foremost among those countries who proposed that in future there should be a floor price for oil below which it would not be allowed to fall.[18]

The Nixon administration was angered at the attempts of the Europeans to negotiate a diplomatic *modus vivendi* with the Arab oil-producing states. The Americans had bitterly denounced the European refusal to support the United States' Middle East client, Israel, both in the 'Seven Days' War of 1967 and, more especially, in the 1973 war which led to the OPEC oil embargo. They were later to interpret the EEC Middle East initiative on Palestine as inspired by little more than a desire to appease the Arab oil states. According to the *New York Times*, Henry Kissinger told a meeting of US Congressmen's wives that during the oil crisis the Europeans had acted 'cravenly' and 'jackal-like'. The European allies disliked that as much as Kissinger's earlier dismissive comment that few of them had 'fully legitimate governments' and that whereas 'Europeans have regional interests—the US has global interests'.[19] In the event, many of America's commercial rivals emerged from the oil crisis and subsequent recession in better shape than America did. This was due, in the main, to the strength of their currencies and a more rapid adjustment to dearer and scarcer energy by the Western European economies. They also benefited from their more successful penetration of Middle East and Eastern bloc export markets.

The US administration adduced the straitened circumstances of the American economy to justify its resistance to international pressure to take the lead in reflating its own and the world economy. In effect America was now abandoning its role as lead locomotive pulling the Western capitalist economies out of recession. Ironically, an unintended side-product of the vast US rearmament programme of the Reagan era has been a super-Keynesian-sized budget deficit which has stimulated faster growth than in most other Western industrialized countries. However, foreign exporters, not US business, have been the primary beneficiaries of this growth.

The advent of the Carter administration marked a change in the style if not in the content of US policy. The Carter years were in part characterized by an attempt by leading US politicians to use the Trilateral Commission—set up to reassert US leadership of the main industrialized Western nations—as a forum for a more co-operative attempt by the United States, Western Europe, and Japan to tackle world problems. It had little real impact, not least because of the growing divergences of interests and perceptions among its leading participants.[20] However, it did help to draw Japan to some degree close into a collective web of Western decision-making. The effect of much of this was subsequently undone in the 1980s with the upsurge of trade-war tensions between Japan and the European Community on the one hand, and the United States on the other.

The Carter administration initially sought improved relations with the Soviet Union, a process which led to the signing of the SALT 2 Agreement in 1979. There was even some support for Western European Social Democrats, such as Willy Brandt in West Germany and Olaf Palme in Sweden who advocated a kind of global Keynesianism involving radical new aid strategies as a response to the growing pauperization of the non-oil-exporting Third World economies.[21] Some 'liberal' business interests in the United States realized that high oil prices, recession in the Western economies, and the increasing costs of borrowing from the Western banks were building up to a major debt crisis which could result in large chunks of the Third World being lost to capitalism and the West. The scale of that crisis became apparent at the end of the decade when countries such as Brazil, Mexico, and some Eastern European states began to hint at a default on their international bank debts.

The new US administration did not secure a markedly better relationship with its European allies. The American response to the events culminating in the fall of the Shah of Iran and the emergence of the Ayatollah Khomeini further eroded European confidence in America's ability to read and respond effectively to international crises, notably in sensitive areas of the Middle East.

Carter's economic failures—and a new deterioration in the US balance of payments—were matched by a series of setbacks to US policy globally. The Iranian revolution, the botched attempt to secure the release of US hostages held prisoner by Islamic militants, and the Soviet invasion of Afghanistan in 1979 were just some of the blows to US prestige. In response America rapidly moved further away from a *détente* strategy which had been downgraded after 1976–7. There was a fresh preoccupation with a new 'Soviet threat' and efforts to force the Europeans to adopt a tougher line against Iran and the Soviet Union.

During the latter years of the Carter administration the United States reverted to an increasingly 'Cold War' approach towards the Soviet Union. Quite apart from Congress's refusal to endorse SALT 2, the Carter administration itself was laying the basis for the ideological swing to Cold War militancy. It was in this propitious climate that Reaganism flourished.

Zbigniew Brzezinski, Carter's security adviser, justifiably pointed to his President's Reagan-like hawkishness. As Brzezinski put it: 'It was President Carter who, for the first time in peace time, increased the defence budget. It was President Carter who ordered the creation of a Rapid Deployment Force. It was President Carter who decided on the deployment of the MX missile. It was he who shaped a regional security framework in the Middle East.'[22] Well before the crisis in Afghanistan the Carter administration had won the agreement of its NATO allies to boost their arms-spending by 3 per cent a year in real terms—the largest deliberate escalation in defence-spending since the early days of the Cold War. Most important of all, the Carter administration, with the overt support of Henry Kissinger and his friends in the West German and British governments, successfully persuaded NATO to adopt the famous Twin-Track decision to deploy new medium-range missiles in Europe.

However, the Europeans refused to endorse the American policy of virtually unqualified support for Israel in the Palestinian dispute, even during the Carter period which included the 'Camp David' settlement between Israel and Egypt. They believed the Americans had lost impartiality in dealing with the problems of the region particularly after the election of Ronald Reagan. They regarded Israel's policies in the area as dangerously bellicose and insisted that its continued occupation of Arab lands posed a major potential threat to Middle East and world peace.

After the 1973 oil crisis, Europe's dependence on Middle East oil supplies did add a material interest to the political one in settling the Palestinian crisis. The EEC governments saw an opportunity in the early 1970s to work with Conservative Arab states to secure a role for the Palestine Liberation Organization (PLO) in the peace-making process (in return for PLO recognition of Israel). They attempted, without success, to convince Washington of the merits of this approach.

The Middle East initiative formed the centrepiece of a more general move by EEC governments in the late 1970s to strengthen their foreign policy co-ordination through European 'political co-operation'. The argument was that only by pursuing a common foreign policy could the EEC act with a political weight commensurate with its international economic power. For a period during the British Presidency of the European Community in 1980 the Council of Ministers attempted to give the Middle East peace initiative top priority. This resulted in the so-called Venice Declaration of 1980 which offered the PLO a role in a peace-making process with Israel, in return for the PLO recognizing Israel's 'right to exist'. Israel and the United States resented European intervention in what the Americans saw as their sphere of interest, and both adamantly opposed any recognition of the PLO. This in effect ensured the initiative would be stillborn.

The ill-fated European Middle East initiative was just one

public expression of diverging American and European interests outside the NATO area. The European Community also began to take commercial and diplomatic interest in other regions where their views did not always coincide with those of the Americans, notably in Latin America (Nicaragua and El Salvador) and southern Africa. There was also disagreement within NATO over the appropriate military stance to take in 'out-of-area' crises. Despite pressure from the Carter administration (which was increased under the Reagan administration) the Europeans dragged their feet over proposals to set up an 'out-of-area' American-led NATO strike force.

However, friction between the Europeans and Americans over foreign policy lessened somewhat in the early 1980s as a result of the swing to the right in European politics (with the obvious but temporary exception of France). This resulted in the election of the conservative Christian Democratic-led coalition in place of the Social Democratic-led government in West Germany and in the election of Mrs Thatcher and the Conservative government in Britain in 1979, and culminated in the defeat of the French Socialist government in 1986.

In private even some of the more conservative European leaders despaired of the crudity and lack of understanding of the Americans in handling the aspirations of peoples in the Third World for social justice and political liberty. They disapproved of US links with some of the unsavoury regimes such as Duvalier in Haiti and Marcos in the Philippines. But in public they maintained a 'loyal silence', rather than encourage the growing criticism of American policy by the radical and peace movements in Europe.

Whatever their conflicts with the United States and whatever their reservations about US leadership of the Atlantic Alliance, a major factor inhibiting the Europeans' response remained their own disunity. This was underlined during the 1970s by the seemingly endemic internal paralysis of the European Community as it grew during the 1970s from six to nine, ten, and, in the 1980s, twelve member states.

During the Carter and Reagan years US–EEC trade conflicts began to grow in number and significance. To America, the European Community's Common Agricultural Policy, with its export, production, and storage subsidies and other financial

aids to European farmers, represented an increasingly intolerable breach of 'Atlanticist' free-trade principles. The Americans were particularly angered by the enlargement of the EEC
which had the side-effect of seriously reducing traditional US
farm exports to the protected European market. The Americans lost hundreds of millions of pounds in grain exports alone
on the accession of Portugal and Spain. Indeed, at the start of
1987, both the EEC and the United States were threatening
each other with import sanctions, following conflict over the
collapse of US grain sales to Portugal and Spain. The conflict
was eventually defused after frantic negotiations which led to a
temporary agreement guaranteeing a proportion of America's
threatened grain sales to the Iberian countries.

On the European side there was growing complaint that,
under the Carter administration, America had managed its oil
taxation to give its industry an effective subsidy and thus an
unfair advantage over competing European goods. But the
Europeans also resented the growing *de facto* protection of sensitive industries such as speciality steel, which had been hard hit
by the worldwide recession in steel and by an overvalued dollar.

As we shall see, it has taken a further economic recession in
the early 1980s to bring many of these tensions to the surface, to
the point where the Atlantic-dominated international monetary
and trade system now stands in real peril. But the actions of the
Nixon, Ford, and Carter administrations, together with the
EEC's seemingly systemic disunity and inability to assert itself,
undermined whatever chance existed for a genuine partnership
of equals between America and its European allies.

The realization that a new 'post-Atlantic' era was dawning
began to be reflected in a new mood among American policy
advisers. As Ronald Steel wrote in 1976: 'The Atlantic Alliance
was built on a reality and marketed on an illusion. The reality
was that the US would not let Western Europe fall into Russian
hands . . . . The illusion was that the alliance would lead to a
true partnership of equals with virtually identical interests. The
illusion has dissipated'—and 'Europeans complain but Americans make decisions'.[23]

Even before the election of Reagan the Atlantic consensus
was already in some disarray. Antagonisms over monetary and
trade policies had been kept in check only through the estab-

lishment in 1979 of regular high-level meetings between US and EEC leaders. But from the early 1980s there was a serious risk of sectional conflicts, for instance over agriculture and steel which had spluttered episodically for some years, developing into open trade war.

On the other hand, the Reagan administration held a fairly firm line against the industrial lobbies pressing for more generalized protection against Japanese, European, and other foreign imports. This in part reflected the strongly free-trade ideological base of much of the President's big-business supporters, located as in large measure they were in those regions of the country least hit by the crisis of restructuring which had devastated so much of the North and East, and among the major international corporations.

But the fact that so much of the successful part of US industry now looked 'west' to the Pacific region for growth of trade and investment reduced the economic leverage which pro-Atlanticists traditionally exercised within the US political establishment. The Reagan administration from the start paid more attention to trade relations with Japan, and has even been willing to negotiate bilateral trade deals with Japan on export restraint, which would push the Japanese export offensive towards Europe.[24]

Ideologically, Reaganism also incorporated the ideas of the 'New Right' Chicago School economic monetarism of Milton Friedman. He had campaigned long against the quasi-Keynesian consensus which had dominated US policy-making since Roosevelt's New Deal. But Friedmanism co-existed uneasily with a quite different and, in the final analysis, incompatible school of right-wing analysis known as 'supply side' economics.

The international economic situation which greeted President Reagan on his assumption of office was gloomy. A new economic downturn had begun in 1979. After a brief recovery, the recession became significantly deeper in 1981 and spread to Europe, Japan, and the rest of the industrialized world during the following year. At the same time the new administration, true to the austerity tenets of monetarism, introduced swingeing cuts in welfare-spending in an effort to reduce the alarming growth in the Federal budget deficit, which was approaching $100 billion in 1982. However, in keeping with the 'supply side' dogma, the administration also cut taxes in order to encourage growth and investment in new industries and services. In that sense, what the President's right hand was doing to implement a monetarist strategy (in part to reduce the federal budget deficit) was being undone by his left hand, implementing supply-side tax cuts which merely added to the deficit. At the same time, the President sanctioned the largest increase ever seen in US defence-spending. This rose from $120 billion in 1980 to $265 billion in 1986 and, according to proposals presented by the administration to Congress, is planned to rise to no less than $344 billion by 1990. A major feature of the new arms build-up has been the massive Pentagon support for high-technology research and development in defence-related projects. European industry fears America is using defence-spending to 'leap-frog' back into an unchallengeable position in world hi-tech leadership over the Europeans and the Japanese.[25]

Nowhere has this umbilical link between American escalation of arms-spending and its strategy to secure worldwide dominance in the high-technology sectors been more apparent than in the SDI (Star Wars) unveiled in 1985. This is projected to absorb no less than $2,000 billion in government-spending on research and development over the next twenty years.

Viewed from a wider economic perspective, the Reagan administration's arms-spending programme resembles the so-called Permanent Arms Economy which played such an important part in stimulating and sustaining the long post-war-boom full employment in US and Western economies for twenty years after the Korean War. As an economic strategy it is seriously flawed. Arms-spending now generates fewer jobs per million dollars spent than twenty years ago, not least because of the changing technological character of the defence industries. Even so, the sheer scale of Pentagon contracts for SDI research and development has made a very real material impact on the prosperity of some politically critical regions of the United States.

The dramatic rise in defence expenditure also ran completely counter to the overall administration objective of reducing its federal budget deficit. Under the impact of higher defence-spending and the administration's fiscal policy, the budget deficit mushroomed rather than contracted in the years following

Reagan's re-election in 1984. The scale of the deficit, which in 1986 was predicted at best to plateau out at around $170 billion in 1987, was seen by the international community as the biggest single obstacle in the way of a world economic recovery.[26]

Meanwhile, the US external deficit reached a record $140 billion in 1986 and in response the international value of the US dollar slumped against the Japanese, European, and other major currencies. This reached the point at the end of 1986 where the export-led growth rate of even the most internationally competitive economies, such as Japan and West Germany, were shuddering to a halt.[27]

Despite the slump in the dollar, there were few signs by the start of 1987 that the US trade-balance would narrow significantly. But in an attempt to finance both the budget and the external trade deficit, the administration pursued monetary policies which underpinned international high-interest rates. These reached historically high 'real' levels (that is, allowing for inflation) during the 1980s when the United States absorbed no less than one-tenth of the gross savings of the rest of the world.[28] Inevitably this had a further depressing and destabilizing impact on the world economy. The high-interest-rate regime imposed further crippling burdens on Third World countries by adding to the cost of servicing their already enormous debts. Although outright default by the major Latin American debtor states was narrowly avoided during the mid-1980s, this spiralling debt crisis cannot continue indefinitely without risk of default and thus a possible collapse of the international banking system. The other advanced capitalist economies will find it increasingly difficult to extricate themselves unilaterally from the worldwide regime of high-interest rates and fiscal deflation as long as the US deficits are not drastically reduced. The Western Europeans are, however, in the paradoxical situation of demanding that America cut its domestic and external deficits—although, if this happened suddenly, European exporters would be very hard hit by the resulting economic depression. In the spring of 1987 there were fears that the combination of the high US budget and external deficits, trade conflict involving the United States, Japan, and the EEC, and greatly decelerating world economic growth, presaged a new international recession, Third World debt crises, and even a collapse of prices on the world's stock-markets.

In the present international environment, no country will readily risk its competitiveness by trying unilaterally to pull out of the cycle of low growth and high unemployment if this means currency devaluation and higher inflation. But, by definition, not all countries can simultaneously improve their competitiveness. During the early 1980s a few 'recalcitrant' governments such as the Socialist–Communist coalition in France and the left-wing PASOK government of Andreas Papandreou in Greece did try to reflate their way out of the crisis. The attempts were abject failures and both governments were quickly brought to heel through pressure on their national currencies. The French government's U-turn in adopting monetarist policies led to more unemployment and industrial failures, and created the political environment in which the Right won the 1986 general election and the neo-fascists achieved their largest ever vote in a post-war election.

The Reagan administration did achieve a striking recovery in production (though not in employment) after 1983 but this was due not so much to market liberalization or welfare cuts as to a budget deficit driven by higher defence-spending and tax cuts. In that sense the Reagan administration was running a kind of 'militarist Keynesianism', but one financed by the rest of the world as more and more resources were drawn in from world capital markets to fund the US deficits.

The persistence and magnitude of the US balance-of-payments deficits meant that by 1985 America had become an international debtor as its total international liabilities overtook its total international assets. In short, the Reagan strategy had not succeeded in reversing US decline, but it had contributed mightily to the destabilizing of the world trading and financial systems and thus eroding much of what remained of the European–American consensus about international economic strategy.

The triangular trade relationship between Europe, Japan, and the United States turned from bad to worse as President Reagan's second term progressed. Already during the first term, in January 1982, the *International Herald Tribune* had carried the headline 'US–European trade "shooting war" feared', and the *Financial Times* has reported an impending 'breakdown of free trade' with Japan.[29] The US administration's commitment to international world free trade, reaffirmed at the start of a new round of GATT trade liberalization negotiations in Uruguay in 1986, lessened as the Congress was won by the opposition and more protectionist-minded Democrats in November 1986, and scandals over arms supplies to Iran weakened the Presidency later in the year. Although the administration was convinced that the overall global interests of US capital remained dependent on the preservation of a liberal, international free-trading order, domestic pressure from US industries hit by foreign competition increased sharply.

In 1977 and again in 1980 the administration introduced a system of so-called 'trigger prices' as a blatant means of shutting out cheaper European and Japanese steel imports. The major US steel-producers justified this by claiming that foreign steel, particularly so-called 'speciality steels' were being 'dumped' on the US markets, and in 1986 the United States took similar action against European synthetic textile exporters.[30]

Between Europe and the United States, farm and petrochemical trade (distorted by the artificially low US oil price) proved particularly contentious. In the summer of 1986, before the opening of a new round of trade-liberalization talks in Uruguay, Brussels and Washington had prepared long lists of retaliatory sanctions against each other in the event of open trade war.[31] Faced with intensifying US competition, the Europeans responded by using the EEC Multi-Fibres Agreement to shut out vulnerable, low-cost textile competitors in Asia and Latin America. Meanwhile, US action to reduce Japanese import penetration in highly sensitive areas, such as cars, through the use of 'export restraint' agreements between Washington and Tokyo, resulted in Japan's concerted export offensive being increasingly directed towards the European market.

One dramatic case in point was the American–Japanese cartel agreement to regulate trade in semi-conductors. The EEC countries interpreted this as gravely endangering their own manufacturers and in April 1987 sought a GATT ruling that the agreement was illegal. Ironically, American charges of Japanese bad faith in observing the agreement regulating the prices of semi-conductor exports led to a decision that month by the

Reagan administration to double import duties on a wide range of Japanese consumer durable exports to the United States.

The United States had long resented and opposed the operations of the EEC Common Agricultural Policy (CAP) which now became the main focus of transatlantic trade strife. Many Europeans share the US view of the CAP system of guaranteed prices, paid to farmers irrespective of production levels or market demand. The subsidies for storing and exporting huge dairy, grain, and meat surpluses is indefensibly costly, as well as being protectionistic and leading to high food prices for European consumers. On the other hand, America spends about $25 billion a year supporting its farmers. It has directly and indirectly subsidized them through grants, cheap bank loans, subsidies to deter production, and other measures.[32] Since the early 1980s, it has taken a much more belligerent view of its traditional food-export markets and fiercely resisted EEC-subsidized export sales of surplus food in those markets. To make matters worse, this Atlantic agricultural conflict and the mounting scale of international agricultural surpluses have seriously distorted world markets, depressed prices, and thus undermined viable agricultural production in some of the poorest Third World countries. 'Cut-price' European and US food imports—together with the officially encouraged conversion from subsistence to cash-crop farming in many of these countries—have helped undermine the viability of indigenous farming in Africa and thus contributed to some of the famine disasters there in recent years.[33]

Towards the close of 1986 a major effort was under way in the European Community to cut production of surplus foodstuffs, threatening to hit hard at farm incomes without immediately abolishing surpluses. Apart from farm-trade conflicts, the United States and the EEC were also heading for confrontation over European exports of machine tools, telecommunication purchasing discrimination, and state subsidies for the European Airbus.[34]

By the second half of the 1980s the picture, then, was one of intensifying commercial and trade conflict between Europe, Japan, and the United States. Specific sectoral conflicts had only been contained by a major effort by diplomats and government leaders. But there were signs of a new international economic recession threatening in 1987, and with it renewed pressures for trade protection.[35]

Japan's current-account surplus is expected to reach $100 billion in 1987 and remain at around $125 billion to the end of the decade. In 1986 the US trade deficit had reached $50 billion with Japan and was running at more than half that figure with the EEC.[36] The EEC trade deficit with Japan was running at around $20 billion. The President sent his Treasury Secretary, James Baker, to warn America's trading partners that if they did not reflate their economies more, import more American goods, and thus reduce the US trade deficit, America would certainly go protectionist.[37]

Little wonder that by the early months of 1987 the US dollar had fallen to a record low level, particularly against the currencies of the largest foreign-trade surplus economies, Japan and West Germany. In spite of pressure on these governments to reflate, reduce interest rates, and increase their American imports, the structural imbalance in trade seemed to have gone too far to be readily corrected by such conventional means.

Even without the swing in the US Congress in support of some 300 trade-protection bills, so-called 'voluntary export restraint' agreements were proliferating between the United States and a number of Asian exporting nations covering sectors such as cars, textiles, steel, shoes, and the new information technologies. The GATT Secretariat itself warned that such agreements were progressively undermining the post-war free-trade system.[38]

The increasingly troubled state of American–Japanese trade relations in 1986–7 was further complicated by the scale of inward Japanese investment in the US economy. In a sense Japan's scale of investment was reproducing the traditional relationship which had operated between the United States and those dependent economies in which US multinational capital invested in the decades after 1945. In addition it became clear that without co-operation from Japanese financial institutions in holding US dollars, it would be far more difficult for the American federal government to fund its enormous spending deficit.

With free trade under immense strains and the world monetary order destabilized by the chronic weakness of the dollar, the international economic system seemed to be evolving towards a new global regionalism. Furthermore, international investment by US multinational companies fell from 66 to less than 50 per cent as a share of total world investment by multinationals during the early 1980s.[39]

The tensions generated by the commercial scramble for world markets and spheres of influence in Africa, Asia, the Middle East, and Latin America are adding to the frictions between America and Western Europe about the appropriate foreign and security policies the West should adopt towards sensitive Third World regions. For politics and commercial interests increasingly march hand in hand. Nowhere does commercial rivalry spill more directly over into conflicting foreign and security policy attitudes than in the Middle East, given Europe's continuing dependence on imported oil from that region.

The Middle East market had in the 1970s offered Europe one opportunity to exploit US unpopularity and offset its trade deficits with Japan, America, and the OPEC states during the 1970s. However, the subsequent collapse in OPEC oil-prices in the 1980s reduced the possibilities of a major expansion in trade and investment in the area. Even so, the United States and the EEC clashed over who had exporting rights to sell grain to Egypt.

Transatlantic commercial rivalries have also influenced Atlantic Alliance policy towards relations with the Soviet bloc. America has sought to extend controls on exports of certain high-technology goods to the Soviet Union, ostensibly to prevent their exploitation by the Soviet military system. This was the excuse used to block European contracts for the construction of the Siberian oil-pipeline in 1982.

American use of the NATO COCOM machinery to restrict Western high-technology exports to the Soviet Union has been largely self-defeating but has angered the EEC states. One EEC Commissioner was even led to declare: 'We are in a state of extreme political and economic tension with Washington.'[40] Despite this, Western Europe (and particularly West Germany) is forging closer economic links with Eastern Europe. Indeed, economically, the two halves of Germany work very closely together and have, with the discreet backing of the Bonn and Berlin governments, achieved a remarkable degree of interdependence.[41]

Economic links across the Iron Curtain in Europe are pro-liferating in spite of the unresolved debt problems of a number of East European states. The EEC and Comecon now have a mutual recognition procedure which could lead to intra-European economic relations being placed on a new footing. In the event of a crisis in international trade, such intra-European commercial links will become even more important. However, Western Europe might find itself called on to mount a Marshall-Aid-type programme to prop up the ailing Eastern bloc economies.[42]

For its part America (and some European states) are suspicious of these links, particularly those between the two Germanies, perhaps seeing in them a threat of a future unified and conceivably non-aligned German state. The Bonn government has already rejected criticism by a senior US official of the provision by the Federal Republic of trade credits for East Germany.[43]

Meanwhile, the extent to which East German farmers are already benefiting indirectly from EEC farm-trade intervention is viewed uneasily by the Federal Republic's EEC partners. The other Western Europeans remain uncertain about the extent to which the growing economic links between West Germany and Eastern Europe will and should be encouraged to lead to closer political ties. In the meantime, EEC taxpayers' money can and does end up in the pockets of East German farmers and farm-trade organizations. As Roger Morgan has commented, in his essay 'Britain's partners in Europe', talking about the German Democratic Republic,

Bonn has won the agreement of her partners, ever since the Rome Treaty was signed, to a special protocol by which trade between the two Germanies is regarded by the whole Community not as external trade but intra-community trade, and thus not subject to the Common External Tariff.

This arrangement not only gives West Germany the economic advantage of extensive dealings with the GDR (though, to be precise, the West German taxpayer heavily subsidizes this one-sided trade, whose direct beneficiaries are the individual firms which do the exporting) but also support for the political aim of keeping alive 'the substance of the German nation' which might one day, in a changed East/West context, provide a basis for re-unification.[44]

For its part, the US administration seems to be relying on the effects of the massive dollar devaluation .to halt the drift to trade-war. Since this has the effect of pushing surplus countries into recession, Washington wants the rest of the capitalist world to shoulder more of the responsibilities of leading the inter-national economy out of long-term 'stagflation'. This the Euro-peans and the Japanese are extremely reluctant to do, partly because they believe that the real problem is caused by the runaway spending deficit of the US government itself; partly because they doubt whether the enormous US trade deficit can be corrected by resort to more inflationary policies elsewhere; and partly because the right-wing governments outside the United States are reluctant to jettison monetarist caution to the extent required by the Americans.

This, then, is the economic background against which major strains over foreign and defence policy have opened up across the Atlantic and within the NATO alliance. The impasse in transatlantic relations is going to be difficult to resolve by treat-ing the economic, military, or political symptoms in isolation from each other. Meanwhile, conflicts of interest in one area—whether economic, political, or security—tend to spill over into others, thus contributing to the erosion of the wider system of shared values which bound the governing élites on both sides of the Atlantic. On neither side has much thought been given to working out either a comprehensive reform of the Atlantic part-nership or an alternative strategy for a post-Atlanticist Europe. It would, of course, be quite Utopian to suppose that any ready-made alternative would command the united support of all Europeans in all countries, from all social groups, and irrespec-tive of political beliefs.

As far as the governments of Western Europe are concerned, there is still a blind assumption that the worst will not come to pass. European politicians seem to be gambling on the restora-tion of the Atlantic economic alliance once the Western econ-omies resume stable and sustained growth. But they also know they are treading a tightrope in urging America to conclude a far-reaching arms reduction agreement with the Soviet Union while, at the same time, seeking to prevent the United States making concessions at their own expense as part of such an agreement.

The transatlantic gulf over both economic and security issues is getting steadily wider. The problems over monetary and trade conflicts would be eased if the developed capitalist world found the road back to sustained and balanced growth and full employment. It is, at the time of writing, a most unlikely scenario.

The intertwined crises of the Atlantic Alliance seem destined to become more, not less, intractable. But what shape is Europe in to face the challenges of this crisis?

4 | Britain—The Reluctant European

The story of Britain's relations with its European neighbours since the Second World War is one of political delusion, missed opportunities, and, on occasion, something close to farce. Four decades ago Britain could claim with some justice to be the single most important economic and political force in Western Europe. In 1960 it could still be considered, in spite of the economic haemorrhaging caused by the war, as one of the 'stronger and richer European countries', with a larger industrial output than that of West Germany, France, and Italy combined. By 1970 Britain's relative economic power had radically declined.[1] Today it ranks as one of the weakest economies in the EEC and has still not confounded Dean Acheson's aphorism that Britain, 'having lost an empire, had failed to find a role'.

The causes of Britain's decline (which pre-date the Second World War) are many and complex. But since 1945 a key factor has been the lack of understanding by successive governments of Britain's ability to survive outside Europe without its Empire. Linked to this was a misreading of the significance of developments in Western Europe from the late 1940s to the middle 1970s. Nostalgia for an imperial world-role and a gross overestimation of its own economic and political influence lay at the core of the British establishment's delusion that the United Kingdom could stand aside from European involvement.

But Britain's obsession with its so-called 'special relationship' with the United States and its ambition to act as European linchpin of an Atlanticist economic, military, and political order also lent force to those delusions. For some thirty years Britain experienced the worst of all worlds: it no longer enjoyed any real 'special relationship' with America, its economic and political power had diminished, it was isolated outside the EEC, and it was seen by many other Europeans, in the view attributed to President de Gaulle, as little more than 'America's Trojan Horse'.[2]

It could all have turned out differently. Most other Western

European countries were initially willing to defer to Britain, in view of its role in the defeat of Hitler. They even tried to persuade the United Kingdom to take the leadership of a reconstructed Europe. The smaller Western European states were keen to see Britain retain the links established with many of their governments in exile during the war, partly to offset the power of France and partly to help exorcise the spectre of a revived Germany.

The Christian Democratic leaders of Italy and West Germany, de Gaspari and Adenauer, also saw Britain as the major pillar of a new political order in Western Europe. They appealed (without success) to British leaders not to retreat into an imperial—or, as it became known, Commonwealth—economic and political laager.[3] More striking, in the light of subsequent friction with Britain, post-war French governments were equally convinced that Britain should take the lead in building a united Europe. Jean Monnet, the French Finance Minister (he and his colleague Robert Schuman, the Foreign Minister, were to win the accolade of being the 'Founding Fathers' of the EEC), began a campaign to involve Britain in the construction of a new Europe little more than a year after the end of the war. As Monnet put it, Britain was 'the one great power in Europe' which could be 'a nucleus around which a European Community might be formed'.[4] The French Socialist Party was also convinced (wrongly) that it could persuade the new Labour government to 'think European'. For French and other European politicians of the period, a leading role for Britain in Western Europe would be a guarantee against any revival of an aggressive Germany and might eventually assure Europe's independence from the two superpowers.

America was committed to the goal of a federal union of Europe as being the best way to assure the future of the liberal international trading system sought by the dominant internationalist factions of US business and banking.[5] With the advent of the Cold War, the Truman administration repeatedly pressed the Labour government and the Conservative opposition to take a positive attitude to European Union. There was strong US support for the establishment of the Council of Europe at Strasbourg in May 1949. Indeed, America even encouraged its Western European allies to consider giving supranational powers to the assembly of the Council. And following the outbreak of the Korean War, America threw its weight behind those French politicians who argued for the establishment of a European Defence Community, including the re-armed forces of the Federal Republic of Germany.

Years of desultory discussion about European union first achieved concrete expression with the Schuman Declaration in May 1950, which advocated the establishment of a European Coal and Steel Community (ECSC). This proposal was prepared in conditions of the greatest secrecy and Schuman made sure that it was known first to the US administration and to the West German Christian Democratic government of Konrad Adenauer before even approaching the British government. The Labour Foreign Secretary, Ernest Bevin, was angered at having been excluded from the earlier consultations. When told of it a little later by the French ambassador in London, Bevin commented acidly but presciently: 'I think something has changed between our two countries.'[6] But the British government was in no real position to complain. It had made a habit of consulting Washington on all major economic, military, and political developments before discussing them with its European allies. This had happened just before the Schuman initiative when Britain devalued sterling without any pretence at prior consultation with other European governments, in contrast to the advance notice provided by the United States.

Even before they launched their *démarche* on the ECSC, Monnet, Schuman, and the other French leaders could not have been too sanguine about the likely British response. Lord Plowden, a wartime friend of Monnet, had already tried to discourage him from the notion of British involvement with, let alone leadership of, a continental European supranational community, saying: 'We have won the war and we are not ready to form any special links with the Continent.'[7] The cool, not to say hostile, reaction of the British government to even this limited degree of European integration was due to the quasi-unanimous instinct in the British governing class that 'continental involvement' was a threat rather than an opportunity. The Labour Party leaders, for instance, believed their management of the British economy would be undermined by too close an association with a supranational and potentially interfering

European economic community. Across the political parties there was also a deep sentimental commitment to the Commonwealth, particularly to what was described as the 'old, White Commonwealth'. And there was an all too material appreciation of the Commonwealth's value in its guaranteed markets and privileged sources of cheap raw materials. Finally, the British were convinced that Britain's world-role would be best assured by allowing nothing to interfere with its special relationship with the United States, including any specifically European encumbrances.

In his memoirs Monnet bitterly recalls the characteristic reaction of British politicians of all parties to France's overtures at that time. Britain, he noted wearily and not without bitterness, 'did not wish to let her domestic life or development of her resources be influenced by any views other than her own, and certainly not by Continental views'.[8]

Even when it came to Marshall Aid, the British were qualified in their enthusiasm. The Labour government leaders waxed eloquent about American generosity when the Socialist International met near London in March 1948. But when the Organization for European Economic Co-operation (OEEC) proposed the setting up of a supranational body to manage the distribution of the aid, the British government was quick to express its opposition. Ministers seemed afraid this might be the thin end of a wedge which could lead to Britain's losing control of the sterling area and what survived of British imperial trade preference.

The official British response to talk of European unity was dismissive. The politicians had convinced themselves that Britain, at the head of its Empire turned Commonwealth, could and should remain a front-ranking world power in its own right and without the inhibitions or constraints arising from any overriding commitments to the rest of Europe. The Foreign Secretary, Ernest Bevin, told the House of Commons in 1947: 'His Majesty's Government does not accept the view . . . that we have ceased to be a great power, or that we have ceased to play that role. We regard ourselves as one of the powers most vital to the peace of the world and we still have our historical role to play.'[9]

The enthusiasm of other states for the idea of a European

Federation was patronizingly attributed by British leaders to the recent experience of military defeat or occupation and to economic and political instability. As Bevin's cabinet colleague, Hugh Dalton, wrote at the time: 'No doubt . . . the experiences of war, including the experience of being occupied by the enemy has broken the back of nationalist pride in many of these countries and this helps to popularise the federalist myths.'[10]

For Dalton and others this disdain for the motives behind European Federalism was compounded by fears of loss of national economic sovereignty. Stating that under no circumstances could the United Kingdom join the ECSC, Dalton said this would mean handing the British economy over to a High Authority of 'European dictators, entirely out of reach of any control by the British government or the House of Commons'.[11]

For the Labour Party leaders this fear of loss of economic control, which was to become such a potent factor in later opposition to membership of the EEC, was not entirely fanciful. The state was more directly involved with the productive economy than it was to be in subsequent decades. But Britain's economy remained unquestionably capitalist, with the government's role largely restricted to providing the infrastructure for recovery and managing conversion from war production. Socialism was not on the agenda. Nor is it the case that, during those years, the French were pursuing significantly more liberal, free-market economic policies. The Fourth Republic was beginning at that time to set up the institutions of what later became known as 'indicative planning'. Although they were economic conservatives, Monnet and his colleagues were keen to extend the indicative planning approach on a multinational basis throughout Western Europe.

Neither the kind of planning favoured by Dalton and his colleagues on the one hand nor that pioneered in France by the new Commissariat du Plan on the other, was aimed at a fundamental Socialist reconstruction of society. But in the discussion which led to the establishment of the ECSC in the late 1940s, there was less emphasis on the free-market, *laissez-faire* approach which subsequently inspired the philosophy of the Rome Treaty and the EEC. In any event, it is difficult to see the post-war Labour government's hostility to European union as deriving from a profound attachment to Socialist principles.

Under American pressure the British government abandoned an early commitment to the nationalization of defeated Germany's Ruhr industries. And in the years that followed, the British government helped ensure that West Germany's economic reconstruction would be on unalloyed capitalist lines, despite the opposition, at that stage, of a radicalized German labour movement.

The opposition of the Labour government to 'entanglement' in continental supranational institutions was shared by the Conservative opposition and by the major leaders of British industry and commerce. One exception was Churchill, who emerged from the war as a passionate advocate of European union which he originally saw as embracing all of historical and geographical Europe. It was his speech at Zurich University in September 1946 which ultimately led to the establishment in 1949 of the Council of Europe. In Churchill's view it was possible to reconcile Europe and Empire (as he continued to describe the Commonwealth) provided that Britain asserted its leadership of both. His enthusiasm was not shared by Anthony Eden or by most of the other post-war Conservative leaders, such as Leo Amery, who cited the opposition of the white 'Dominions' as justification for keeping Europe at arm's length.[12] By 1950, while still arguing that Britain should 'sponsor and aid in every way the movement towards European unity', even Churchill had come to recognize that 'with our position at the centre of the British Empire, we could not accept full membership of a federal system of Europe'.[13] It was a position supported throughout the post-war period by most leaders of British industry and finance.

Among the Labour leaders only Bevin originally entertained any real hopes for European unification which he saw through very 'British imperialist' spectacles. As early as the 1938 Labour Party conference Bevin had urged that 'the great colonial powers of Europe should pool their colonial territories and link them up with a European Commonwealth, instead of being limited British, French, Dutch, or Belgian concessions as is now the case'.[14]

Interestingly, the British leaders took the view, in the immediate post-war period, that the Soviet Union would look benevolently on British leadership of a Western European federation. Dalton recounts that Stalin said as much to him in direct conversation: 'Stalin agrees to OUR being the dominant power in western Europe—which he as good as says might be federated under our direction and control—and thinks, very wisely, that Germany should be broken up.'[15]

In Dalton's view the Americans might also agree to this but at a price, namely the transfer of 'our South American or Far Eastern positions' to the United States. Dalton concludes: 'Essentially, the situation is that we can maintain our position as a World Power either by being the centre (economic and political) of the British empire, including the Dominions, OR by leading some European bloc.' It was a conclusion only opposed by small minorities of the Left, including a very few advocates of a 'Socialist United States of Europe'.[16]

The fervour of Labour's commitment to the Empire-turned-Commonwealth, above all to the White Dominions, was striking. The 1950 Labour National Executive Committee statement on European unity, prepared among others by its young International Secretary, Denis Healey, underlined the 'spiritual unity' of the Commonwealth, echoing an earlier argument of Hugh Dalton that 'we are very much closer, in all respects except distance, to Australia and New Zealand than we are to Western Europe'.[17] Speaking to the 1950 Labour Party conference, Hugh Dalton went on to contrast the superior economic, cultural, and political virtues of the White Dominions with the more backward Europeans who, in addition, were quite likely to fall under the thrall of 'reactionaries' who would try to 'decree that we in Britain shall go back to the inter-war years of trade depression and all the rest of it'.[18] In his speech Dalton articulated a variety of reasons, some mutually contradictory, for keeping out of Europe. Appealing to the Left, he referred to the danger from 'European reaction', for the Right he underlined Britain's world role in the struggle against Communism. Addressing the Left he warned of the threat to Labour's 'commitment to planning', while he invited the Right to consider the vastly more profitable economic opportunities opened up within a British-led Commonwealth rather than a semi-bankrupt Europe. Dalton made only one potential half-concession to the advocates of European federalism within the Labour Party. Progressive integration in a new Western

European federation might have more to recommend it, he said, if the other European states could ensure that their colonies were included, in order to 'provide the foodstuffs and raw materials' needed by Britain. But, he went on, this was anyway better assured from Britain's own Commonwealth.

A year earlier, in a document entitled 'The Labour Party and European Unity', Denis Healey had employed Britain's commitment to 'Democratic Socialism' specifically as a useful ideological weapon for the West to employ in stemming the challenge of pro-Moscow Communism in the rapidly developing Cold War. But he went on to cast doubt on the potential of some Western European states (including France and Italy) to follow Britain's lead because of the conflict between planning and a seemingly endemic 'civic irresponsibility and administrative inefficiency'.[19]

After the 1950 election the British government continued to react with the greatest caution to the Schuman plan, the Paris Treaty establishing the ECSC (1952), and proposals to give the Parliamentary Assembly of the Council of Europe wider powers. The strategy was not fundamentally challenged by the Conservative opposition.

Determined to shape the economic and political character of post-war Europe, the Americans made it clear they believed that this reluctance of Britain to respond to the European challenge was a serious error. But with so many other economically and politically unstable European allies, successive US administrations opted to press the European option on the British in private rather than unleash their full armoury of public persuasion and pressure.

The Eisenhower administration took a rather more robust stand and Eisenhower's hawkish Secretary of State, John Foster Dulles, did not disguise his view that Britain was 'the weak sister' in the Atlantic Alliance. He even took the view that the British ruling-class's obsession with playing an independent imperial role was fundamentally in conflict with America's own political and commercial interests. After the Suez episode Dulles said: 'The United States cannot be expected to identify itself 100 per cent either with the colonial powers or [advocates of colonial] independence. There were, I admit, differences of approach by the three nations to the Suez dispute, which perhaps arise from fundamental concepts.'[20] In 1956 Eisenhower refused to back the Anglo-French invasion of Egypt and effectively sabotaged the military operation by refusing to support sterling when it came under pressure on world currency markets before the British had agreed to a ceasefire and withdrawal.[21]

In the early 1950s, however, the British government gave strictly qualified support to the various initiatives for a European political and military Cold War bloc. While being militantly anti-Communist and supporting collective Western defence in the Cold War, the British government insisted that European economic, political, and security co-operation be 'inter-governmental', not federal, in character. And its 'European' aspirations had to be subordinate to the Atlantic Alliance.

The situation in Europe after the expulsion of the Communist ministers from the government in Paris and the completion of Stalin's takeover in Eastern Europe deteriorated rapidly. The British government signed the Brussels Pact in 1948, which led to the formation of NATO. It also took the decision to develop British nuclear weapons, partly because America had earlier decided to deny the British its nuclear secrets. Britain also welcomed the return of US forces to Europe. As Bevin told the Cabinet in September 1948, the original idea was for the United States to send three groups of B29 bombers for the duration of the Berlin crisis.[22] The presence of the proliferating 'temporary' US bases was not regularized until 1950 by which time Britain had joined NATO, which led to a further influx of US forces to the United Kingdom.

To this day the papers relating to the 1951 agreement negotiated by the Labour Prime Minister, Clement Attlee, with the United States over the use and control of American bases in Britain have not been released. The following year, however, Churchill (now Prime Minister) and Truman stated: 'We reaffirm the understanding that the use of these bases in an emergency would be a matter for joint decision . . . in the light of the circumstances prevailing at the time.'[23]

However, under the US Constitution, the American President has sole authority to authorize the use of US nuclear weapons sited in American bases in Britain and can delegate that authority only to other American citizens. The situation is more complex when those weapons are being used on behalf of NATO, but the British input appears to come down to its participation in a 'Combined Chiefs of Staff Committee [including] a representative of the UK Chiefs of Staff'.[24]

While remaining within the Council of Europe, the British remained firmly opposed to its being given real executive power. Dalton characteristically chose the outbreak of the Korean War in 1950 to boast to the Council assembly that Britain alone possessed the worldwide naval and military resources to provide effective support for the UN force (itself overwhelmingly American). The British message to the rest of Europe was clear: 'You need us; we do not need you.'[25]

The gamble of the British political establishment was twofold. First, it assumed that, in practice, the Americans would prop up, rather than directly undermine, Britain's Empire-centred world role. Secondly, it assumed that Britain would broadly maintain its relative economic and industrial position *vis-à-vis* the other European states. It was only during the Macmillan Conservative government of the late 1950s, in the aftermath of the Suez débâcle, that it began to dawn on the establishment that Britain could neither afford to stay outside the EEC nor put its complete trust in a continued 'special relationship' with America.

The Labour Party Left in general was no better at grasping reality during that period. For many on the Labour Left and in the trade union, Dalton's hybrid nationalism, combined with his defence of national 'planning' and invocation of the Commonwealth, had great appeal. Their obsessive concern was to prevent backsliding in the stance of the Labour leadership towards Europe. The grasp of reality by the British Left was hardly more inspiring. There were broadly two tendencies within the Labour Left, the first associated with the Keep Left group and the second a smaller and more nebulous band of European Socialist Federalists; and both played some role over a brief period in questioning the general thrust of official policy during the late 1940s. The group that later formed Keep Left were originally sympathetic to the concept of European unity but saw it covering the whole of Europe. Their bitter opposition to US rearmament policy and to the Cold War division of Europe initially led them to take a similar position towards the

Soviet Union as the Western Communist parties. Both were bitterly critical of Labour's pro-American stance.

However, as Cold War divisions deepened in Europe there was a parting of the ways between most of the Keep Left group and the Communist Party, particularly after the Prague *coup*. Although the Keep Left group had worked on some issues with so-called 'Fellow Travellers', who continued uncritically to parrot the line of the Communist Party and the Soviet Union, it declared its support both for Tito and for other dissidents within the Eastern bloc. In the early post-war period it also expressed support for European federal union which might, or might not, be Socialist from its inception. Arguing that Britain must not allow itself to be separated from Europe, Keep Left insisted:

If we permit ourselves to be separated . . . from the rest of Europe, and if we take cover under the mantle of America, we shall not only destroy our own and Europe's chances of recovery, but also make a third world war inevitable. A socialist Britain cannot prosper so long as Europe is divided.

The goal we should work for is a federation which binds together the nations now under European domination with the peoples of Western Europe. But this is a long way off. For the present it would be wise to concentrate on less spectacular forms of European collaboration designed gradually to remove the Iron Curtain.[26]

For a period after 1947 the Keep Left group took a similar stand on the European issue to the outright Federalists and a third faction, composed of ex-members of the old Independent Labour Party, the Committee for a United Socialist States of Europe. This latter group was opposed to what it saw as the aggressive Cold War stance of US imperialism as well as to the emerging Stalinist dictatorships of the Eastern bloc.

With the worsening of the Cold War in 1948 some of the Keep Left leaders, notably Richard Crossman, effectively abandoned any attempt to hold a 'Third Force' position between the United States and the Soviet Union. The majority of the group, disillusioned with Stalinism, became zealous advocates of NATO membership and the alliance with the United States. The Left Labour weekly paper *Tribune*, which was closely associated with the views of Aneurin Bevan, went so far as to argue that the Soviet Union was 'now the main danger to peace' and urged support for the launching of NATO and for British membership. Ian Mikardo was one of the very few to protest.

The polarization of attitudes within the Left, generated by the heightened tension of the Cold War, particularly after the outbreak of fighting in Korea, highlighted the isolation of the advocates of Socialist European federalism. The idea was seen by some left-wingers as a creature of American anti-Soviet strategy and by others as a threat to Britain's own world role for peace. In the two decades which followed, support for a united, Socialist, 'third-camp' Europe was confined by the pressures of Cold War politics on the labour movement to tiny factions of Trotskyists and other independent Marxists.

The Conservative government which succeeded Labour after the general election of 1951 maintained the policy of bi-partisanal Atlanticism. Indeed, the new government of Winston Churchill was barely a few months old when the Foreign Secretary, Sir Anthony Eden, cautioned the United States not to push Britain towards Europe since this ran 'counter to its instincts'. Eden spelled out his misgivings quite explicitly and said that he spoke 'as an ally on whose effective co-operation you depend'. Referring to 'frequent suggestions that the United Kingdom should join a federation on the Continent of Europe', he was clear as to the outcome: 'We know that if we were to attempt it we should relax the springs of our action in the Western democratic cause and in the Atlantic association which is the expression of that cause.'[27]

Britain was now in an acutely ambiguous position. It was the European NATO state which, more than any other, preached loyal adherence to the alliance and to US leadership of NATO. At the same time, however, British governments refused to accept the US view that Britain should work actively for European union as the cornerstone of Europe's contribution to the Western anti-Communist alliance.

It was possible for Britain to straddle this uncomfortable divide in its loyalties through the 1950s in large measure because America's other European allies, at least until the return to power of General de Gaulle as President of the Fifth Republic in 1958, proved pliantly reliable. Moreover, Western Europe was taking the first increasingly confident steps towards unity without any help from the British.

The 1950s were also the Indian Summer years when it seemed to many in the British establishment that an almost Edwardian-era world-power role had been restored to it. The US government was still prepared to indulge British delusions about the Anglo-American 'special relationship'. British leaders visiting Washington were accorded a protocol status appropriate to being *primus inter pares* among America's client states. However, with the one, still historically controversial instance of Attlee's successful mission to Truman in 1950 to dissuade him from using nuclear weapons in Korea, there is little evidence of any specific British influence over the course of US foreign or defence policy.

Britain might well have been propelled into having to make the kind of choice between Atlanticism and Europe it had so strenuously sought to avoid in the past, had the European Defence Community come to anything. When the proposal was narrowly defeated in the French National Assembly, the British government breathed an almost audible sigh of relief. However, in a compromise designed to assure the association of West Germany with the core European NATO states, the Western European Union was subsequently established. But the WEU never took effective decisions on defence policy as such.

By the mid-1950s the world situation was beginning to change. Quite apart from the shattering of illusions after Suez, these were also the years when the true fragility of Britain's post-war economic recovery was becoming apparent. In the late 1940s and early 1950s British industrialists remained in general as sceptical about the potential of an integrated European market as the politicians were. Their confidence in British industry's dominance over its European rivals was as fervent as it was misplaced. British industry still looked to export markets in the United States and the Commonwealth to sustain the stuttering motors of British growth. As late as 1962 British Conservative MPs such as Peter Walker were still campaigning for stronger Commonwealth trade ties which would rule out the very possibility of Britain's entering the EEC which they said would be 'a great gain for Communism'.[28]

The scale of Britain's decline as an economic and political world power only began to dawn on the British establishment when Harold Macmillan succeeded Anthony Eden as Prime Minister. Two factors seem to have influenced the change of course which was pursued, cautiously and inconsistently, by Macmillan. The first was the growing evidence of British industry's diminishing share of world markets. The scale of the remarkable industrial recovery and potential competitive threat not just from West Germany but from other European economies was also becoming clearer.

There was considerable pressure on the government to reduce the non-productive 'overheads' borne by the British economy as a result of its surviving imperial military commitments. That these were still maintained was in part due to an outdated doctrine of protecting Britain's trading 'lifelines'. But an 'East of Suez' military presence was also justified in responding to any threat of aggression towards, or 'subversion' in, former and still-existing British colonies and protectorates.

The new Colonial Secretary, Ian MacLeod, was given the green light to speed up agreements giving the bulk of the remaining colonies their independence. In addition, the first steps were taken to reduce the enormous costs of maintaining the 'East of Suez' commitments. However, when Labour took office again in 1964 it found these still running to about £100 million a year.[29]

There was a second legacy from Empire—the world-trading and reserve-currency role played by sterling on the international money markets. This was hugely profitable to the banks and other finance and investment institutions in the City of London. They rigidly advocated the primacy of a strong and unchanging exchange rate for sterling in British government economic policy. The result was to saddle the weakening productive sector of the British economy with a grossly overvalued currency, thus precipitating a continuing loss of international competitiveness.[30]

The Macmillan government, like others before and since, was ready neither to confront the power of the City nor to impose the priority of industrial modernization which de Gaulle so avidly pursued after 1958. The result was that episodic attempts to reflate demand in the British economy invariably led to balance-of-trade and payments deficits, and consequently damaging sterling crises. In reaction, the government felt obliged to impose deflationary policies which only weakened British industry further.

Britain was gradually abandoning its remaining imperial commitments, but without being forced to confront the need for an alternative, modernizing strategy. Worse than that, governments maintained other figments of an imperial past, notably a world-banking role, and also perpetuated the myth of Britain being an independent nuclear power.

Operating on his own maxim, 'We must rely on the power of the nuclear deterrent or we must throw in the sponge',[31] Macmillan pleaded with President Kennedy, at the Nassau summit in December 1962, to sell Britain the Polaris missile system. Kennedy was sceptical about the value of a British nuclear capacity but was unwilling to force a crisis over the issue.

Macmillan's stubbornness owed something to pressure from the politically influential armed-services chiefs, and something to the need for a national virility symbol, to avert attention from his wider strategy of disengagement from the responsibilities of Empire. What he did not realize was how this new expression of Britain's 'special relationship' with the Americans would be interpreted in Paris. Suggestions within the Macmillan cabinet for specific Anglo-French co-operation over nuclear arms were never followed through.

It may be that de Gaulle would have found some other excuse for vetoing Britain's first serious bid to join the EEC in 1963, but the Nassau agreement was excuse enough. In the view of the French it proved that Britain would never be a 'loyal European', given its continuing and craven dependence on the Americans. Even West Germany and the Benelux states were now anxious for some belated recognition by the British of the economic and political significance of the EEC and of the role they had always assumed would fall to the British within it.

The French suspicions about Britain's real loyalties were not assuaged by the continuing, if now less public, enthusiasm which the Americans continued to express for British participation in the EEC. Britain, the French believed, could not but act as a Trojan Horse for America's Atlanticist interests within Europe, and was unsuited to membership of the EEC. Matters were made worse by the vain attempt by British governments in the 1950s and early 1960s to erect an alternative Western European economic grouping. This was seen by an increasingly self-confident EEC as another example of the British penchant for misreading the dynamics of European development. No sooner had the Messina Conference of 1955 cleared the ground for the launching of the EEC than the British government backed the creation of the seven-nation European Free Trade Association (EFTA). By 1960, however, the limitations of what a purely free-trade association could achieve were obvious, and after what seems to have been a relatively brief internal debate the Foreign Office, recognizing the inevitable, recommended an early approach by Britain for full membership of the EEC.[32]

The decision to join the EEC was therefore inextricably part of Britain's belated recognition of its economic weakness and decline as a world power. But this was equally apparent to Britain's future EEC partners. It could not but weaken the bargaining hand of British negotiators in the successive attempts to agree terms for full British membership of the EEC. What was less obvious was the subtle change beginning to overtake American enthusiasm for European unity at about this time, in part because of the external tariff barrier erected around the EEC.

It took the full force of that economic decline which hit (and nearly derailed) the Labour government after the sterling crisis of July 1966 to force a change in Labour attitudes. Until that point Labour's strategy towards Europe had consisted of broad support for Conservative attempts first to discourage and then to dilute the supranational element in European institutions, whether the Council of Europe, the ECSC, or the EEC, and to remain outside after 1958. Labour was even more insistent than the Conservatives that any attempt—for instance through the Western European Union—to evolve a more coherent European defence policy should be subordinate to wider NATO and US strategy. The Labour Party was only too ready to seize, from faltering Conservative hands, the banner of the British Commonwealth as the point of orientation for British economic and foreign policy.

Through the 1950s and 1960s Labour had only the scantiest grasp of the significance of the economically dynamic European market. Labour leaders seemed blind to the decline of Britain's commercial dominance, even within the Commonwealth. Political independence, while it perpetuated the former colonies' economic subordination to the industrialized economies, did mean they were no longer obliged to buy from Britain or sell raw materials to Britain at privileged prices.

The former African and Asian colonies used this newly won opportunity to buy in the most competitive market for industrial goods. As a leading banker noted in 1964, 'The signs that Britain is in danger of losing her share of traditional Commonwealth markets are there for all to see . . . . One cannot blame any country for shopping in what it considers the best market. But when one thinks of . . . our long association with the Commonwealth countries, the same language, a sterling currency and common habits as a result of colonisation or administration from this country, this trend can only be described as disappointing.'[33]

British industry found itself increasingly hard pressed by more competitive rivals not only for its share of the expanding European market (where it faced the additional disadvantage of trade tariffs) but, increasingly, in what industrialists had traditionally regarded as their commercial backyard, the Commonwealth.

The 1950s and 1960s were the decades when British capitalism failed to seize its last opportunity to reverse its protracted decline as a world economic power. But while the US economy was only just beginning to be drained by its enormous expenditures on its worldwide military role, Western Europe and, less obviously, Japan were exploiting the potential for export-led growth in a booming world economy, unencumbered by arms-spending burdens. Britain, meanwhile, staggered fitfully from one stop–go crisis to another.

In the period after the ill-fated attempt by the Macmillan government to enter the EEC, the Labour Party leadership was uncertain what its strategy should be. A special committee set up by the Labour Party National Executive Committee to recommend a policy towards the EEC met and weighed the evidence for and against entry for several years without being able to agree a unanimous report. It was clear, however, shortly after the return of the Wilson government in 1964, that there had been a shift of opinion among a section of its leadership in favour of EEC membership. Even so, it remained an issue which deeply split the dominant Labour right wing within the

Parliamentary Labour Party through the years of the Wilson governments of the 1960s and into the 1970s.

One faction, associated with a number of disciples of the then 'revisionist' Labour Party leader, Hugh Gaitskell, and led by Roy Jenkins (later to become President of the European Commission), strongly urged an end to British hesitation and a rapid conclusion of negotiations for EEC entry. They ridiculed traditional Labour arguments that EEC membership was incompatible with Socialism, emphasizing that in the EEC Labour could lead a concerted strategy for economic growth and social justice which would be supported by other progressive EEC governments.

The Labour Left, notably those who looked to the leadership of Aneurin Bevan but also those sections of the wider Labour movement influenced by the attitudes of the Communist Party, remained strongly hostile. Their grounds for opposition had changed little from those advanced more than a decade earlier by Hugh Dalton.

In their most sophisticated form, the misgivings of the Left were set out by the Hungarian-born economist Nicholas Kaldor.[34] He directly challenged the fundamental economic tenet of both Conservative and Labour pro-marketeers, that import liberalization in the EEC would 'dynamize' British industry. The Left warned that exposure to free trade within the EEC would undermine an already enfeebled British industry while the Common Market bureaucracy would be hostile to the kinds of state economic intervention that were needed to protect and strengthen key sectors of the British economy.

In truth the case of the Labour Left against the Common Market was drawn from a mixture of democratic, 'class', and purely nationalist arguments. But in the final analysis the strategy had greatest popular resonance where it was least explicit about the 'anti-capitalist' as opposed to supranational character of the Rome Treaty and the EEC institutions. But at that level the arguments of the British Labour Left had no real point of contact with even the most militantly anti-capitalist sections of the Left elsewhere in Europe.

There is no doubt that the pro-Market Labour right wing were as convinced that exposure to the 'douche of competitive cold water' in the EEC would reverse the decline of the British economy as were the Conservatives under their new leader, Edward Heath. In a note to the Labour Party NEC, Roy Jenkins complained that in recent years Britain had 'been encouraged not to worry about its economic sluggishness. Going into Europe would make it more difficult to go on with this easy going course.'[35]

Thanks in part to Gaullist-inspired declarations of Europe's separate 'destiny' to that of the United States, Labour opponents of EEC entry were less preoccupied with European unity as a mere Cold-War-inspired manoeuvre of American imperialism than they had been in the late 1940s. But the Labour Left had lost nothing of its fervent attachment to the Commonwealth and to entrenched notions of national parliamentary and state sovereignty which they saw threatened by the Brussels bureaucracy and the supranational EEC institutions. These were concerns shared with many on the right of the Party, including Hugh Gaitskell. This explains the ecstatic reaction of many of his erstwhile left-wing critics to his panegyric to all things British in his speech to the 1963 Labour Party conference where he warned that EEC membership would threaten the existence of the Commonwealth and be a betrayal of 'a thousand years of British history'.[36] The Gaitskell group were opposed to EEC entry unless the British government could secure sweeping changes in the system under which EEC rules applied to Britain and in the future relations of both the Commonwealth and EFTA to the EEC. Tactically they concentrated on opposition to the terms which the Conservative government was seeking from the EEC, and by 1962 the Labour Party had come down against membership on the terms available.

The use of openly nationalist and patriotic rhetoric in opposition to the Common Market produced a popular echo in the country. Meanwhile, however, opinion had swung the opposite way in both the Conservative and the Liberal Parties. In those parties anti-EEC feeling was reduced to relatively small groups of right-wing nostalgics and jingoist opponents of links with continental Europe. One Tory MP, Edward Du Cann, later to become chairman of the influential 1922 Committee, accurately predicted that EEC membership would push up prices. But he displayed an all too typical chauvinism of the period when he asked: 'Shall we surrender the right to decide our destiny for ourselves—delegating it instead to other nations less politically stable?'[37] More significant in the long run, 1958 was the last year when the Federation of British Industries (FBI), the principal voice of big business, was to declare itself against membership of the EEC.[38]

The Labour government which was returned in 1964 was still deeply divided about entry. Since Labour's opposition to the Macmillan application had, after much argument, ended up as opposition to the actual terms sought, some ministers were encouraged to reopen the question. The problem as ever was securing conditions which could be sold to a majority of the Parliamentary Party and avoiding a second veto by France.

Some former opponents of EEC membership, such as Richard Crossman and, temporarily, Tony Benn, were converted for reasons of industrial-modernization strategy into Common Marketeers. The Prime Minister, Harold Wilson, conscious that time was running out for British exporters to secure their position in Europe, decided to risk a new application in 1967. This new overture to the EEC was firmly opposed by many of Harold Wilson's former comrades in the erstwhile Bevanite Left and by former Gaitskellites such as Douglas Jay, who resigned from the government in protest at the new bid for membership. But a second de Gaulle veto, even before formal negotiations had begun, effectively scuppered the attempt.

Most leading Labour politicians now realized that membership of EFTA and possession of a Commonwealth were powerless to reverse the continuing and accelerating decline of the British economy. The British industrial and political establishment was now increasingly desperate to secure a place within a still booming EEC to help lift the British economy out of its slowly spiralling decline. They were by now willing to settle for quite modest and mostly temporary concessions from the rest of the EEC, notably on the Common Agricultural Policy (CAP), on EEC budget contributions, and on access to the European market for certain Commonwealth exports, such as New Zealand lamb and West Indian sugar.

The pro-marketeers shared the Conservative view that EEC membership would have a positive, dynamic impact on the

British economy and on manufactured exports in particular. They assumed that, like the Federal Republic, British manufacturing companies were still large enough and competitive enough to win a major share of the still growing EEC market. The costs of phasing out cheaper Commonwealth food and the anticipated payments to the EEC budget were seen at that point as a matter of secondary importance compared to the increase in trade, production, and employment which must follow on access to the EEC market.

This was the goal which the Heath Conservative government pursued with single-minded determination after it was elected in 1970. With de Gaulle removed from the political scene, after his resignation on his defeat in a constitutional referendum, protracted negotiations were completed with the Treaty of Accession in December 1972 followed by actual membership in January 1973. A little over a year later, Labour and Harold Wilson were returned to power, in the wake of the crisis over the miners' strike, power shortages, and the four-day week.

The Labour government subsequently went through the charade of renegotiating membership terms, which culminated in the Dublin summit agreement and only very minor changes in those terms. Then Wilson, aware of the growing strength of the pro-marketeers and the uncertainties of some former opponents, agreed to put the whole issue to the electorate in a national referendum.

The pro-marketeers easily won the day, supported as they were by the government and all the resources at its disposal, the national media and the weight of supposedly expert testimony that economic growth and full employment could best be assured inside and not outside the market. It was a campaign almost exclusively focused on bread-and-butter issues, for instance the impact of the EEC on jobs and pay. Little attention was given to the wider political issues, such as the palpable lack of real democratic accountability of the EEC decision-making institutions, or to the significance of the changing American–European relationship.

By 1967 American enthusiasm for European unity was waning, partly because of the emergence of economic frictions, and partly because of the political conflicts between Washington and Gaullist France which had culminated in France leaving

NATO's integrated military command and expelling its head-quarters from Paris in 1966. In 1969 the US Commerce Secretary, Maurice Stans, warned that America intended to 'mount a full scale counter attack' on EEC non-tariff trade barriers.[39] A year later the US ambassador to the EEC spoke of the 'irritation, frustration and brooding sense of apprehension' over Europe's attitude to the 'economic problems and the political and military burdens carried by the US'.[40] The same year a senior White House aide said he did not 'see any way to avoid an economic Cold War between a growing EEC and ourselves'.[41] The outcome was that in 1973 Britain joined the Community which was already drawing away from the United States. It would be much more difficult in future for Britain to remain with one foot on each side of the Atlantic. Moreover, Britain joined the EEC too late either significantly to influence its institutional and political evolution or to benefit from the promised economic bonanza. The experience of the past decade of membership has been a bitter one, in which the worst fears of the anti-marketeers about Britain's economic performance and the rigidity of key policies, such as the CAP, seem to have been borne out.

The reality is more complex. The continued decline of the British economy owes little, in itself, to the operations of the Common Market. Being in the EEC has rather exposed the appalling long-term underlying weaknesses of the British economy. The hopes held out for British industry in the EEC were simply too ambitious given its long-term atrophy. Speaking at the Lord Mayor's banquet in the City in 1972, Edward Heath had promised that Britain could now 'break out of the depressing circumstances which have confronted us for so long; the gradual decline in our economic strength and the decline in our traditional markets and outlets. We can now, at last, take advantage of our European partnership to win new influence and greater prosperity.'[42] By the end of the 1970s these hopes were seen to be a chimera. Britain's trade deficit with its EEC partners rocketed, unemployment rose, and the gap between UK and EEC living-standards widened.

The ultimate irony was that Britain finally managed to secure EEC membership at almost the precise moment when the long post-war boom in the Western capitalist economies was giving

way, in succession, to monetary instability, rampant international inflation, major increases in oil prices, recession, and
mass unemployment. The Labour governments of the 1970s
made little effort to rally European governments to a concerted
economic recovery strategy. Although the global scale of the
crisis was unmistakable by the mid-1970s, Labour was indifferent to the need for a recognizably European Socialist alternative strategy. Both the Labour government and the new
Conservative government led by Margaret Thatcher, elected in
1979, continued to oppose sterling's participation in the
exchange-rate mechanism of the European Monetary System
(EMS), launched in the same year.

The inability of British industry to exploit its access to a 250-
million-strong market meant that the entry costs of membership, notably the costs of the CAP and the related issue of
Britain's annual net payments to the EEC budget, loomed large
in the decade after accession. Mrs Thatcher launched a strongly
nationalist campaign to get a ceiling on Britain's payments
which was conceded after a bitter and divisive series of negotiations in 1984.

It was only by the end of 1986 that EEC farm ministers took
the first steps to bring the CAP under control. But the EEC still
faced 1987 with a likely budget deficit of more than $2 billion,
and it was far from certain whether the belated farm-spending
curbs would make an impact on the Community's astronomic
financial deficit.[43]

After ten years' experience of British membership of the
EEC, the more idealistic expectations of Britain's partners had
been disappointed. The combination of an enfeebled economy
and an inability to choose between an Atlantic and a European
role had prevented the United Kingdom from playing an effective role within the Community.

Successive British governments have taken a 'minimalist'
position on key issues of institutional reform such as majority
voting in the Council of Ministers, while the Thatcher Conservative government has been foremost among the member
states denying the Community the financial resources it needs
to address key industrial, technological, social, and regional
problems.

The British have been keen on greater political co-operation among member states but an unwillingness to confront American opposition to important European foreign-policy initiatives has resulted in many of them, such as the Middle East initiative of 1979, being stillborn. The British government has been among the most supine in the EEC in the face of the American injunction against any serious attempt by the Europeans to formulate a separate policy on arms control. Along with West Germany Britain was the first to acquiesce in the restrictions placed by the United States on security and disarmament discussions within the Western European Union.

Britain has certainly not been the only country to drag its feet over developing an independent European economic, political, or security policy. The West German Christian Democratic/ Liberal coalition, led by Helmut Kohl, has proved equally obstructive to attempts to achieve internal institutional reform and equally weak-kneed in challenging US policy within the Atlantic Alliance. It remains to be seen whether the election of self-proclaimed 'Socialist' governments in Western Europe in the years ahead will result in greater European autonomy in economic, political, and security policy. The precedents, to judge from the failures of the French, the Greek, and the Spanish Socialist-led governments, are not encouraging. The moral seems to be that failure to make radical changes in domestic policy sooner rather than later undermines the will and capacity to carry through radical changes in foreign and defence policies. That could well be the fate of European governments whose courage in the face of US hostility does not match their reforming ambitions at home.

The British Labour Party has obviously altered its general stance towards the EEC since the defeats of 1979 and 1983. The leadership openly and realistically accepts that withdrawal is not a viable economic or political option, not least given its wider acceptance of the economic status quo. Indeed, it would like nothing better than to see an end to the argument about withdrawal and to concentrate on developing some kind of economic and social reform programme in co-operation with the other Socialist parties within the EEC. The Labour Left, too, has had second thoughts about the largely nationalist and isolationist nature of its past opposition to Common Market membership. There is far more interest now in developing closer contacts with like-minded Socialists in the European peace, feminist, and trade-union movements. European trade-union support for the British miners during their long strike in 1985 revived left-wing enthusiasm for closer contacts in Europe and even for tentative attempts—which we will discuss later—to hammer out a common Socialist strategy for the whole of Europe.

Ironically, the British Labour Party is in danger of moving from a narrow-minded opposition to all things European to a superficial infatuation with the institutions of the EEC. While a serious involvement in the work of those institutions would be a great step forward, there is a danger that Labour will ignore the restrictive impact of the Treaty of Rome on even the most modest strategies for national economic revival where these conflict with EEC rules on competition or the free movement of capital.

A review of the Rome Treaty and the changes which need to be made to its more extreme free-market provisions, in the light of Europe's deep-rooted structural industrial problems, is long overdue. A new European Treaty would, of course, be a major project. It could only be attempted on a supranational basis, rather than on a nationalist one. However, none of the established parties of the Confederation of European Socialist Parties has yet even raised this issue seriously, partly because they envisage few radical alterations to the EEC status quo. But without fundamental changes in the Rome Treaty, it is going to remain an obstacle, if not the major obstacle, in the path of any radically Socialist government which is obliged to take purely national action to protect jobs and key industries, in the absence of an agreed, collective strategy by governments across the Community to achieve the same goals.

However, outside the orthodox political structures, the women's movement, the ecologists, the peace movement, and the trade unionists have all raised questions of policy and strategy which can only be addressed on an all-European basis. None of the mainstream political leaderships has yet responded to this new constituency for European development. It could, ironically, fall to the radical Left to take up the banner of European unity, in the period ahead.

ㄅ | Dawn in the East

The end of the war against Hitler saw the Soviet Red Army and its allies in occupation of virtually all of Central and Eastern Europe. The Kremlin's erstwhile allies were quick to interpret Russia's absorption of these states as fulfilling long-laid plans by the Soviet Union to extend its frontiers westwards. Many of them were convinced that expansion reflected Stalin's commitment to the Bolshevik Party and Communist International goal of spreading the Communist Revolution to the rest of Europe.[1]

It soon became obvious that the Soviet Union would maintain its *de facto* military occupation and political control of most (though not all, as the case of Finland showed) of the territories it had originally helped to liberate from the Nazis or regimes allied with the Nazis. But was this evidence of any Messianic revolutionary mission? The final proof for the increasingly influential anti-Communist ideologues in the United States and Western Europe during the 1940s was the sweeping Stalinization of Eastern Europe unleashed by Moscow in 1947.

All surviving elements of political pluralism, whatever the juridical formalities about 'people's democracies', as well as the remnants of private capitalism, were swept away. A despotic dictatorship and a monolithically centralized, state-owned, and state-controlled economy were installed in their place.

Forty years on we can see more clearly how the Stalinization of Eastern Europe owed much more to the conservative geopolitics of the Soviet bureaucracy than to any commitment to revolutionary international political change. From the mid-1920s, when Stalin consolidated his grip on the Soviet Communist Party and the state machine, his foreign or domestic policies were already inspired by 'Realpolitik' calculation, not by any residual revolutionary Bolshevism.

Joseph Stalin headed a new bureaucratic class which had seized power in a Russia whose economy had been all but destroyed and whose revolutionary political ideas had been politically subverted by the isolation of its revolution and the terrible civil war which followed. Stalin proceeded to purge the Communist Party and the state machine of the generation of Bolsheviks who had made the revolution and replace them with a privileged caste of acolytes, opportunists, and political career-ists, many of whom were themselves subsequently to be liquid-ated in the 1930s.

A profoundly conservative despot, Stalin legitimized his nationalist strategy for the building of an independent industrial economy in the Soviet Union in a new doctrine of 'Socialism in one country'. This dogma replaced the Leninist belief in the essentially international character of the Socialist revolution, for want of which, they believed, workers' power in Russia would ultimately be doomed.

More than a decade before the Second World War, the policy of the Communist International and pro-Moscow Communist Parties was basically determined by the foreign-policy interests of the Soviet state as Stalin saw them, not by any strategy for international revolutionary change. This policy led Stalin to make alliances with virulently anti-Communist forces such as those of Chiang Kai-shek and the Kuomintang in China, even though this led directly to the near liquidation of the Chinese Communist Party.[2]

To anyone who cared to listen to him during the war years it was clear that Stalin would seek a post-war order in Europe that left the Russian bureaucratic ruling-class free to consolidate its power. An almost totally isolationist economic autarchy was deemed necessary to force through the rebuilding of the Soviet Union's shattered industry to the point where it could secure the independence and security of the Stalinist system from international rivals as well as domestic subversion. In that sense the perspective and outlook of Russia's rulers was comparable to the xenophobic isolationism and suspicion of foreign influences which marked Shogunate Japan after the first contact had been made with the West in the seventeenth century. There were even some parallels with the political isolationism which marked the United States after the First World War.[3]

Stalin was prepared at Yalta to abandon any pretence of sup-porting Communist revolution in the rest of Europe. Hence the understanding whereby he gave the British a free hand against the anti-Fascist and anti-Royalist partisans in Greece, who were led by the Greek Communist Party, in return for non-interference in Russia's reorganization of the internal affairs of the occupied territories in Eastern Europe.[4] At Yalta the three allied leaders even went through the farce of confirming what precise degree of influence each might exercise in the countries of divided Central Europe. But in essence Moscow's objective was to achieve recognition of its domination of a line of buffer states between itself and a potentially 'revanchist' Germany or an over-ambitious America.

The Russian bureaucracy initially displayed no interest in transforming the Eastern European states into mirror-image replicas of the Russian system. Provided that Moscow, acting directly and through subservient local Communist parties, decisively controlled foreign and security policy, they were content to leave whole sectors of the economy in private hands. They actually preferred governments of pliant non-Communist Social Democrats, peasants, and even far-right parties to governments based on the popular anti-Fascist resistance forces.[5]

Any popular revolutionary movement which looked as if it might threaten the established state and a private-property-based economy, the Soviet authorities moved to crush. This even applied in cases where anti-Fascist partisans moved against known wartime collaborators.

Reporting on the revolutionary upheavals in Bulgaria during the liberation from the occupying Nazis and their right-wing Bulgarian collaborators, *The Economist* reported that the situation vividly recalled 'the picture of the Russian army in 1917. Soldiers' councils have been set up, officers have been degraded, red flags hoisted, normal saluting has been abolished. Molotov intervened declaring: "If certain communists continue their present conduct we will bring them to reason. Bulgaria will remain with her democratic government and her present order . . . "[6] The *New York Times* reported that the Russian authorities had ordered local Communists to hand back control of city halls to officials of the wartime regime.[7]

In Romania the local Communists were ordered into a co-alition led by right-wing, anti-Semitic politicians such as Georges Tatarescu. As late as 1947, Prime Minister Groza made it known that on advice from Moscow the government 'did not intend to apply either collectivisation of land or nationalisation of banks and industries'.[8] The leader of the Communist-controlled National Democratic Bloc pledged himself and the government 'to fight together for the consolidation of the monarchy, because we are convinced the King is the strongest factor that rallies all Romanians. We shall fight for the consolidation of the national church and of private property, the source of all private enterprise.'[9]

The story was much the same in Hungary where the political report to the 1946 congress of the Communist Party insisted: 'This is not the time for transition from capitalism to socialism . . . but of the struggle between democracy and reaction within capitalism.'[10] There were even cases of private estates being handed back to their owners.

In Czechoslovakia land was redistributed (but only collectivized after 1948). Much of industry and finance was also taken into state control, but most of the enterprises so nationalized belonged to capitalists from the German-speaking minority which was in the process of being brutally evicted from the country. Both the expropriations and the mass evictions of the German minority were carried through with the enthusiastic support (and in some instances instigation) of the Social Democrats and other non-Communist parties in the post-liberation coalition.[11]

In Poland, too, the bulk of the decrees nationalizing industry applied to enterprises abandoned by the eight million Germans expelled when Poland was allowed to annexe part of Eastern Germany in compensation for the loss of territory on its eastern borders with the Soviet Union. But in Poland, more than elsewhere in Eastern Europe, the occupying Soviet power was faced with the bitter opposition of a people who retained vivid memories of the Hitler–Stalin Pact and the subsequent partition of their country.

It was more difficult for the occupying Russians to ensure 100 per cent subservience by Polish ministers. Some individual members of the post-liberation government did protest about the loss of lands to the Soviet Union, the absence of genuinely free elections, and overweening Soviet domination. But as early as 1943 the United States and, especially, Britain had decided to let the Soviet Union have its way in Poland. After 1945 the Western allies did little more than mutter disapprovingly.[12]

For the first few years after the occupation of Eastern Europe the Russian interest was narrowly material, almost piratical: the expropriation of wealth by both direct physical and indirect trading means justified as legitimate war reparations as agreed at Yalta. According to authoritative studies Russia extracted resources worth some $20 billion from Eastern Europe between 1944 and 1953.[13]

As well as the dismantling of plant and machinery and its transportation to Russia, the bureaucracy also rigged the terms of its trade with its East European clients and until 1954 used the means of jointly owned companies to achieve a similar resource transfer. But the Soviet leaders were vigilant in preventing any moves towards economic, let alone political, federation which might strengthen the relative position of the Eastern European satraps *vis-à-vis* the Soviet Union itself.[14]

During this period the working class in Eastern Europe, theoretically the agency of Communist revolution, was not allowed to play any independent political role, let alone encouraged to secure fundamental economic or political change. After the outbreak of open Cold War in 1947, comprehensive Stalinization was imposed from above, through the existing state machinery and without any independent action by the workers or their organizations.

The rulers of the Soviet Union, while insisting on its unchallenged hegemony of Eastern and part of Central Europe, would probably have continued to operate through the buffer states and allow them varying degrees of formal independence but for the drastic deterioration in East–West relations through 1946 and 1947. The conflict between Washington's increasingly self-confident global strategy after 1947 and Stalin's paranoid isolationism sealed Europe's fate. The Kremlin not only opposed popular upheavals or revolutionary change in their Eastern client states, they insisted that the pro-Moscow Communist parties in Western Europe collaborate with (and, in the case of France and Italy, actually participate in) 'bourgeois' post-liberation governments. As a result the French and Italian Communist parties loyally disarmed the wartime partisan forces and opposed demands for workers' occupation of the factories to establish their power. Stalin even persuaded the French Communist Party to support the reassertion of French control of

Indo-China.[15] In Britain this temporarily produced the bizarre result that prior to the 1945 general election the Communist Party actually opposed the return of a majority Labour government and urged instead a coalition to include 'progressive' Conservatives such as Churchill and Eden.[16] At the same time the Soviet leaders were determined not to be forced into the American 'open' world economic system which, they were convinced, would condemn Russia to economic and ultimately political subordination. This would have prevented the rebuilding of Soviet autarchic economic power as well as rendering the Stalinist system vulnerable to political 'subversion'.

The single issue, then, which more than any other led to the Cold War and sealed the division of Europe was the refusal of the Russians to participate in the American-envisaged post-war world order. The mere existence of a powerful Soviet state, albeit one without any serious commitment to the overthrow of international capitalism, standing outside (and in economic rivalry with) the new Atlanticist world order, was an affront to many in the US political establishment. From early on President Truman took a more uncompromising line over relations with the Soviet Union than his predecessor, Franklin Roosevelt. His self-confident belligerency in handling the Soviet leaders was enhanced by the outright American monopoly of nuclear weapons, after the bombing of Hiroshima and Nagasaki. Although Poland was already a subject of dispute, after the Potsdam summit East–West relations steadily deteriorated.

The predictable Soviet rejection of Marshall Aid confirmed the determination of the Soviet Union and its satraps to remain outside (and increasingly suspicious of) the emerging economic and political order in Western Europe. As economic conditions deteriorated in 1947 the Communist parties were thrown out of the French and Italian governments. In response Moscow sanctioned a superficial and temporary left turn, involving support for militant trade-union action by the Western Communist parties. This, in turn, was interpreted by America and its allies as evidence that Moscow was seriously planning to 'subvert' Western Europe as part of a strategy to ensure its ultimate domination. The negotiations with the Russians over the future constitution of Germany, seen by Stalin as a Western plot to unleash the forces of 'German revanchism' against the Yalta settlement and thus directly threaten the Soviet Union, broke down. In an atmosphere of near-military confrontation, Moscow made a drastic turn of policy towards the Eastern European states, unleashing a total takeover by the local Communist parties and so completing the comprehensive Stalinization of those regimes. There followed a clumsy attempt to force the Western powers out of Berlin and a *de facto* Soviet economic blockade of Berlin. This in turn led to a highly organized Western airlift to the city and an eventual Soviet climb-down.

The rearmament and remilitarization of both sides during this period ensured the finalization of the European division not only into two ideological, economic, and political camps but into two armed blocs.[17] In that sense the Stalinization of Eastern Europe was a defensive response to what the Soviet leaders saw as a growing threat in the West to weaken and ultimately undermine the very basis of Russia's separate development and independent power and to draw its buffer states in Central and Eastern Europe into the American economic and political orbit.

That said, the Prague *coup*, the Berlin blockade, and the elimination of any residual political freedom in the Soviet-bloc states contributed directly to the finalization of the division of Europe.[18] Even Western Europeans hostile to the United States and sympathetic to the Soviet Union were aghast as the tentacles of bureaucratic despotism extended into every aspect of social and political affairs in the Eastern bloc. Not only were the state apparatus and the political system purged of all elements with any genuine independence of the Communist party, but even within the Eastern European Communist parties purges and liquidations from 1948 onwards ensured the elimination of all independent or potentially independent factions. The zealousness of these purges was intensified by Moscow's horror at the one successful case of resistance, by the Yugoslav Communist Party leadership.

Tito's defiance of Stalin was made possible by the unusual circumstances in which the Yugoslav Communists had come to power. The liberation of Yugoslavia from the Nazis was accomplished almost solely by domestic partisan forces under Communist leadership and owed virtually nothing to external support. Furthermore, the Red Army had been withdrawn from Yugoslavia before 1948 and, despite US indifference to the fate of the Titoites, Stalin had no effective means of imposing his will on Yugoslavia.[19] There was, in fact, no fundamental conflict between Moscow and Belgrade over the kind of economic and political system which should exist in Yugoslavia. Rather the split was due to important factions within the Yugoslav leadership, which had long experience of Russian nationalist arrogance towards other pro-Moscow parties and their willingness to submit and sacrifice Yugoslav interests at Moscow's whim. The pretext for the purge of so-called Titoites in the other Communist states was a totally fictitious series of conspiracies. There is no doubt that the purges bred deep national resentments and an ultimate ambition by the Eastern European regimes to exercise greater autonomy. Indeed, it was the origin of the persistent tensions that have existed between the pro-Moscow and more nationalist factions in the Eastern European Communist leaderships ever since.

Although the end of the first phase of the Cold War eased some of the worst features of Stalinist repression, notably after the dictator's death, the revolt of the East German, Polish, and Hungarian workers in the 1950s was followed by the crushing of all open dissent. It was not until the mid-1970s that many of the national Communist leaderships felt they had the space and opportunity to pursue (cautiously at first and with an eye permanently on Moscow) a more independent strategy.

The post-war decades confirmed that the Stalinist economic system itself was ridden with profound contradictions. Within the Soviet Union in particular bureaucratic privilege, monstrous waste, chronically low industrial productivity, the systemic failure of agriculture, and above all, the massive distortions and the economic burden of the arms race, generated deep internal strains in the system. They were, of course, a source of acute vulnerability in the struggle with the United States. For their part some influential US arms strategists have always regarded the destabilizing impact on the Soviet economy of any new generation of weapons systems or technologies as a key argument in favour of their development and deployment.

Many of these features were reproduced in the other Communist states of Eastern Europe and reflected in the Council for

Mutual Economic Assistance (Comecon) set up in 1949 to co-ordinate the development of the Eastern European economies. Long after the immediately post-war direct transfer of industrial and other assets to Russia had ceased, the internal terms of trade between the Soviet Union and its partners remained in favour of the former.[20]

By the early 1960s the strains arising from the low productivity and technological backwardness of the entire Communist bloc was becoming apparent to the authorities. The economies of the Soviet bloc were experiencing increasing difficulty in matching the high-technology-based US arms developments, particularly after the advent of intercontinental ballistic missiles and more sophisticated anti-ballistic missile defences.

The death of Stalin, fears of workers' uprisings over living standards, and the opportunities of *détente* all pushed the Eastern-bloc regimes towards economic 'liberalization' involving the reform but not the dismantling of the bureaucratic command model of national planning. The Eastern European economies were allowed to increase their trade with the West, which was already expanding faster than trade with the Soviet Union, in order to acquire the high-technology products so desperately needed to modernize industry.[21]

However, liberalization necessarily had to involve some degree of political reform as the Czech events of 1968 illustrated, when an initially economic programme of reform led to the 'Prague' spring of political liberalization. It was extremely difficult for reformist factions of the bureaucracy to control this process so that it did not trigger popular expectations for a more fundamental transformation of the system. But over the past decade the different Eastern European governments have acquired, to varying degrees, greater autonomy from Moscow.

The Eastern European states have even occasionally challenged Russian policy within Comecon. At the same time several Eastern European governments have frequently pursued commercial (and implicitly political) links with the West further and faster than Moscow wished, at least until the emergence of Mr Mikhail Gorbachev.[22]

Apart from the special position of Yugoslavia, Hungary has particularly close trading links with the EEC countries and it is there that market liberalization has been taken furthest.

Moscow has conceded the EEC's right, which it did not 'recognize' for many years, to negotiate detailed commercial cooperation agreements with Russia's satellite states. This may well reflect at least a tendency in Moscow to accept that the Comecon bloc as a whole, including the Soviet Union, must forge closer economic and possibly political links with Western Europe if only to acquire urgently needed Western technologies.[23]

The progressive integration of the Eastern European economies into the world economy has now reached a very advanced point and some of them are as a result significantly dependent on Western European markets. But this integration is Janus-faced. On the one hand it has enabled the Eastern-bloc economies to effect a degree of restructuring and modernization; on the other, it has made them dangerously vulnerable to the cyclical and other crises of the international system. Yugoslavia, Hungary, Romania, and Poland have been hard hit by the successive international inflations and recessions from the early 1970s. They have also been burdened by their accumulation of enormous bank debts to cash-rich Western banks. Servicing these debts is crippling some Eastern European economies, particularly since the worldwide increase in interest rates. However, the regimes have so far opted for austerity and lower living standards rather than risk Western disapproval by defaulting on those debts.[24]

These developments have temporarily driven the Eastern European states back closer to the Soviet Union. But their basic objective is to manoeuvre between East and West without having to make a fundamental choice. This policy has been pursued avidly by the Ceauşescu regime in Romania. While internally the most Stalinist state after Albania in Eastern Europe, Romania has publicly and sometimes provocatively pursued an independent foreign and security policy, perhaps in part because of—certainly in spite of—its parlous economic crisis, probably the worst in Eastern Europe.

The story of Eastern Europe since 1945 cannot be reduced to one of bureaucratic tyranny punctuated by episodes of managed liberalization. Through the past forty years the peoples of Eastern Europe have episodically sought to shape their own destiny. Even during the most repressive phase of Stalinization, deep currents of opposition and revolt have flowed beneath the surface and on occasions dramatically asserted themselves. Since the early 1950s there has been an almost cyclical sequence of mass protest movements, revolts, and outright revolution, and their influence remains potent today. All these oppositional movements have had three striking characteristics: they were infused with profound opposition to the Soviet Union's oppression of their countries; they reflected the deep alienation of the mass of the working people from the Stalinist economic system; and, lastly, they explicitly envisaged a future reunification of Europe outside the Cold War alliances.

The first of these movements was the revolt of the East German workers in June 1953, which was only put down after several days of bitter street fighting between striking East German workers and Soviet tank forces. The spark which exploded the powder keg was a revolt by factory workers against a new increase in the crushing work norm imposed by the regime. However, this was suffused with a barely concealed resentment of the all too visible presence of the occupying Russian forces. Official propaganda put out by the East German leadership at the time attempted to discredit the revolt by suggesting it had been organized by 'right wing, revanchist circles in the West supported by the United States'.[25] In fact the West, including the West German workers' movement, stood by as an impotent witness to a revolt which none had predicted, let alone instigated, and felt powerless to help.

As shown in the leaflets and other material put out by the strikers at the time, the revolt was as opposed to any return to capitalism as it was to totalitarian Stalinism. Indeed, one theme which emerged during those few days and which was to recur in Hungary and Poland was the notion of industrial self-management, of democratic workers' control of new forms of social ownership distinct from both the capitalist corporation and the Stalinist bureaucratic model of planning and production.[26]

Another feature of the East German revolt was the presence among its leading militants of many former or actual Communists. Many of these had joined the Communist Party during the 1930s and 1940s, genuinely believing that it was the only consistent force fighting Nazism and that the advent to power of the Communist parties would lead to profound political and social liberation, not the monstrous, nightmarish caricature of Socialism which emerged.

Just three years later, Soviet hegemony in Eastern Europe was confronted with a far greater challenge. The Hungarian revolution of 1956 did not come completely out of the blue. It had been preceded by bitter protests, including strikes, in a number of Eastern European countries, most notably Romania. But the climate which made the Hungarian movement possible was brought about in large measure by a partially successful movement for reform in neighbouring Poland.[27] Although the protests in other countries had been effectively suppressed, the Polish movement was on such a scale that it could only be met by concessions on the part of the government and the Soviet authorities. The emergence of a 'reform' faction of the ruling Polish bureaucracy in place of the most unpopular figures most closely associated with the worst Stalinist excesses, was designed to buy time by meeting some of the immediate demands of the people. The initial demonstrations by workers and students in Hungary were in solidarity with the Poles but also sought the removal of those Hungarian leaders responsible for earlier purges. As Gomoulka appeared as a 'reform' leader in Poland, so in Hungary Imry Nagy replaced ultra-Stalinist leaders such as Matyas Rakosi. But by then the initiative for the protests had passed to more radical workers and students determined to achieve the removal of the Russians and fundamental, rather than merely cosmetic, changes in the system.[28]

The story of the revolution is well enough known, but one fundamental feature which has never received proper attention was the emergence of workers' councils as embryonic centres of dual power and an alternative democratically self-managed economic system. Not only were workers' councils set up to give expression to the demand for democratic social ownership and control of industry, but they were becoming increasingly co-ordinated, through the Budapest-based Central Workers' Council, when the Soviet leaders decided on military intervention to crush the revolution.[29]

While there were undoubtedly many diverse political currents present in the Hungarian movement, two key features do stand out. The first is the notion of an independent and non-aligned Hungary, free to associate with like-minded states elsewhere in Europe.[30] The second is a commitment to a 'third road' form of economic and political development, distinct from both Western capitalism and Stalinism.

Although its challenge to the prevailing order was initially limited, the movement thrown up by the 'Prague Spring' of 1968 was radicalized after the Soviet invasion. In the Czech case, however, the popular movement initially played a purely supportive role to the manoeuvres of reform-minded politicians within the regime, led by Dubcek, who were willing to mobilize the working population within defined limits to press for concessions from Moscow.

In the great strike movements in Poland in the early 1970s and again around the birth of the Solidarnosc trade-union movement after 1980, the element of popular and potentially revolutionary mobilization was dominant. Whereas the early challenges to the prevailing order in Eastern Europe were successfully suppressed or apparently defused by the Soviet Union and its allies, the Polish movement remains a smouldering fuse capable of igniting again in the future. Solidarnosc, and the radical Polish oppositionist tendencies within it, have developed a sophisticated analysis and ambitious ideas both on internal economic and political change and in Poland's relations with the outside world. Some of these were set out in the early 1970s by the Committee for the Defence of Workers (KOR) militants, like Jacek Kuron, who has played an influential role as adviser in the Polish movement since.[31]

Apart from Solidarnosc in Poland and the Charter 77 in Czechoslovakia, which have so far defied efforts to destroy them, there are openly oppositionist peace, ecological, and human-rights groups operating both in East Germany and in Hungary. Dissent in countries such as Romania and Bulgaria is still confined as far as can be judged to isolated individuals, while Albania, even post-Hoxha, remains the most totally Stalinized of the Eastern European states. But some opposition groups, including independent Marxists, operate in 'liberal' Yugoslavia only with difficulty and subject to episodic and arbitrary repression by the authorities. However, outside Poland, the largely activist base of the small dissident groups has not yet achieved anything like the status of mass movements.

Prominent individuals in the Polish opposition have articulated an advanced strategy not only for a new Poland but also for a new Europe. Domestically, the Polish opposition advocates economic and industrial self-management and political pluralism. Groups of right-wing Polish nationalists are also active. Some, perhaps influenced by the Church hierarchy strategy, are sympathetic to the 'patriotic' stance of the Jaruzelski military regime.

Although it would be wrong to speak of the complex Polish movement as having an agreed policy, some conclusions have been spelled out by Jacek Kuron and others.[32] Kuron insists that the demand for a 'sovereign' Poland must be part of a political settlement involving superpower recognition that both Germanies, Poland, and other Central European states should be free of all nuclear weapons and bases and neutral as between NATO and the Warsaw Pact. In this sense the Polish movement has firmly twinned the issues of peace and non-alignment in Europe with the issues of social and political change at home. This mirrors the concerns of many Western Europeans who believe that a post-Atlanticist future must involve not just radical changes in foreign and defence policy but fundamental changes in Europe's own economic and social development. What the Eastern European dissidents are saying is that peace is inseparable from freedom, independence, and non-alignment for their countries.

Writing from prison in June 1984, Kuron suggested that, along with Poland, both West and East Germany, as well as other Central European countries, should be 'denuclearized' and leave the two superpower-led blocs. In an echo of the approach of the more radical peace groups in Western Europe, Kuron argues that while both superpowers might oppose such a demand, it could provide the engine for generating unstoppable political pressure in both parts of Europe.

Summarizing these views two years later, Kuron wrote of the goal of central European 'non-alignment':

I am aware that this programme is unrealistic and unacceptable to eastern politicians as well as western. It is unacceptable to western leaders, since the Federal Republic of Germany is the fundamental military power of Europe in view of which the west would be giving up a lot more than the east.

The USSR, however, would lose central Europe, not only strategically but ideologically and politically. Soviet leaders have reason to fear that self government . . . will be a dangerous example. The central European project of neutrality and demilitarization can, however, become a programme for socio-political movements in the Soviet bloc as well as in the West. The stronger these movements, the greater the direct influence will be . . . on what politicians describe as realistic.[33]

More recently there has been the remarkable advent of the 'Peace and Freedom' (WiP) organization which openly sympathizes with the general approach of the Western peace movement. As an interview with *END Journal* spelled out, the WiP have moved beyond isolated protests. 'They fast, march, sit down in the street with banners and petitions—all with impunity. Some 100 of them are currently refusing the oath [for military service], yet after the amnesty no one is in prison.'[34]

While some oppositionists privately believe that Western military strength creates a situation which makes it possible for them to act, others disagree. The END interviews with WiP activists showed them to include outspoken opponents of US policy towards, for example, Nicaragua. Many are pacifists while for others non-violence is a tactical issue. Most are alarmed at Poland's ecological crisis and are sympathetic to the underground workers' movement demands for industrial self-management.

The radical opposition forces in Eastern Europe are gaining in self-confidence in spite of fitful repression by the authorities. Something of this more assertive spirit was reflected in the declaration issued by Czech, East German, Hungarian, and Polish dissidents on the thirtieth anniversary of the Hungarian revolution, in November 1986, in which they recommitted themselves to the goals of that revolution: 'independence, democracy and neutrality'.[35] Significantly, the declaration by more than 100 militants of diverse backgrounds and political views asserts their 'joint determination to struggle for . . . the peaceful reunification of a divided Europe'. They restated their position on disarmament and the disengagement of the superpowers, but also touched on a variety of economic and social ills including the ecology, an increasing source of concern in Czechoslovakia and Hungary.[36]

Undoubtedly the conditions in which the Eastern European opposition operates improved markedly during 1986. All remaining Polish political prisoners were released and the curbs on dissidents and 'unofficial' peace activists eased significantly, seemingly as part of a deliberate policy of liberalization and relaxation sanctioned by the Soviet leadership itself. Indeed, in the months after the abortive Reykjavik summit in November 1986, a number of human-rights prisoners, including Andrei Sakharov, were released in Russia.

Neither the strength nor the homogeneity of the Eastern European opposition should be exaggerated. Even in Poland Solidarnosc has been, at least temporarily, marginalized. But, as we have seen, opposition groups are becoming more influential and their ideas are being circulated and debated far more widely than ever before in Eastern European society.

While the Solidarnosc organization itself is being rebuilt, there are also a number of diverse political groups and even embryo political parties emerging within the broader organization and canvassing their own programmes and perspectives. Among these, openly leftist groups are proliferating. Their publications spell out in some detail objectives which include the transfer of the 'factories to the workers, land to the peasants, power to the self managed society for an independent nation'.[37]

Non-Stalinist Socialists are active in the Czech Charter 77 organization which also includes a number of individuals who might be described as liberals or even fellow thinkers of the Western European Cold Warrior right wing. Many of its members agitate around issues which might be thought of in the West as 'apolitical', such as the right of artists and musicians to self-expression. The extent to which this is, in fact, an important political issue was revealed by the arrest by the Czech State Security Police in the summer of 1986 of members of the Jazz Section of the Prague Musicians Union.[38]

The Hungarian movement is equally heterogeneous and writers and artists are equally prominent in its leading samizdat journals *Beszelo* and *Hirmondo*. One leading spokesperson of the Hungarian movement, Andras Hegedus, argues that the question of peace transcends political issues, and he is not sanguine about any evolutionary convergence of the two Europes without profound social changes. But he fears that such changes could threaten stability in relations between NATO and the Warsaw Pact and thus threaten peace.[39]

The extent to which 'dissidents' in Eastern Europe and the radical peace movement in Western Europe share an identical outlook, while both are opposed to the respective domination of their continent by the Soviet Union and the United States, must not be overstated. Suspicions have been, and to some extent still are, entertained by some radical Eastern European dissidents about the Western European peace movement.[40]

Some Western European radicals either still do not understand or choose to ignore the scale of human-rights denial in the Eastern bloc and the intimate and organic link in Eastern Europe between the issue of peace and that of justice and freedom. This has led to criticism of the West German Social Democratic Party (SPD) for maintaining contacts with Eastern European governments, to the exclusion of the unofficial peace and dissident groups, in pursuit of better relations with the official regimes as part of its Ostpolitik.[41]

On the other hand, there are close links between Eastern European oppositionists and European Nuclear Disarmament (END), a Western-European-based, multinational radical peace umbrella organization. END supports demands for human rights, freedom of expression, and national self-determination in the Eastern bloc. It takes a similar stand to the organizers of the Eastern European 'Hungarian Revolution' declaration on the goal of European reunification and nonalignment.

Some governments and the radical opposition groups therefore have an interest, albeit for different reasons, in seeking to disengage their countries to a greater or lesser degree from Soviet hegemony and form closer links with the rest of Europe. The extent to which the more nationalist regimes travel down this road will, in the final analysis, be determined by the state of the international climate, by the extent to which the Soviet leadership tolerates or encourages such moves, but above all by their ability to control the challenge of the 'dissidents'. Thus far, for example, Hungary has moved further down the reform road than any other East European state.

The political environment in which the Eastern-bloc opposition operates is crucial. Eastern European peace activists have an obvious interest in a climate of maximum *détente* between East and West, and specifically within Europe. The unofficial peace movement has always feared that any return to a new Cold War would strengthen the most reactionary and repressive features of bureaucratic tyranny.

Initiatives by Western European countries to disarm unilaterally, to remove US nuclear bases, or to distance themselves from NATO may not automatically or immediately produce a matching response by the Eastern bloc. But such initiatives would encourage even the more conservative and repressive of Eastern European bureaucracies to press for reciprocal action by the Soviet Union and the Warsaw Pact.

There was such a 'reciprocity' after de Gaulle's decision to take France out of NATO's integrated military command and expel NATO headquarters from Paris in 1966. A series of measures taken by the Ceauşescu regime in Romania included not merely the establishment of closer commercial links with the West than the Soviet Union wanted at that stage, but also the denial of transit rights to Soviet forces to take part in Warsaw Pact exercises in other member states and the pursuit of a blatantly independent and even to some degree 'non-aligned' foreign policy.[42]

A number of other Eastern European leaderships have been emboldened in recent years to put their own 'national' gloss on Soviet and Warsaw Pact policy. They have also not been deflected from their chosen national economic strategies. The Kadar government in Budapest has indicated that, whether the Soviet Union approves or not (and under Mikhail Gorbachev it appears to approve), it will persist with policies designed to restore a far greater role for internal free markets.

More significantly, even an ultra-loyalist with an impeccable Stalinist pedigree, such as the East German leader Erich Honnecker, has let it be known that he regrets Moscow's decision to implant tactical nuclear weapons in Eastern Europe.[43] This may, in part, reflect the regime's keen awareness of the extent of silent support for the outspoken advocates of the withdrawal of Soviet and American missiles and troops among the militant peace leaders of the East German Protestant Churches.[44] So far the East German regime has adopted relatively more flexible economic policies while remaining politically immobile.

The fundamental question is, what will be the attitude of the Kremlin to a more assertive Eastern Europe? Just how much rope will the Soviet Union allow its client states in pursuing autonomous foreign as well as economic policies? Would it ever really be willing to permit even an uncertain drift of the Eastern European states towards Western Europe with the inevitable loss of control that would imply?

Clearly these are issues at the heart of the Soviet Union's own longer-term strategic thinking, and there are signs that there is more than one point of view among Russian policy-makers. It would be wrong to generalize too far from the tactical line adopted by the present Gorbachev leadership, but the Kremlin does seem to recognize that reform and some political liberalization are unavoidable if the neo-Stalinist system is to master its deep-rooted economic crisis.

That said, the present Soviet government does appear to be signalling a greater degree of flexibility in its international strategy than for many years past. Clearly the Gorbachev administration has staked much on a considerable liberalization of the Soviet economic system. There have also been some concessions towards the regime's internal critics, with the release towards the end of 1986 of leading human-rights activists and the granting of permission for some Jewish activists to emigrate.

In the aftermath of the Reykjavik summit, Moscow was anxious to proclaim its 'reasonableness'. This is despite the Reagan Administration decision to persist with SDI, thus threatening a blatant violation of the ABM Treaty. Other planned American strategic arms developments will violate the SALT II Treaty. The Soviet leaders did warn in late 1986 that they would not continue indefinitely with their unilateral nuclear-test ban in the face of continued US nuclear testing and, in fact, resumed a limited number of such tests early in 1987.[45] This may be no more than a tactical propaganda move, designed to win the sympathy of Western European public opinion and thus drive a wedge between the United States and its European allies over arms negotiations. But since the present European NATO governments believe that America went too far in conceding possible arms reductions in Reykjavik, such a strategy is unlikely to achieve quick results.

There may well be a great deal more to the Soviet position

than mere propaganda. Although Western Cold War propagandists naturally have a vested interest in exaggerating the extent and significance of the systemic crisis within the Eastern bloc, Soviet apologists equally try to underplay its true significance.

There is no doubt that the economic system is in deep trouble: economic growth is stagnating; productivity (particularly in the Soviet Union) is lagging well behind the West; living standards in many Eastern European countries are under severe pressure; international indebtedness is worsening; and technological backwardness remains critical. What lends all of these problems a deeply political character is the widespread and increasingly publicized resentment of the Eastern-bloc populations not only at the failures of economic management but at the still considerable social and economic privileges of the 'Nomenklatura'. Indeed, one consequence of the market-liberalization reforms of recent years has been to increase that sense of injustice, since they are leading to greater discrepancies of income and wealth. This is just one way in which the involvement of the Eastern European economies in the world system has increased both their opportunities to modernize and advance and their vulnerability to the problems of inflation and recession 'imported' from the world economy.[46]

The investment priorities of the Soviet economy are determined principally by the irrational and externally imposed compulsion of the international arms race with the United States. This bizarre dynamic is largely responsible for both the scale and the lopsided pattern of the industrialization of the Soviet economy.[47] Although America's defence-spending is greater than Russia's, Soviet arms expenditure absorbs a bigger share of the smaller Soviet economy.[48]

These distortions in the Soviet economy are a source of chronic instability. Defence-driven heavy industry uses up the system's all too scarce technological resources while highlighting the scientific, technological, and productivity gap with the United States. This gap will widen further if the Soviet leaders cannot dissuade América from pursuing SDI. They may conclude they have to boost SDI research themselves.

The arms-race-induced industrial and economic competition with the West has also exacerbated disagreements about economic strategy within Comecon. The Soviet leadership has called for a 'new economic mechanism in our co-operation', and the Hungarian government newspaper *Magyar Hirlap* has said that 'the slowdown in the economic growth of the socialist countries indicated that co-operation was not really taking place'.[49]

The extent to which the Soviet Union will countenance greater autonomy for their satellite states depends crucially on two further factors, over which neither Moscow nor its client bureaucracies have complete control. The first is the state of East–West relations; the second is the need to keep control of oppositional, above all worker-based movements seeking radical transformation of the whole system.

Failure by the United States and the Soviet Union to secure agreement on arms control could lead to a renewed arms race and Cold War confrontation. Such a development would make it more difficult for the Eastern-bloc rulers to pursue political liberalization. It would also be bound to strengthen all those factions within the Soviet ruling system who are suspicious and afraid of even limited political reform.

At the same time there appear to be two conflicting schools of thought in the Soviet Union towards the very idea of European unification. These seem to reflect the two basic options for the Soviet Union in conducting its policy towards the West: whether or not to give absolute priority to trying to achieve a global agreement on arms control and *détente* with the United States. Whether or not Moscow ultimately judges that such a global agreement is possible with the United States will determine its basic attitude to a new political and security settlement in Europe with all that that would inevitably imply for Soviet hegemony over Eastern Europe. For as long as Russia's rulers believe a global deal with the United States to be feasible they are likely to adopt a basically sceptical and even occasionally hostile attitude to European integration. This is reflected in policy statements over the years which basically attempt to prove that European unity is an American-backed stratagem to undermine the Yalta settlement and to 'roll back' Soviet influence in Europe and thus threaten Soviet security.[50]

Such a strategy would not necessarily prevent the Soviet government exploiting contradictions and conflicts within the Atlantic Alliance for tactical reasons. There is no doubt this has been an element in Soviet policy at least since the 1979 NATO decision on cruise and Pershing missile deployment. The Soviet Union has also tried to persuade Western Europe to dissuade the United States from persisting with SDI development, and it would welcome any disarray within the NATO alliance over any American decisions if this changed US policy and thus relieved the pressure on the Soviet Union to match the US arms build-up.

There have, however, always been limits to Soviet exploitation of disagreement within NATO. The Warsaw Pact authorities have always disapproved as much of particular states unilaterally leaving NATO as of suggestions of Eastern European clients unilaterally withdrawing from the Warsaw Pact. This has always been the line taken by pro-Moscow Communist parties in the West who support the formula of eventual 'mutual dissolution of the military alliances' rather than withdrawal by individual countries.[51]

If a global understanding with the Americans is possible, the Soviet Union would have no interest in encouraging European unification since this would always risk undermining Soviet hegemony in Eastern Europe. But as the 1980s draw to a close the auguries for such a comprehensive agreement between the nuclear superpowers appear uncertain.

The Reagan Presidency was seriously weakened both by the failure at Reykjavik and by the 'Irangate' affair. America retreated, under European pressure, from earlier ideas about the elimination over ten years of all strategic nuclear weapons and it was uncertain whether there would be a superpower agreement on the complete elimination of European-based intermediate-range missiles. At the start of 1987 the Soviet Union still refused to complete a strategic nuclear arms reduction agreement without concessions by the United States over future SDI research and development. But America seemed determined to stick with SDI.[52]

Suddenly, in the middle of April 1987, the Soviet leadership abandoned the linkage between SDI and the issue of European missiles. Mr Gorbachev offered President Reagan an agreement eliminating all medium- and shorter-range intermediate nuclear missiles and negotiations for drastic reductions in battlefield nuclear weapons, chemical weapons, and conventional forces. The first reaction of the Reagan administration

was more positive than that of some European NATO governments, who feared the abolition of the intermediate nuclear
weapons would increase the risk of an eventual 'decoupling' of
Western European from American security. Furthermore, the
negotiating gap on strategic nuclear forces, including SDI,
remained as large as ever.

If the Soviet government does eventually conclude that comprehensive arms agreement is not possible in the foreseeable
future, it may well be tempted to 'play the European card'. This
might go far beyond short-term propaganda to divide the
NATO allies, and in effect signal a willingness to review the
whole basis of the Yalta agreement.

What might such a 'European card' consist of? It could
involve a direct approach to the European NATO states to
negotiate the elimination of European-theatre-based nuclear
weapons, leading to the Western Europeans sending back US
nuclear missiles and bases and phasing out the British and
French national deterrents. In return the Soviet Union might
dismantle all its European-based nuclear weapons and make
significant reductions in its conventional forces.

It might, alternatively, consist of a direct approach to West
Germany (and any other NATO states interested) to negotiate
a Central European nuclear-free zone. This would involve not
only the removal of nuclear weapons but the withdrawal of the
states involved from their respective military alliances. It could
even lead to a mutual security pact between the Soviet Union
and its allies and all of European NATO. But this would imply
a more radical break-up of the two military alliances than either
Moscow or the majority of Western European governments
seem likely to contemplate for some considerable time.

Even a partial withdrawal from the NATO integrated military
command by West Germany would obviously represent a fundamental transformation of the situation in Central Europe. It is
not imaginable except in the aftermath of a widely perceived
breakdown in negotiations on arms control between Moscow
and Washington which also coincided with a generalized and
deep-rooted conflict over economic and foreign policy.

Clearly the prospects of such a deal will depend to some
extent on the political complexion of the Western European
governments. The possible election during the early 1990s of

Labour or Socialist governments in West Germany, Britain, and the Benelux and Scandinavian states on the basis of the current defence policies of the Socialist parties would be a development of major significance.

However, even the centre-right coalition in Bonn was, in the early months of 1987, displaying considerable interest in a much improved relationship with the Soviet Union. This went far beyond prospective agreements on nuclear and, possibly, conventional arms reductions in Central Europe. Federal German politicians and industrialists were excited by Soviet proposals for much expanded German–Soviet trade and the encouragement of joint investment ventures in the Soviet economy. The West German foreign minister, Mr Hans-Dietrich Genscher, revived ideas for a major programme of economic aid for Eastern Europe. Early in 1987 there were even greatly increased official contacts between the Christian Democrat-led authorities in West Berlin and those in East Berlin.

In the persistence by the present right-wing Christian Democrat-led coalition government in Bonn with the SPD Ostpolitik some see evidence of a hard-headed realization that a new Central European settlement could be in German interests. Some East European dissidents have become alarmed at such a possibility lest it lead to a deal between governments in Europe that ignores the political and human rights of the peoples of Eastern Europe. Some have even warned of the dangers of a 'new Rapallo Pact'.[53] By this is meant a West German understanding with Russia which opens the way for progressive German reunification but leaves Soviet hegemony and the internal political system elsewhere in Eastern Europe basically untouched. It is compared with the Rapallo Pact signed between the Soviet Union and nationalist right-wing politicians during the Weimar Republic in 1922.

Although they dismiss talk of a new Rapallo, some policy-makers in London and Paris are concerned at a possible eastward orientation in West German foreign policy. This is one reason for their interest in a more active Anglo-French-based European security system. Privately some British and French leaders argue that such a European security power would help ensure that West Germany does not 'drift eastwards'. They fear that otherwise, if America does over the next few years signal its determination to withdraw from Western Europe, West Germany will be encouraged to seek an accommodation with Moscow.

Such a development would be welcomed by those in both Western and Eastern Europe who believe that a phasing-out of the security and political 'patronage' of Moscow and Washington is long overdue. The one single development which, more than any other, could be relied on to break up the forty-year-old political geography of Europe would be some new Central European economic and political consensus involving both Germanies. However, there are profound economic and political interests tying West Germany to Western Europe. For the time being it is almost certain that the Federal Republic will attempt to achieve its economic and political goals in Eastern Europe through and with the EEC and without any drastic changes in its relationship with NATO.

But could a transformation of Europe's geopolitics occur without a parallel reconstruction of the political and economic system in both parts of Europe? It may be that the economic crisis which is now disrupting the post-war Atlantic settlement will place just such radical changes on the European political agenda of the 1990s.

These and other far-reaching possibilities are already being debated. While it is true that the debate is, thus far, mainly taking place in the smaller, radical parties of the Western European 'Green' and New Left, it is also being given prominence by the increasingly assertive voice of the Eastern European opposition.

The longer the superpowers are perceived to be holding the world—and specifically Europe—to ransom in the pursuit of a systemic global and nuclear rivalry, the more likely post-Atlanticist alternatives to the Yalta agreement will begin to feed into the mainstream European political debate.

5 | European Disunion

Europe and America are very different entities. America is a single state with a single federal government, a single foreign and defence policy, a completely integrated national market, and widely accepted national constitutional, political, educational, and other institutions. Europe is a continent divided in two by a superpower conflict which may have had its origins in Europe but whose dynamic and *raison d'être* have long since become global. Not even Western Europe is united. And the EEC towards the close of the 1980s falls well short of the aspirations for its future which inspired its Founding Fathers thirty years ago. It is still 'L'Europe des Patries'.

The reality of a Europe fractured by economic, political, and security divisions is as relevant in understanding Western Europe's subordinate relationship to the United States in the post-war years as either the fact of American power or the manner in which that power has been deployed. The United States would no doubt have felt resentment, and perhaps been driven earlier to a divorce from its European client-allies, had Western Europe been united and not divided. But America has not, in recent decades at least, had the power to obstruct that unity had Europe willed it to be.

The failure to create a united Europe has therefore, first and foremost, been a European failure. Even today 'European Community' is somewhat of a misnomer for a body which embraces only Western Europeans, and by no means all of them. For as long as the Eastern Europeans, to say nothing of the peoples of Austria, Switzerland, and most of Scandinavia, remain apart, 'Europe' will have an uncertain claim to be taken seriously as a global region. And even that leaves on one side those with more hesitant, qualified, or ambiguous 'European' aspirations, such as the Cypriots, the Maltese, and the Turks.[1] The greater part of the responsibility for the arrested development of the EEC must lie with the three major 'core' states— Britain, France, and West Germany. However, they and the other EEC states cannot be blamed for the fact that some Western European countries still remain outside the EEC.

The remaining members of the European Free Trade Association (EFTA) have thus far refused the option of Common Market membership. They have sought, instead, to exploit their specific international economic advantages. But all the EFTA states have been careful to retain a close *de facto* association with the EEC without having to incur the financial and political burdens involved in maintaining its institutions and funding its common policies.

The EFTA states have had a variety of other motives for not opting for full membership of the EEC. For Switzerland, the banking controls and other financial conventions expected of EEC member states would have compromised its idiosyncratic national banking regime which affords international business a degree of protection from scrutiny that is unacceptable in other European states.[2] Iceland and Norway remain outside the EEC primarily because of the importance of their national fishing industries. It was suspicion that the EEC common fisheries policy would lead to other European fishing fleets being given access to Norway's rich fishing waters that, more than any other single factor, ensured the 'no' decision in the 1973 Norwegian national referendum on the terms of Common Market membership.[3] But given the rift in the Atlantic Alliance it would not be surprising if Norway revised its attitude to EEC membership in the not too distant future. Swedish governments have claimed that joining the EEC would compromise their traditional neutrality in foreign affairs, not least because all the EEC member states, apart from the Irish Republic, are also members of NATO. Swedish political independence from Cold War bloc politics is long-standing. But it also allows Swedish industry a degree of flexibility in its international operations which, the Swedes feel, EEC membership might compromise. Finland, of course, has a special relationship with the Soviet Union which has ruled out even indirect links with a political and economic grouping thought to have any Cold War affiliations. But this position could conceivably be affected by the increasing commercial and even political links being forged by individual Eastern European member states of Comecon with the EEC. The extent of Finland's *de facto* independence to pursue its own interests in spite of its geopolitical circumstances should not be underestimated.

The EFTA states as a whole—now minus Portugal and Spain, which became full members of the EEC in 1986—have in some ways the best of both worlds in their relationship with the EEC. EFTA and the EEC have negotiated a more or less comprehensive industrial free-trade agreement which offers EFTA countries privileged access to the EEC market. But the EFTA states, which, were they members of the Community, would be substantial net contributors to its budget, incur none of the direct costs of membership.

Those links continue to grow. The currencies of Austria, Switzerland, and the Scandinavian EFTA countries are indirectly linked to the fixed exchange-rate mechanism at the heart of the European Monetary System (EMS). They are now *de facto* associates of a European monetary bloc with what that implies for future economic co-operation.

The relationship between EFTA and the EEC is, officially, purely commercial and economic. In practice it is about much more than that. Behind the scenes there is much informal political consultation between the EEC states and individual EFTA governments and the issues which appear on the EEC 'Political Co-operation' agenda are also likely, for example, to figure on the agenda of the Nordic Council, not least because Denmark is a member of both.[4] Moreover, at its own request, Norway is becoming more intimately associated with the attempts through European Political Co-operation to forge a common foreign policy. Norway now receives special briefings before and after the regular meetings of EEC foreign ministers and political directors. Given the uncertain dividing line between 'EEC' and 'NATO' issues in political co-operation, there are obvious limits to the extent to which the non-aligned EFTA states will want to be publicly associated with the EEC. However, this could change in the future should Europe and the United States draw apart. It should also be added that the European Community consults the other Western European states, including the 'neutrals', to co-ordinate policies within the Conference on Security and Co-operation in Europe set up after the Helsinki conference with the Soviet Union and the Eastern European states. This conference produced the Helsinki Human Rights Declaration of 1975.

What drew the EEC and EFTA together originally was a mutual interest in exploiting the advantages of creating a *de facto* Western European free-trade area. The EFTA states are aware that their economic interests could be hit if they stand apart from the EEC goal of creating a full internal market by 1992. The emergence of a series of potentially hostile economic world blocs has underlined for both groups of European states the old adage 'better that we hang together than that we hang separately'. If in the coming years what remains of the Bretton Woods international monetary and free-trade order gives way, at least temporarily, to global 'regionalization', the EFTA states will want the benefit of the collective strength which a more united Europe can deploy in an uncertain world. Already the EFTA steel firms co-ordinate their prices and output in step with the EEC steel-crisis management regime. They also actively sponsor broader European industrial and technological co-operation projects such as the EUREKA initiative, designed to reduce European dependence on 'foreign' (that is, American and Japanese) technology.[5]

The same harsh international economic climate which is uncertainly drawing the EEC and EFTA closer together is also creating pressure on the twelve EEC member states to push faster towards greater integration. But, simultaneously, conflicts of national interest and the arrested imbalance in the Community tend to push them apart. Moreover, in the Community's complex decision-making processes, insufficient weight is still given to broad strategic issues and common interests and too much to differences over issues of secondary importance. Conflicts over fish quotas or lorry weights loom larger in the popular consciousness than issues such as unemployment or technological backwardness where there is, at least potentially, a common EEC interest. The system by which decisions are reached in the Council of Ministers and its subsidiary bodies is, moreover, one of multilateral bargaining in which national (even minor national) interests are given overwhelming weight.

But the political failure to build a European Community which can treat on a basis of relative equality with the United States is primarily the failure of the three 'core' countries of the

EEC: Britain, France, and West Germany. Theirs is the primary responsibility for the political stagnation, lack of direction, and political impotence which have afflicted the EEC in recent decades.

The other states are, of course, not without responsibility, but at least until the late 1970s the Benelux countries and Italy were moved to a considerable degree by the now dated ideals of the Monnet–Schuman vision of European union. In latter years it has been the inability of the Centre and Right throughout the EEC to conceptualize a united Europe beyond the Rome Treaty which has been at the roots of the political drift of modern Europe. However, the parties of the orthodox Social Democratic Left have no better record. While certain initiatives at a European level were made by the Euro-Communist parties, notably the Italian Communist Party, in the 1970s, the political decline of this current seems related to its overly close identification with the existing institutions of the EEC, and even NATO. The non-aligned, radical Left, notably the West German Greens, are only now beginning to think through the implications of a supranational European strategy on issues such as ecology, peace, employment, and women's rights.

Hopes were high at the birth of the EEC that within a decade or two Western Europe would be well down the road to economic and, indeed, political union. Monnet and Schuman always regarded the mundane business of creating a tariff union and comprehensive 'common' market as a preliminary step towards a fully federal, united Europe. Their Europe would have co-existed in close but equal partnership with the United States in a wider Atlantic Alliance.[6] They were strongly supported by Western Europe's Christian Democratic leaders, notably Konrad Adenauer in West Germany and Alcide de Gaspari in Italy. Indeed, the post-war influence of Christian Democracy was crucial in giving the ECSC its strongly federal character and in building into the EEC social policy features designed to achieve a broader social consensus in support of the European institutions.[7] This was very much in line with US policy at that time, which saw social welfare reform programmes and partnership with organized labour as crucial means of combating the influence of the Communist Party and the Left and consolidating a Europe open to America's broader commitment to liberal free trade. The US attempt to create a post-war Europe based on liberal economics and Rooseveltian social policies depended heavily on working with and through both the Christian Democratic and, to some degree, the Social Democratic parties to encourage them to abandon residual elements of Marxism in their programmes.[8]

The EEC's constitution was less unambiguously federalist and more inter-governmentalist than the ECSC. This was partly due to the relatively stronger position in 1957 of the more 'nationally' minded Western European Social Democratic parties and the relatively weaker position of the Christian Democrats. Of course the idea of extending the interventionist ECSC approach to European industry as a whole would have been a very radical, almost a revolutionary, innovation. This hybrid character of the EEC institutions was to prove a serious weakness from the 1960s.

Even so, the immediate dynamic behind the Treaty of Rome and the launching of the Community was political rather than economic. The shock created by the failure of the French Assembly to endorse the proposed European Defence Community in 1954 led directly to the calling of the Messina conference in 1955 and, subsequently, to the Rome Treaty.[9]

The other great error made by the architects of the EEC was the belief (naïve, with the benefit of hindsight) that a dynamic free market would propel Europe not only towards economic integration but also towards parallel political integration. Important though the economic changes were which occurred during the first ten to twenty years of the Common Market, the creation of a customs union fell significantly short of a full common market.[10] The failure was for a while disguised by the effects of the worldwide boom which was in full flood during those years.

Economic boom plus trade liberalization and the increasing freedom of movement of capital did create a new breed of European multinational firm. But it took awareness of the scale of American big-business penetration of Europe from the mid-1960s and of the slower economic growth and more intensive international competition in the following decade, to renew efforts to eliminate proliferating national visible and invisible barriers to a full Common Market.[11]

By 1970 even the Confederation of British Industry had come to realize that 'successful European industrial policy will require very substantial capital resources, which will only be forthcoming through a mechanism which permits savings to be mobilised on a Continental scale'. But during those years national governments frequently conspired with industry to protect national markets (particularly where defence interests were involved) and actually to block some transnational company mergers, even though the result was to surrender European markets first to American and then to Japanese multinationals.

The Commission's first President was the West German Walter Hallstein, a dedicated European federalist whose Commission was widely regarded as a sort of embryo of the fully fledged European government of the future. By the mid-1960s it was clear that his belief that the Community was establishing 'the role of the state' was misplaced.[12] In less than a decade after the establishment of the EEC, some national governments were determined to restrict the Commission's role in initiating, let alone seeking to 'manage', Community economic strategy. European integration had initially drawn political strength from a popular reaction to twentieth-century internecine European war and a desire to transcend the bigotries of narrow nationalism. By the 1960s this mood had begun to wane.

The ECSC itself declined in influence after the years of chronic steel shortage in the early 1950s. While lip service was paid to social objectives, national governments tended to be dismissive towards Commission-initiated plans for new common social policies and were reluctant to find the necessary budgetary resources. It was only on the accession of Britain that it was agreed to give a regional development function to the Community.

Economic boom and full employment had strengthened the bargaining hand of the organized labour movement, and in the 1960s the Social Democratic parties were bidding for political power (notably in West Germany) while powerful mass-membership Communist parties remained a major political force in France and Italy. But while the EEC and its institutions espoused a philosophy of co-operation between the 'social partners', the focus for the politics of consensus remained overwhelmingly national rather than European.

The only area where the Commission inherited powers of direct intervention in the economy, apart from the steel sector, was agriculture. The CAP, established in 1962, was intended in part to balance the advantage which the more industrialized countries, such as West Germany, derived from EEC free trade with a system of price support and production aids for farmers, politically of great importance in France and Italy. Unlike most other areas of policy, the CAP was unashamedly 'dirigiste' from its inception in 1962. It was based on the establishment of a single market with annually agreed common prices covering a wide range of agricultural products. The unique assurance was given that 'those working on agriculture will enjoy a standard of living comparable to that enjoyed by workers in other sectors; preference for Community produce; financial solidarity through a European Agricultural Guidance and Guarantee Fund.'[13] The management of the CAP has proved to be an increasing source of conflict within the Community. The persistent and massive overproduction of some key temperate foodstuffs (notably grain, milk, and beef, as well as wine) is the dual consequence of the extraordinary growth in European agricultural productivity and of politically cowardly decisions to defer structural reform long after it was obviously necessary by the mid-1970s. The principal beneficiaries of the CAP bonanza have not been the smaller or poorer farmers, in whose cause the policy has been defended, nor the poorer agricultural regions, but the superproductive large farmers of northern Europe. Industrialized agriculture has boosted output by the indiscriminate use of pesticides and chemicals. It has despoiled the environment by destroying hedgerows, draining marshes, and turning whole areas of the European countryside into a grain-growing imitation mid-West.[14] The EEC has proved unable to regulate guaranteed prices at a level where supply and demand are kept more or less in equilibrium. The policy of food stockpiling and subsidized exports has become financially crippling because of the scale of the European Community's food surpluses. The financial drain on the Community's budget has contributed to the warping of the Community's wider policy evolution. In the late 1980s the EEC farm crisis, if unresolved, could produce a state of *de facto* budgetary bankruptcy and bring all development to a halt.

It was a plan by Walter Hallstein, Commission President, in 1965 to find additional sources of revenue for the budget and the CAP which led to the first major political crisis in the Community. The plan involved taking over the levies charged on imports from non-member states at the EEC's frontiers and giving the appointed members of the European Parliament powers to scrutinize both the revenue and the expenditure of what was now the Community's own budget.[15] The French government under President de Gaulle, who had come to power after the collapse of the more European-Federalist-minded Fourth Republic, was bitterly opposed to giving such powers to the Community and to the European Parliament in particular. The whole Community was thrown into a constitutional crisis when, on 30 June 1965, the French Foreign Minister stormed out of a meeting of the Council of Ministers on agricultural-policy financing and refused to return. For the next seven months, despite appeals from its EEC partners, France maintained an 'empty seat' policy. The crisis was only resolved the following year when, at a meeting in Luxembourg, the Council agreed that in future an individual government could veto majority decisions of the Council when it claimed that a 'vital national interest' was at stake.[16]

Although few people realized it at the time, the so-called 'Luxembourg compromise', while it defused the immediate crisis, introduced a major obstacle to further progress towards European union. It condemned the EEC to move at the speed of the slowest member state. In the years that followed most national states, including some committed in theory to supranationalism, were not above the use of the veto, sometimes over issues of marginal significance. The political pendulum had been pushed decisively away from a federal Community to one controlled by intergovernmental institutions.[17] The subsequent loss of momentum towards European economic and political union arose from more than just the effective surrender of majority decision-making in the Council of Ministers. By the mid-1970s economic and political factors—notably inflation and then recession—were at work which were sapping and undermining the political will to achieve the goal of Economic and Monetary Union by the original timetable deadline of 1980.

Apart from the loss of federalist zeal, few people still believed that the only thing stopping France and Germany going to war again was the existence of the EEC. Nor was Germany any longer feared in quite the way it had been.[18] Europe's vulnerability to challenge by American and Japanese industry was not yet apparent. The 1970s were years of complacent drift and indecision. The impetus given to Western European unity by the onset of the Cold War had also weakened by the end of the 1960s. The advent of *détente* and 'Ostpolitik' shifted the focus of political attention and aspiration from internal to external issues. And while domestic European economic and social problems became more pressing, the EEC institutions lacked clear powers or 'locus standi' to determine the collective responses so clearly needed.

Something of the resentment felt in national capitals at the role of the Commission under Hallstein before the 1965 crisis can be gauged from the observations of President de Gaulle. In his memoirs of this period he wrote:

[Hallstein] made Brussels . . . into a sort of capital. There he sat, surrounded by all the trappings of sovereignty, directing his colleagues, allocating jobs among them, controlling several thousand officials who were appointed, promoted and remunerated at his discretion, receiving the credentials of foreign ambassadors, laying claim to high honours on the occasion of his official visits, concerned above all to further the amalgamation of the Six, believing the pressure of events would bring about what he envisaged.[19]

The decline in the status of the Community's institutions began to be reflected in the prestige attaching to the European Commission itself. In its first decade, member governments tended to appoint politicians of the first rank to the Commission because they saw them playing a crucial role of European political leadership. In the years which followed, and notably after the successive enlargements of the Community, some national governments used their power of patronage to ensure that no one was sent to Brussels who would challenge 'intergovernmentalism'[20] in the community.

Chastened by their eminent predecessor's bruising confrontation with de Gaulle, the new generation of Commissioners tended now to be less prepared to challenge national governments on major policy issues. As the years passed, the Commission came to accept that a new balance had been struck between the competing claims of supranationalism, intergovernmentalism, and national sovereignty.

It was quite apparent by the Hague European summit meeting in October 1969 that without a determined push towards faster economic integration the achievements of the previous thirteen years might be imperilled and the Community unable to absorb new member states. A plan, named after the then Luxembourg Prime Minister, Pierre Werner, was agreed under which the Community would move in pre-ordained stages to full economic and monetary union, including a common currency, by 1980.

The ink was no sooner dry on the agreement to implement the Werner plan than the EEC found itself in the eye of the world monetary storm unleashed by the dollar crisis. The US government suspended convertibility of the dollar into gold, thus beginning the process of unravelling the Bretton Woods international monetary system. It was also a moment which symbolized the passing of the apogee of American world power.

In the summer of 1971 the exchange rates of the European currencies began to diverge wildly from each other and thus from any 'norm' which might form the basis of a fixed EEC currency system. National governments, central banks, and the EEC authorities held a series of crisis meetings during the year, which resulted in a series of devaluations and revaluations and an agreement to limit future fluctuation of EEC currencies (including those of the candidate member states, Britain, Denmark, and Ireland) against each other and against the US dollar through an EEC currency, 'Snake'. The agreement did restore the objective of monetary convergence. But for progress to be maintained, the national authorities would have had to agree closely to co-ordinate their national monetary policies. This would logically have implied eventual harmonization of their national fiscal and expenditure policies as well. National governments were firmly opposed to this notion. Resistance to any transfer of authority to Community bodies for economic policy was intense among the national bureaucracies, notably the Finance Ministries and Treasuries. While continuing to pay lip service to the idea of economic and monetary union, most national governments secretly feared that the increasingly dominant West German economy would use union to impose its ultra-orthodox financial hegemony over the rest of the Community.[21]

This was a theme which was frequently heard in the years which followed. Developments in the international economy—in particular the protracted decline of the US-dominated international monetary order—did renew interest in monetary union. But the sheer power and international competitiveness of the West German economy (based on its very low inflation and consequently strong currency) was regarded apprehensively by the British in particular as the mould to which all other EEC economies would have to conform, irrespective of national circumstances or interests.[22]

The Nixon administration's New Economic Policy led to a temporary strengthening of the US dollar, but this only produced new problems for Europe. An over-strong dollar now produced strains between the EEC currencies which led to the French Franc, British sterling, and Irish Punt having to withdraw from the EEC currency 'Snake' system, limiting exchange-rate movements.

The dollar crisis of the early 1970s was followed first by inflation and rising oil and commodity prices and then by recession. In 1973 and 1974 the now ten-strong EEC attempted to counter the crisis by introducing a common energy policy and a common industrial and social strategy. But here, too, differences between oil producers such as Britain and the oil-consuming states limited effective unity.[23] At the same time the Belgian Prime Minister, Leo Tindemans, was asked to prepare a report on how the EEC could recover the impetus to achieve not merely economic and monetary integration but full political union. It was a symbolic gesture, however, and was not followed by any serious commitment by the member state governments to implement the recommendations of the reports.[24]

During the 1970s the economic crisis exacerbated the divergence in the economic performances of the member states. With the costs of unemployment rising, national governments began to get alarmed about levels of state expenditure and budget deficits. The climate for radical measures of EEC economic integration, especially those dependent on greater collective expenditure on common industrial objectives, turned increasingly sour. The Commission and national governments found their hands full dealing with a succession of short-term crises in particularly hard-hit industrial sectors such as textiles, shipbuilding, and steel. Crisis management, rather than longer-term strategic and economic planning, now dominated EEC decision-making. The situation in the Community took a turn for the worse after 1977 when the failure to control spending on the CAP produced a full-scale crisis in the Community's own budget.[25]

As early as 1971 there were fears even in core Community 'loyalist' states such as West Germany that the EEC was drifting dangerously. A West German Commissioner went so far as to write an anonymous article in a national newspaper, claiming that the Commission was

an illiberal and bureaucratic Leviathan, obsessed with harmonising things for the sake of harmonisation . . . the Common Agricultural Policy is threatening to fall apart . . . the check to economic and monetary union [is] a result of disagreement between France and West Germany . . . . It is time to abandon the idea that the Brussels Commission is the embryo which will one day grow into the government of Europe.[26]

On the other hand, left to themselves, market forces tended to lead away from rather than towards European integration. In this maelstrom of conflicting pressures and despite the Community's internal economic and political disarray, the EEC took one decision in 1975 which reflected the continuing pressures for faster progress towards union. A Community summit meeting in Rome agreed to convene the first-ever direct elections to the European Parliament, to be held in 1979, fulfilling the long-standing commitment of those who had launched the EEC to a supranational system of democratic control. But by putting the Tindemans report on ice the EEC governments denied the parliament the context in which it could play a more meaningful role.

Those who originally pressed for the European Parliament to be given a direct mandate by the electorate of the Community did so in the belief that by the time it came to pass the Common Market would have reached something close to economic and political union. There would then, they assumed, be a need to subject a powerful European executive to democratic control by European voters rather than indirect scrutiny by national Parliaments through appointed members. Ironically, the directly elected European Parliament came into being without there being anything remotely like a Community government in the making. The elected assembly was left as a purely consultative assembly without a clear executive interlocutor. The politically diminished Commission has proved more often than not to be an ally of the Council of Ministers rather than an adversary.[27] Far from acting as a catalyst to greater popular 'European' consciousness, the elected Parliament has floundered in a political vacuum, without a clearly defined function or real powers beyond limited entitlement to amend the annual budget (or, *in extremis*, to throw it out). It has, therefore, very little influence and no real authority over the Council, where the real executive power lies, and its advice, though it has to be sought by the Commission, does not have to be heeded by the Council of Ministers. It has failed to establish itself as a serious force in European politics.[28] This is bound to be the case until it has a powerful supranational executive over which it can seek to assert itself. That is also a prior condition for the development in the European Parliament of consistently ideological, rather than national, political discourse and conflict. In the meantime the European Parliament has gained some very marginal increases in its rights to amend Commission proposals, as part of the constitutional reforms introduced under the EEC 'Single Act' amendment to the Rome Treaty in 1987.

In theory the all-powerful Council of Ministers is answerable to the twelve different national Parliaments. The reality is very different. Effective national Parliamentary control is minimal, with the one exception of the Danish Folketing which has the power to mandate Danish ministers attending Council meetings.

There is, then, an unfilled democratic void at the heart of the EEC which will only be overcome by an agreement to give the elected European Parliament very much more substantial legislative and scrutiny powers. At present the Council is the real legislative body in the Community and, amazingly, is allowed to meet and pass laws in secrecy, shielded from scrutiny by the public or by the media.[29]

To date the major political groups in the European Parliament have allowed themselves to be overshadowed by their national Parliamentary colleagues. Too many of them are happy to settle for a quiet and pleasant life. This is unlikely to change until the whole debate about the future of the EEC is repoliticized in a way that it has not been since its foundation. Until that happens the political groups will not be in a position to develop programmes for the future of the EEC or be able to win serious support for their ideas among the mass of what is, at present, an almost totally indifferent electorate.

By the late 1970s the members of the Council of Ministers were increasingly operating to rigid national mandates and, with the national veto, were capable of blocking even the most modest moves towards integration. A large measure of effective power has passed to the Committee of Permanent Representatives (the ambassadors of the member states) known by its French acronym, COREPER. An increasingly frustrated Commission found itself with an ever-long list of proposals for common European policies ignored by member states.

The British and French showed the greatest distaste for anything smacking of 'supranationalism'. The third core member state, West Germany, has also given ineffective leadership during the past two decades. Content to reap the benefits of industrial free trade, Bonn has appeared to lose interest in the Community as such during the 1980s. For this reason the Federal Republic has the reputation of being Western Europe's 'economic giants, but political pygmies'. Worse still, West Germany has proved itself as narrowly short-sighted as any other state in defending the privileges of its own farmers against pressure for CAP reform.[30] The European Commission was sufficiently alarmed at the scale of frictions and misunderstandings between the Community and the Federal Republic to hold an unprecedented meeting of the full European Commission and the West German cabinet in April 1987 in an effort to 'clear the air' and solve the Community's mounting budget crisis.

During the late 1970s and early 1980s there was even some speculation about whether the EEC might break up. A variety of alternatives were canvassed. These included an à la carte Community which would not require all members to accept all common policies and might repatriate much of the remaining powers left with EEC institutions back to the national states.[31]

It was not an approach, however, which seemed to offer any easier route to European co-operation and little was heard of it during the 1980s.

One institution which was influential in preventing any centrifugal tendencies in the Community during these years was the European Council, the now twice-yearly summit meetings of the heads of state and government of the EEC. It was able to resolve the long-standing dispute over Britain's complaint about its EEC budget rebate in 1985. However, its influence has, at the same time, worked to reduce the standing of the decision-making bodies created by the Treaty of Rome, notably the European Commission itself.

It was the internal CAP and budget crisis which overshadowed all other internal tensions during these years. This was brought to a head in 1977 by the British government which announced it could no longer accept a situation in which, although one of the economically weakest member states, it ended up as the second largest net contributor to the annual EEC budget. There was eventual agreement about the unfairness in the contributions and benefits paid to and derived from the common EEC budget by different national member states. This primarily arose because the growth of Community spending on agriculture had not been matched by a strengthening of common policies and expenditure on other key Community policies such as industrial and technological development and common social and regional development. Britain, as a food importer rather than a major agricultural producer, did particularly badly out of the CAP which was already unpopular for the rise in food prices to UK consumers after the phasing out of cheaper Commonwealth imports. The fact that Britain would end up a net contributor to the European budget, like West Germany, had always been foreseen by those who negotiated the terms of membership. But they had assumed that, like West Germany, Britain would profit through exploiting EEC markets for its manufactured exports by far more than the cost of its annual budget payments. Few had expected that a few years after EEC entry Britain would have a massive and growing trade deficit, not a surplus, with the rest of the Common Market. This discredited one of the fundamental planks for EEC membership advanced by successive British governments since that of Harold Macmillan.

A series of ill-tempered and bitterly divisive EEC summits failed to resolve the British budget crisis, although awareness that the EEC budget itself could be bankrupted by the constant increase in the cost of the CAP did gradually produce a consensus in favour of radical reform. By 1984 a partial solution was found which put a ceiling on Britain's future net payments to the EEC budget but left the fundamental issues of agricultural reform unresolved, despite the fact that EEC farm production and export subsidies had now brought the Community to the brink of trade war with the United States. The budget and farm rows had the effect of turning attention inwards and inflaming national rivalries and nationalist attitudes within the Community just at the time when Europe needed to adopt a collective stand to face the growing international crisis and the strains in relations with the United States. The budget dominated EEC ministerial and summit agendas for five years during which the crises of mass unemployment, de-industrialization, and technological decline received scant attention.

One step towards the original goal of monetary union during this period was taken in December 1978 when EEC heads of state and government finally agreed to establish a European Monetary System (EMS). This had four main components: a European Currency Unit (ECU), an exchange and information mechanism, credit facilities, and transfer arrangements. At its heart was a fixed exchange-rate mechanism which all the EEC states joined, apart from Britain and subsequently Greece. The British kept their distance from the EMS for a mixture of reasons, worried that as an 'oil currency' sterling could not be easily contained in the exchange-rate mechanism. Whitehall feared loss of control of credit and monetary policy to the West German central bank because of the dominating role of the Deutschmark in the EMS, while the Labour leaders feared they would be forced by Bundesbank conservative orthodoxy to deflate rather than devalue sterling if the UK economy hit trouble.[32] National governments remained reluctant either to pursue common economic recovery strategies or to accept disciplines which derived logically from their adhesion to the EMS. However, the early 1980s saw a rightward swing of the political pendulum in the majority of EEC member states, bringing to power governments determined to impose monetar-

ist, anti-inflationary policies despite mass unemployment. The
result was a kind of harmonization of national economic strategies but one biassed to deflation rather than to recovery.

The 'New Right' European monetarist governments were
willing to risk deepening the economic recession and the
already very high levels of unemployment in the Community in
order to reach the goal of reduced inflation and increased international competitiveness for European industry. Any Community government attempting a unilateral expansion of its
economy and resisting the deflationary bias in the EEC became
all the more vulnerable to pressures on its currency within the
EMS and the international money markets. As already noted,
the French Socialist–Communist coalition was, for this reason,
driven to abandon its attempt to expand out of crisis and mass
unemployment. A similar fate befell the Greek left-of-centre
government of Andreas Papandreou in 1985–6. The Socialist
government in Spain fell into line with the deflationary orthodoxy even more rapidly, jettisoning its original programme
soon after being elected.[33]

The New Right orthodoxy reinforced an existing bias in public expenditure, above all increases in EEC budget-spending on
common industrial and social objectives. But at the same time
governments had to face the stark reality that industrial Europe
was falling further and further behind its major international
rivals, Japan and the United States.

The decline of the EEC among the developed industrial
economies can be measured in a variety of different ways. In
common with the United States, for example, the Community's
share of world trade has fallen since 1973. The decline has been
particularly severe for manufacturing and especially for trade in
the 'high technology' sectors. This betrays a more general European problem of backwardness in high-technology research and
innovation.[34] As a result a competitivity gap has opened up
between Western Europe and the United States and, especially,
Japan. Europe supplies only 25 per cent of its semi-conductors,
it has a $10 billion deficit in main-frame computers, and a cur-
rent surplus in telecommunications equipment is thought by
some experts to be heading for a deficit of as much as $16 billion
by 1990.[35]

During the early 1980s European governments, industrial

leaders, and the EEC authorities were left in no doubt about the way in which the technology gap was, in turn, leading to the subordination of some of Western Europe's most important multinational firms to American and Japanese interests. As a result of a new wave of international mergers and take-over and technology exchange agreements from the late 1970s the independent existence of an advanced European industry was being called into question in key sectors.[36] In the early 1980s leading European industrialists came to the conclusion that European industry would have to be encouraged to restructure with the direct help and involvement of the EEC and its member states if it was to survive in an ever more competitive international market. The idea was that the restructuring should be carried out through deliberate co-operation among European multinationals, otherwise the grip of American and Japanese companies would actually increase and Europe would eventually descend to a dependent industrial status.

It was this preoccupation which led to initiatives such as that of the chief executive of Volvo, Pehr Gyllenhammar, to establish the Round-table of European Industrialists in April 1983. This 'top club' of leading European multinationals had the active support of the European Commission and set itself the objective to 'help strengthen and develop Europe's industrial and technological base', principally by promoting transnational frontier business and co-operation.[37] The idea was to encourage European big business to seek European rather than non-European partners for collaboration, particularly in the high-technology area. At the same time the Commission attempted to encourage the process by renewing efforts to remove remaining internal barriers to free trade within the EEC, by urging a European rather than a national preference in public purchasing policy, and by backing major new high-technology innovation and development schemes. As a result the EEC and national governments established or participated in a number of projects known by their acronyms, such as EUREKA, ESPRIT, FAST, and RACE, designed to encourage high-technology research and innovation with particular emphasis on key high-technology sectors such as informatics, telecommunications, and bio-technology projects of both a commercial and a pre-commercial character. Some of these projects, such as

EUREKA, involve eighteen different European countries and not just the twelve-nation EEC. The European Community has approved some fifty major joint development projects, mainly in computers, semi-conductors, and telecommunications.[38] There has been some debate about what relationship, if any, EUREKA should have with European NATO defence development programmes. There have even been suggestions, reportedly favoured in France, to use EUREKA as an umbrella for co-ordinating research and development of a Western European version of the American SDI. But, thus far, it has retained a non-military character.[39]

The whole subject of the scale of funding of these projects is still a matter of intense dispute within the EEC, and the question of a future link between EUREKA and future European defence research cannot be regarded as totally closed. There are also differences of basic strategic philosophy such as the extent to which European research programmes should be purely 'market-driven'. Many professionals urge a longer-term and more socially based view of the priorities for European research.

Some modest progress has been made in reducing the remaining barriers to a fully integrated European market, but the harmonization of common industrial and other standards may still be some considerable time away. Attempts to secure an end to discrimination in favour of 'national' suppliers in the allocation of public-sector contracts have not been made easier by the near-bankrupt state of some major firms and by mass unemployment. There are many national interests opposed to the creation of a common market in financial and other services.[40] This explains why Italy, Greece, and other countries have tried to block Commission plans to integrate and reduce internal airfares. The West Germans have opposed an integrated market in banking and insurance, while France has dragged its feet on moves to eliminate indirect or hidden trade barriers. For its part Britain has been unenthusiastic about proposals to harmonize indirect taxes, notably VAT.

Sparse results have so far been achieved by the attempt to foster intra-European restructuring by European multinationals. A study prepared for the European Commission in 1986 on corporate agreements in the telecom and related sectors showed that the number of agreements or at least contacts between European and outside firms outnumbered those between European firms themselves by a factor of three to one.[41]

Towards the end of the 1980s, therefore, the EEC still faces the prospect that conventional free-market strategy, even one bolstered by state or EEC support for high-technology development, may not be capable of reversing Europe's industrial decline. There is, however, equal confusion about Japanese and American direct investment in European industry and about the wisdom of technology co-operation.

Some have argued that 'European companies stand to gain from alliances with the Americans and the Japanese that give them access to those companies' experience, research and, if possible, markets in return for advantages in Europe'.[42] Against that it is pointed out that unless European governments 'co-ordinate their approach, especially on the terms on which participation is to be accepted, the US will attempt to pick up only those technologies where European companies or research establishments have a lead over the US. This could leave many companies whose work could be competitive with their US counterparts with no role to play.'[43] Either way, European big business intends to exercise a much greater influence over policy-making in the EEC in future. Another European Research Associates report predicts that in future 'the European Commission will act as much as a service agency for business as an initiator of laws and regulations'. It also suggests that, in the interest of building stronger international corporations within the EEC, less may be heard about anti-trust policy. Companies headquartered outside the Community will 'have to deal with a European strategy geared to meeting the competitive threat of its rivals' and the encouragement of a 'European political/industrial complex'. This approach will be 'challenged strongly by the United States and the GATT'.[44]

But it is not only over commercial and industrial policy that the Europeans have displayed an incapacity to think through and execute a strategy towards the changing character of the Atlantic partnership. The European response over defence and foreign policy issues has been equally confused.

Since the 1979 NATO decision on cruise and Pershing missiles, there has been much talk about the need to build a stronger and more self-supporting 'European pillar' within NATO. This means a number of different things, including greater European interdependence in defence-equipment production and procurement; a more assertive European voice on key strategic issues such as arms control; and a more vigorous promotion of European interests in out-of-area issues affecting NATO states, primarily in the Middle East and Africa.

In theory the European governments in NATO accept the logic that having a bigger voice in policy may have to be accompanied by paying more of NATO's budget. There is even some willingness to contemplate European forces taking up some of the slack created by possible future reductions (or even the total departure) of US troops based in Western Europe. The reality is rather different. All the European NATO states talk of the need for greater European self-reliance but they seem—to date—incapable of willing the means.

Far from signalling their willingness to increase defence spending, virtually all the European NATO governments are slowing down the rate of increase in defence expenditure between now and the end of the 1980s. Most are under severe budgetary pressures because of mass unemployment, while the British and French are having to cut back on conventional defence spending because of the escalating cost of their national nuclear weapons systems.

Nor is it the case that the Europeans have been able to agree on a comprehensive European defence procurement policy. National military and industrial interests have so far limited the areas of genuine European co-operation on arms production and procurement. But the cases of the £20 billion European Fighter Aircraft project, bedevilled by disagreements between the British and the French, and the troubled Franco-German joint tank project, are all too typical.[45]

The European NATO governments have shown even less resolution in developing a common-policy arms-control strategy. Indeed one reason why Britain, France, Italy, and the Benelux states revived the Western European Union in the 1980s was to have a forum for such exchange that was not overshadowed by the presence of the Americans. The participating governments also went a long way to reassure the Americans by excluding not only neutral EEC states, such as the Irish Republic, but dangerously free-thinking NATO governments, such as Denmark and Greece. Even so, America objected to what it saw as an attempt to influence alliance strategy on arms control behind their backs, and after strong representations from Washington the WEU effectively abandoned any attempt to work out a distinctively European position on issues of sensitivity.[46] But the Europeans did not disguise their anger when it emerged after the Reykjavik summit that America was willing to contemplate far-reaching strategic and intermediate-range nuclear weapons concessions without even prior consultation with the governments most affected.

But if the European NATO states have been unwilling or unable to stand up for their own interests with the Americans, their track record on agreeing common foreign policy positions outside NATO is no more impressive. There was the protracted disarray of the EEC states during 1986 and 1987 over South African sanctions when the British and West German governments, ignoring the clear position of the majority, were determined to dilute the sanctions so as not to hit potential industrial interests in South Africa. Again, when the British called for sanctions against Syria because of its alleged support for terrorism, some EEC states held back, partly because of doubts as to whether terrorism was really favoured at the highest levels of the government in Damascus, but partly because of specific national commercial and political interests in the region.

The contrast between the rhetoric of all the EEC governments on 'European solidarity' and the record in practice is the more striking because the great majority of governments share a similar Right-wing political philosophy. But this limited European foreign policy consensus will surely be put under much greater strain if the European political pendulum moves back to the left.

Despite its set-back in the general election of January 1987, the election in a few years of a West German Social Democratic government committed to radical changes in NATO's nuclear strategy, especially if dependent on support from the Green Party, which is now firmly opposed to West German membership of NATO, would pose a serious challenge to existing European NATO orthodoxy. And the return to office of the British

Labour Party, which is pledged to remove all US nuclear bases from Britain and also secure far-reaching changes in NATO strategy, including a pledge for 'no first use' of nuclear weapons, would be an even bigger shock to the system.

In summary, commercial conflict with America and Japan is pushing Europe to a more aggressive and partly protectionist industrial counter-strategy. But there is little evidence for believing that a strategy determined by European big business and shaped by essentially free-market considerations will be capable of resisting, let alone reversing, the de-industrialization of Europe and its subordination to non-European interests.

Meanwhile, disillusion is growing with the failure of the European Community either to tackle its major internal problems, such as the CAP, or to confront the central economic issues of de-industrialization and unemployment. In consequence there is in most EEC countries a growth of narrow-minded parochial nationalism, which means that there is no strong political constituency for arguing a 'Europeanist' strategy.

As far as defence and foreign policy are concerned, the governments of Western Europe seem incapable either of challenging America for control of NATO strategy or of developing a credible European alternative security strategy of their own. There is growing awareness of the gulf dividing Europe and America but no capacity to respond to the challenge of a post-Atlantic world. It seems that parties and governments committed to free-market economic policies will have the greatest difficulty in devising alternative foreign and security strategies to those which rest at present on the Atlantic relationship.

The question remains—is it too late for an independent Europe to assert itself? Is there an alternative to the Balkanization or the subordination of Europe? Might there yet be a different basis for organizing Europe's economy and society? It is to these alternatives that we finally turn.

7 | After Atlanticism—Agenda for a New Europe

The Atlantic Alliance, defined in its wider political sense, could now, in the late 1980s, be facing a period of potentially terminal decline. The long-term trends in the world economy towards a new global regionalism, the bifurcating evolution of American and European geopolitics, and the deepening conflicts over both trade and defence, all seem to prefigure either a rupture or, at least, the slow decay of Atlanticism. Yet, as we have seen, Europe is ill-prepared to tackle the consequences of these developments.

There have been earlier periods marked by transatlantic tensions over a variety of issues. The period between 1971 and 1974 was particularly fraught and there were frictions between 1961 and 1964 and even between 1953 and 1955. But they are not to be compared with either the scale or the complexity of the differences which have opened up across the Atlantic in the past decade.

It would be foolish, however, to write any premature obituaries for the Atlanticist system. Any political structure or set of ideas which has held sway for as long as the Atlantic Alliance and has had such apparently close correspondence with deep-rooted historical and political forces in both the United States and Western Europe will not readily disintegrate.

It would also be foolish to underestimate the importance of the close personal and political ties which still bind many of the present generation of politicians and policy makers in office on both sides of the Atlantic.[1] Even given the swing towards a new globalism in US strategic thinking—personified by the advocates of SDI and, at the economic level, giving priority to the Pacific Basin over Europe—there are influential 'Atlanticists' to be found in American public life. Equally, there are politicians in power in Western Europe who, whatever the anxieties and conflicts with Washington, are anxious to preserve as much of the Atlantic relationship as possible. If they feel, as many do, that a break with the United States might encourage European neutralism in foreign and defence policies and might lead to a revival of anti-capitalist values in economic and social policies, they will be ready to make some sacrifices to preserve the primacy of the Alliance.

These men and women grew up and received their political education during the 1940s and 1950s, in a world largely enclosed by the assumptions of the Cold War and the Atlantic Alliance. They are to be found not only in politics and government service but also in the universities, the media, and other decision-making and opinion-forming institutions in America and Europe.

On the other hand, even within those political parties which have been historically most committed to Atlanticism, a generation is emerging which is less moved by references to post-war or early Cold War history and shared experiences. They now look at the costs and benefits of the Atlantic partnership in a colder, more calculating light.

In the United States this hard-nosed reappraisal of the Atlantic Alliance is typically reflected in an article, written by a leading American industrialist, entitled 'Should the US pull out of NATO?'. The writer compares Europe's declining economic significance for US capital to the growth of the Pacific Rim economies and concludes, 'When we measure the near optimised markets of Europe and its 250 million persons against the near unoptimised 1.5 billion to 2 billion people of the Pacific Basin, Europe seems a puny affair.'[2]

We have seen the extraordinary rise of the 'anti-Atlanticists' —sometimes known as the 'new globalists'—within the Republican Party and among key government advisers in the United States. Often to be found on the right wing of the Reagan administration, these policy-makers are deeply sceptical about the primacy traditionally accorded to the alliance with Western Europe and they resent the constraints it imposes on America's freedom of action.

Whatever their other differences with the Republican Right, many of these frustrations with the Europeans are shared by the new leaders emerging in the Democratic Party. The Democrats are as angry as is the Republican administration at what they see as the reluctance of the Europeans to pay a 'fairer share' of the costs of running the NATO alliance.

Indeed, the Democratic Senate leader, Sam Nunn, who could be his party's next Presidential candidate, has demanded increases in NATO conventional force goals as well as radical changes in burden-sharing. He has not disavowed the implicit threat that America will reduce its forces in Europe if the Europeans do not collaborate. He has already warned that 'the American poor and working class are getting fed up with having to pay for the defence of the European rich and middle class'. (One US official chided the Europeans, 'We have gutted our social programmes. You have not.')[3]

In the looming economic confrontation and trade war with Western Europe, a Democratic administration may prove more, not less, belligerent than a Republican one. During its years in opposition to Reagan, the pressures of de-industrialization and the economic decline of many electoral strongholds on the north and east coasts of America have had their impact on the Democrats. The Democratic Party has moved a long way from the traditional American bipartisan consensus in favour of free trade and against protectionism.

At the start of 1987, negotiations to settle the long-standing conflict between the United States and the EEC over American grain exports to Spain and Portugal broke down. More ominously, both sides were preparing a series of escalating sanctions and countersanctions and only last-minute concessions by the EEC prevented open trade warfare. The US telecommunications authorities had initiated action to hit European imports and the EEC had protested over moves in Washington to try and curb machine-tool imports.[4]

It is too soon to say how quickly and how radically a Democratic President, if elected in 1988, would sanction a general move to protectionism. Certainly the Democrats now support sweeping powers being given to the US government to hit countries deemed to be trading 'unfairly' with America. Short of an economic miracle, an increasing number of American politicians will find there are many more votes in protectionism than in free trade in the years ahead.

The irony, then, is that the Democratic Party which, since 1945, has been most consistently Atlanticist in its foreign policy could yet trigger a major breach with allied European governments by initially withdrawing perhaps 100,000 of the 325,000

US troops currently stationed in Europe. Some Democrat strategists, alarmed at America's mounting budget crisis, have already raised the possibility. Others, such as Zbigniew Brzezinski, have suggested that some American forces assigned to Western Europe be redeployed to the Middle East, specifically to the Persian Gulf.

Three other critical factors will bear on the fate of Atlanticism. They are the health of the world economy, the prospects for agreed reductions in the nuclear arsenals of the superpowers and thus for the future of *détente* between East and West, and the extent to which the European political pendulum swings towards the pro-disarmament and even neutralist European Left. A new economic recession, deadlock over arms control, a reversion to Cold War relations across the Iron Curtain, and radical political changes in Europe will toll the knell for Atlanticism.

Short- and medium-term forecasts about international economic trends are notoriously unreliable. But by the start of 1987 the clear weight of evidence suggested that several key Western industrialized capitalist economies, including the United States, Japan, and West Germany, were heading for another recession of uncertain intensity and duration. Mainstream official international economic agencies such as the OECD were convinced that unemployment would remain above 31 million in the industrialized economies as far ahead as could be reasonably forecast and were fearful of the risk of recession by 1988.[5]

Even before the 1988 US Presidential election, the Democrats' success in the November 1986 Congressional elections had, by the end of the year, increased the prospects of Congressional trade legislation of a protectionist character before 1988. In what commentators see as a last-ditch effort to head off outright protection, the Reagan administration has unveiled a series of measures designed to improve the competitiveness of US industry through a variety of support measures and a *de facto* import curb.[6] Further legislation, involving curbs on imports from countries which fail to reduce their trade surpluses with the United States as Washington demands, seems primarily aimed at Japanese, South Korean, and other Asian 'superexporters'.[7]

The basic international trade conflict is now triangular, with the United States, Western Europe, and the countries of the

Pacific Rim increasingly pitted against each other. American action taken to deter Japanese and other Asian exporters will tend to have the (possibly) unintended side-effect of deflecting the Japanese/Asian export drive towards European markets. Although in theory, and over a long period, the Asian exporting nations could increase home demand to produce more balanced growth, this cannot be achieved overnight, so that to reduce export growth is, for those countries, to risk shutting down the motor of economic growth itself.[8] At the same time the yawning US budget deficit was still, at the start of 1987, distorting the international pattern of savings, investment, and trade.

There were few signs that the fall in the US dollar would rapidly eliminate the trade deficit or that any foreseeable US administration would be politically strong enough to take the kind of domestic action which would result in a speedy elimination of the domestic budget deficit. Indeed, to do so might be to risk not just a recession but an outright slump in the US economy which would be bound soon to spread to the rest of the world.

The Democrats may cut back the Pentagon's more extravagant planned increases in arms-spending, but they will be less willing than the Reagan administration to reduce federal nonmilitary spending. They will also have very limited scope for major increases in taxation. Unless, therefore, a totally unexpected economic boom appears from nowhere, both the external and the budget deficits look set to remain at crisis levels. The Gramm–Rudman bill requiring a balanced budget by 1992 seems doomed.[9] One alternative might be for the Europeans, as well as Japan and the other Pacific Rim economies, to reflate their own economies to an extraordinary degree or, in other words, to shoulder virtually all the sacrifices in correcting the American deficits. The Europeans and the Japanese are willing to make modest concessions to US demands for reflation and interest-rate reductions, but they insist they cannot go as far as some in Washington are demanding for fear of triggering a new inflation in their economies.[10]

Acute imbalances of trade and persistently high unemployment provide a poor environment in which to defend the GATT system of world free trade or to secure the degree of currency co-operation between the regional world monetary powers necessary to guard against the possibility of an international banking crash. The spectre of a world banking crisis cannot be ignored as long as major developing nations may yet be forced to default on their international banking loans. Little wonder that the EEC is seeking to strengthen the EMS as a self-contained regional currency system which seeks, as far as possible, to insulate Europe from the perils of too close and subordinate a relationship with the US dollar.[11]

One immediate flashpoint is transatlantic conflict over agricultural trade. At the start of 1987 both the EEC and the United States stood ready to impose sweeping sanctions because of the loss of markets to the United States when Spain and Portugal joined the EEC. Outright farm-trade conflict would be bound, in turn, to call into question the entire future of the GATT free-trade negotiations.[12] There are, moreover, already some signs of a slow-down in overseas investment by large US multinational companies, some of which are already starting a disinvestment programme in Europe and repatriating key overseas projects, including some with the more advanced technologies, to the United States. This was an issue which led to protests by European trade unionists working for the American Kodak Corporation in 1984 and 1985. A decision by the American Caterpillar Tractor company to close a profitable Scottish plant with the loss of more than 2,000 jobs at the end of 1986 and concentrate production within the United States, led not only to widespread protests in Britain, supported by some Conservative government ministers, but to a protracted occupation of the threatened plant by its workers.

One remarkable feature of the 1980s was the greater flow of European investment to the United States than vice versa. While much of this investment has gone into Federal government securities, and this has helped fund America's enormous budget deficit, there has also been a sharp increase in direct European investment in US industry. This has not, however, always been welcome and it has sometimes resulted in protests by local communities and workforces, on occasions backed by local and state authorities, angered at what they fear may be the loss of American jobs in a foreign-controlled rationalization process.[13]

Overshadowing these commercial and financial disputes is the overriding issue of the future of Western European security policy. On the one hand the apparent determination of the United States to pursue SDI (a dangerous chimera in the eyes of many Europeans) could yet lead to the undermining of the Soviet–American ABM Treaty and of the prospects of agreement with the Soviet Union on major reductions in (let alone the elimination of) strategic nuclear forces. At the same time the speed with which in early 1987 the United States seemed ready to move to an agreement eliminating all American and Soviet land-based intermediate-range nuclear missiles in Europe was further eroding the confidence of even the most loyal European NATO governments. In the eyes of many right-wing European Atlanticists, the beginning of the end of the American nuclear guarantee for the defence of Western Europe seemed to be in sight.

For all these reasons it was impossible to be confident that a comprehensive breakthrough in East–West arms-reduction negotiations was finally within grasp. Although after Reykjavik in the autumn of 1986 the prospects for reductions in medium-range 'Euro missiles' did appear brighter, the two nuclear superpowers appeared further apart than ever on the crucial question of long-range strategic nuclear weapons.

In a sense the Americans are caught in a Catch 22 trap where they cannot satisfy the conflicting aspirations of all their European allies. Failure to meet Soviet objections to the development of SDI or to agree to make deep cuts in strategic nuclear forces in negotiations with the Soviet Union is bound to expose Washington to deep criticism, even from European NATO governments, as well as to condemnation by a remobilized European peace movement which already sees the United States as the primary obstacle to disarmament. American obduracy over strategic nuclear weapons, above all SDI, could also have the effect of weakening the internal political authority of those sections of the Soviet leadership, around Mikhail Gorbachev, who have offered far-reaching concessions to the West in arms-reduction negotiations.

On the other hand, if Washington does agree to scrap virtually all shorter-range as well as medium-range intermediate nuclear missiles in Europe, some European governments will fear the 'abandonment' of the defence of Europe by the United States. The British and French governments will also resist any implicit understandings between the United States and the Soviet Union which could imply a halt to the expansion of their own national nuclear forces. In so far as the British government in the late 1980s was counting on replacing its Polaris nuclear missiles with the newer American Trident D missiles, it was vulnerable to a possible Soviet–American consensus on these lines.[14]

It is unclear how the Americans will react to this 'damned if we do and damned if we don't' dilemma in managing their future alliance with the Western Europeans. In the short run Washington may agree to moderate its negotiating tactics with the Soviet Union so as not to offend right-wing European susceptibilities over the intermediate-range balance or over supplies of nuclear weapons to sustain Britain's 'independent deterrent', even if this should delay an overall arms agreement.[15] But if budgetary pressures to curb defence-spending increase, a future US administration might feel obliged to clinch the best deal it can with the Russians, whatever the fears of the Europeans. One trigger for a possible agreement between a future US President and Moscow might be further concessions by the Soviet Union on the size and deployment of the Warsaw Pact's conventional forces in Central Europe. These might be offered either in the Soviet–American negotiations on Mutual and Balanced Force Reductions in Vienna or in the wider Conference on Security and Co-operation in Europe.[16]

It is more likely, however, that US insistence on the continued space-testing and development of SDI, even at the expense of a strategic arms deal with the Soviet Union, will force a different kind of crisis in relations between the United States and Western Europe. Sooner or later the European NATO states will make their opposition to SDI more public, and if SDI were really, over a period of years, to imperil an agreement with the Soviet Union, a major breach between the allies would surely follow.

This combination of a worsening international economic environment and growing divergences in European–American security interests may also exacerbate transatlantic differences over foreign policy. The Europeans already resent what they see as an unacceptable degree of American unilateralism in the formulation and execution of major foreign-policy initiatives, sometimes without elementary consultation with the Europeans. Recent examples include the covert decision of the Reagan administration during late 1986 to reopen diplomatic contacts with the Khomeini regime in Iran and to dispatch arms supplies to Tehran directly and through its Israeli surrogate. This was in blatant contravention of agreed Alliance policy not to supply offensive weapons to either side in the Iran–Iraq Gulf War, as well as violating the agreed policy of the NATO partners not to send arms to regimes designated (above all by the Americans) as practising 'state sponsored terrorism'.

The question for the Europeans is whether the Atlanticist system can be repaired, and if so how. Alternatively, if the present combination of economic, political, and security differences implies an inevitable 'separation' between the United States and Western Europe, how should Europe handle the changed relationship?

There are a number of sharply different and some fundamentally conflicting perspectives on offer. They can be roughly grouped into four separate categories: Atlantic reformism, European reformism, European Gaullism, and, finally, a non-aligned Socialist Europe. Although the different approaches do not yet correspond exactly to any existing European political formations, they do mark the most obvious poles of future discussion about European alternatives.

What I have called 'Atlantic reformism' approximates, at present, to the official policy of most of the European NATO states. Some European politicians believe that 'Atlantic reformism' should take precedence over 'European reformism'. Many others still believe it is possible to pursue both objectives and, as a result, restructure the entire Atlantic relationship. But while in the past there was no overriding contradiction between the two positions, this is less and less true today. In future, European states may have to make their first priority strengthening and reforming the EEC.

The main premiss of the Atlantic reformists is that a powerful 'European pillar' can and must be developed within the Alliance and that this will ensure a greater coherence and evenhandedness in the evolution of Alliance strategy on all key issues, notably on arms control. According to the Atlantic reformists it is up to the Europeans to get their act together on policy formulation and integration of the European defence industry and arms procurement. They point out that the so-called 'Euro-group' was formed in NATO at the end of 1968 to improve specifically Western European Co-operation in the Alliance. However, France does not participate since it is not a member of NATO's integrated military command. France is, however, a member of the Independent European Programme Group, set up in 1976, to facilitate rationalization of defence equipment procurement. To date the Western Europeans are a long way from having achieved a genuinely common European arms procurement policy or the rationalization of the European defence industry. The tendency persists, therefore, either to 'buy American' or to encourage (or at any rate permit) European firms to negotiate deals in which they are relegated to being junior partners with US corporations—as witness the Westland affair. The trouble is that too great a technological/industrial gap exists between many US arms manufacturers and their European counterparts readily to justify preference being given to the European as opposed to the US product. This was, for instance, clearly the determining factor in forcing the British government to abandon development of the British GEC NIMROD airborne early-warning system in favour of an immediate purchase of the rival American AWACS system made by Boeing. In theory nothing stops the Europeans asserting themselves more strongly in policy formulation. But even the larger Western European NATO states buckled quickly under American pressure in 1985 to prevent the Western European Union becoming a Europeans-only forum to hammer out common European arms control policies. Although a further effort to revive the WEU as a European caucus within NATO got under way in 1987, it remained unclear to what extent the Europeans would assert their views in open defiance of American thinking.

But if the Europeans did opt for a policy of defiance, what would be the likely American response? Not all US policymakers are opposed, in principle, to the Europeans having a bigger say in the formulation of policy, and some are even willing to allow the Europeans a much bigger say over the shape and direction of US negotiations with the Soviet Union. But any US administration which might be persuaded to go down this road might demand a heavy price of the Europeans. This would surely include the Europeans making a bigger direct financial contribution to the cost of the US forces kept in Europe. The scale of what might be involved in a more 'equitable' share of costs should not be underestimated. Although the European NATO states are committed to supplying 85 per cent of the ground forces and 80 per cent of the aircraft on the outbreak of war, about 30 per cent of the entire US defence budget is attributable to the defence of Europe. Some estimates put the incremental operating costs of stationing US forces in Europe at about $2 billion and the total costs, including early reinforcement, at $90 billion. According to this view, 'Europe will cost the United States $2.2 trillion' over the next ten years.[17] Some US politicians believe privately that the Europeans may have to replace a minimum of a third or a half of the present just under six US divisions stationed in West Germany with their own forces over the next few years. They also insist the Europeans must spend more on NATO's longer-term force goals, possibly including highly controversial objectives such as chemical warfare capacity and logistical back-up for the US Rapid Deployment Force for use outside Europe. Any remaining net US costs arising from America's European commitment might even then still have to be offset by US arms sales to Europe. At the start of 1987 there was a veritable chorus of leading Democratic party leaders, including Senator Sam Nunn, Senator John Glenn, and Zbigniew Brzezinski, calling for an immediate withdrawal of 100,000 of the 300,000 US troops in Western Europe. This was resisted by the Reagan administration both because it would 'undermine the confidence our allies have in NATO' and because withdrawal itself would be a costly business, incurring a one-off expense of $5 billion, which would not be recouped for five years.[18]

The Americans will also want assurances that there will be no flagging in the willingness of the Europeans to carry out the 'nuclear tasks' and other military duties allotted to them in NATO's current war-fighting strategy. The United States would not want to hear any questioning of NATO doctrines such as 'Follow on Force Attack' and 'Airland Battle' in conditions where the Europeans were being given an equal voice in shaping Alliance policy. In addition the Europeans might be required to swallow their reservations about current NATO strategy which envisages the possible use of nuclear weapons fairly early on in any conflict. All of these conditions would be extremely difficult to sell politically in most if not all of the allied states. Indeed, some European NATO states are already discussing decreasing their allotted roles within NATO strategy. There is general agreement within the Netherlands on a scaling-down of its existing nuclear tasks while the government has signalled it may even reconsider its agreement to site cruise nuclear missiles in view of the disappointing outcome to the Reykjavik summit. The Danish opposition parties have now adopted a 'defensive defence' policy which calls for the withdrawal to Denmark of some Danish forces now under joint command with the West Germans, the disarming of the bomb-carrying capacity of their F16 aircraft, and the phasing out of their naval combat capacity.[19]

The biggest problem of all would be to persuade the European governments about (and for the European governments to win electoral support for) an increase in defence-spending, particularly on greater conventional forces, to replace some at least of the American forces withdrawn from Europe. If the alternative was to share the burden of the existing commitment with the United States more 'equitably', this would also inevitably involve greater levels of European defence-spending. As long as the Europeans do not abandon the entire concept of a serious (if not imminent) Soviet military and nuclear threat they will be vulnerable to arguments which logically require them not to decrease but to increase defence-spending, and to undertake some of the nuclear military roles currently undertaken by the Americans. Virtually all the NATO European states fulfilled their promised contribution to the annual 3 per cent growth in arms-spending laid down by NATO in 1979, but more recently the rate of defence-expenditure growth has decelerated or even gone into reverse in many Western European NATO countries. This is even true in Britain, although the situation there is complicated by the growing drain on the British defence budget as a result of the planned acquisition of the US Trident nuclear submarine system.

In both France and Britain the cost of sustaining a separate nuclear deterrent seems certain further to erode conventional defence commitments. This has encouraged the British Labour Party to adopt a policy whereby the savings made by cancelling Trident are added to the country's existing conventional defence budget. However, there is considerable internal opposition within the Labour movement to any further increase in defence-spending at a time of economic crisis, high unemployment, and underfunded social services in Britain.

One may take leave to doubt whether significant increases in arms-spending would, in practice, be delivered by any of the European NATO governments in the event of a major withdrawal of US troops over the next few years. There are still powerful financial and political pressures on all the Western European governments to curb the overall growth of public spending. In most countries the social and political tolerances of cuts in non-military spending have already been tested to their limits.

Governments attempting to divert further resources from the social to the defence budget might expect to have to pay a heavy political price. At a time when popular belief that Western Europe faces a tangible threat to its security from the Soviet bloc appears to be waning, it is likely to be very difficult in the late 1980s and 1990s to persuade voters to accept the sacrifices involved in maintaining, let alone increasing, defence-spending. In the absence of such commitment by its European allies, however, it is doubtful whether any US administration will concede genuine parity in policy-making within the Alliance, whatever the superficial niceties about 'improved consultation'.

The programme of reform of the NATO structures and strategies sought by the mainly conservative European NATO Alliance members has so far achieved little. But what would happen if Western Europe elected governments pledged to far-reaching changes in NATO's overall nuclear and war-fighting strategies in the future as well? There is no doubting the scale of the challenge to American views about NATO's future which is spelled out in the current defence programmes of the British Labour Party and, to a lesser extent, of the West German SPD. These parties seek not just the removal of US medium-range missiles but, in the case of Britain, all US nuclear bases.[20] They are committed to a drastic alteration in NATO's basic war-fighting posture from 'follow on force' and other deep-penetration and forward-defence strategies to a much more non-offensive stance. They would also eliminate the possession of battlefield nuclear weapons and outlaw NATO's existing policy of nuclear 'first strike' in the event of NATO forces being unable to repel a Soviet conventional attack. Both parties are also resolutely opposed not just to Star Wars development but also to other US planned weapons systems such as the MX and Trident D–5 missiles.

The Americans have already said that the Labour Party and SPD proposals, if pursued in government, could lead to the collapse of NATO. Speaking on British television on 28 September 1986, Mr Richard Perle said: 'while there is a great deal with which we disagree in the programme of the SPD, the programme of Neil Kinnock is so wildly irresponsible, so separate and apart from the historic NATO strategy . . . that I think that a Labour government which stood by its present policies . . . would, if it did not destroy the Alliance, at least diminish its effective ability to do the task for which it was created.'[21] In the same programme the US Defence Secretary, Caspar Weinberger, made clear that the United States would not readily tolerate even the milder reforms sought by the right-wing European governments in the creation of a 'European pillar' for NATO. Commenting on this approach, Weinberger said: 'I think the NATO Alliance is one of the best ways of keeping us all united. I do not think it is a good idea to break into two blocs—one European and one American.' Henry Kissinger also warned against an independent European foreign policy on crises outside the NATO area. Referring to European criticism of the US bombing of Libya, Dr Kissinger said: 'If this kept going on, if the United States felt obliged to intervene in many places and if the Europeans . . . participated in the opposition against us, then the Alliance . . . would lose support in the United States.'[22]

Although there are formidable barriers on the road to moderate, let alone radical, reform of NATO, the Europeans have yet even to begin to hammer out a common strategy for reform. The Western European Union (WEU) remains transfixed by the US veto on its being used to work out specifically European policy lines on disarmament. The result is that the Europeans are all too often reduced to making *ex post facto* responses to shifts in US policy.

Those European political parties who want to 'denuclearize' NATO have yet to explain how they plan to convince the Americans. It is also far from clear how they would prevent a confrontation with Washington leading to the imposition of possible sanctions by the Americans and a direct split inside the Alliance. This is by no means a fanciful scenario. When the New Zealand Labour government banned visits by US warships carrying nuclear weapons in the early 1980s it was summarily expelled from the Anzus security pact and denied US military supplies and intelligence.[23] Precedent suggests that America might not put itself out to discourage a flight of American capital from European countries which defied it in a similar fashion.

Some in the Labour Party foresee circumstances in which the Europeans might eventually have to accept the 'resignation' of the United States from NATO. But what would then remain that was recognizably NATO at all, as opposed to a rump organization which might conceivably be transformed to execute a purely European security policy? Could the Americans leave NATO without the whole Alliance crumbling?

The question would still remain, even in these circumstances, what assumptions a purely 'European' version of NATO would make concerning the alleged Soviet 'threat' to Western Europe. For without a drastic change in that 'threat assessment' the new European NATO would, as we have seen, face identical choices about nuclear strategy and overall force goals as NATO currently does. The choice facing Western Europe after a progressive American withdrawal might be between a continuing nuclear-based strategy, but one which would have to be executed by governments without the same military resources as are available to the United States, and a fundamentally different strategy based on achieving a new political settlement in Central Europe. This might be aimed at securing the parallel withdrawal of Soviet forces and nuclear weapons from Eastern Europe. Least credible would be a non-nuclear strategy resting on an unchanged Soviet threat assumption and depending on politically unobtainable levels of overall defence-spending. Put another way, the only real choice in the long run may be between Europe remaining trapped in a subservient role within an American-led nuclear-based alliance, and the adoption of policies leading to progressive European non-alignment as between the nuclear superpowers.

Difficult as the issue of NATO reform might seem, it is relatively straightforward compared with the task of reconstructing the world of economic Atlanticism. At present governments on both sides of the Atlantic have their work cut out fire-fighting particular currency, trade, or other economic conflicts and preventing them from escalating into general economic warfare.

Extemporized, short-term agreements to defuse specific trade disputes or to curb currency upheavals will no doubt continue. But experience suggests this is a Sisyphean task in that the underlying international economic environment is pushing America and Europe apart faster than they can be drawn together. In their turn these transatlantic conflicts are really just part of an overall pattern of intra-regional global economic conflicts involving the Japanese and the Asian Newly Industrialized Countries as well as other actual or embryonic regional economic blocs.[24]

Bilateral agreements also tend to exacerbate tensions elsewhere. Thus the US–Japanese effort to stabilize the relationship between the dollar and the yen tends to put the European currencies under greater speculative pressure on the world foreign exchanges. And the better America succeeds in forcing through agreements with Japan about 'voluntary restraint' in its sensitive exports to the United States in sectors such as microchips—the subject of a Japanese–American agreement early in 1987—the more the resulting export surpluses tend to be directed towards the European market.

There are few signs that the chronic imbalance in world trade and payments and the related deficit in the US government's own budget will respond on the scale and at the speed required to the hesitant and inconsistent approach of the US administration. The other developed industrialized economies are increasingly unwilling to bow to US pressure and to carry the primary responsibility for correcting the US deficit by reflating on the massive scale demanded of such 'surplus' economies as Japan and West Germany.

We have seen the extent to which protectionist pressures are on the increase, not just in the United States. There are potential alternatives both to free trade on the one hand, and to national or regional import controls on the other. It is possible to envisage a system of international trade-planning under which imbalances in trade could be limited within an agreed international framework which would also be based on agreed objectives for world economic growth and employment. Between them doctrinaire free traders and nationalist protectionists have blocked any such development to date. So, too, with capital movements and currency exchange rates. Financial orthodoxy insists that all Western countries should seek a balance, or preferably achieve a surplus, in their commercial dealings with others—a mathematical impossibility. It would make far more sense to recycle particular surpluses through a recycling system which had a deliberate bias in favour of their use by the poorest developing countries. It is precisely these countries which have the greatest potential to restimulate world economic activity because of the vast unfilled needs of their peoples.

Under the present system the whole relationship between the rich and poor countries is being stood on its head. The poor countries are denied resources because they are poor and, from a profit-making investment standpoint, risky. We end up in the obscene situation where, despite short- and medium-term financial loans and official 'aid' to some poor countries, the net flow of resources is from the poor to the rich countries.[25] The International Monetary Fund (IMF), the World Bank, GATT, and even the OECD seem paralysed in the face of the structural imbalance in the world economy. But time is running out. A future international recession, caused by America's inability to reduce its massive deficits and the rest of the world's inability to organize a compensating expansion, will further undermine the remaining economic foundations of the Atlantic order.

The second school of thought, European reformism, accepts that the gravity of the crisis and the implications of the continuing drift apart of the Europeans and the Americans require new thinking. Some go so far as to believe that the EEC must now evolve into a Federal Europe. Only in this way will Europe, they argue, have the political as well as the economic clout to defend its interests in the new, harsher post-Atlantic world climate.[26]

Most European reformers are deeply reluctant to make a formal choice between Europe and America as such, and hope that even if Europe does become a more self-sufficient international politico-economic power it will be possible to preserve at least the key elements of the Atlantic Alliance. They are aware not just of the ideological, defence, and other links across the Atlantic but of the complex pattern of international corporate investment (including European investment in the United States) which might be imperilled by an angry rupture in the Atlantic system.[27]

At least some of the European reformers share with the European 'Gaullists', notably the present French government, a belief in at least contingency planning to give Europe an independent security capacity. The British Social Democrats (and some Conservatives), the French Socialists, and some other European Christian Democrats and Liberals, particularly those associated with the Luxembourg-based European Defence Institute, take this view—some because they believe a progressive withdrawal of American troops from Western Europe, though regrettable, may now be inevitable. This tendency is willing to confront the challenge of eventually replacing all (and not just some) of the American forces stationed in Europe and even to replace US nuclear weapons with a European nuclear capacity. A first step, they argue, might be for the British and the French to agree on the co-ordination of the targeting and maintenance cycles of their 'national' nuclear forces, eventually leading to their formal integration.[28] There are, however, formidable problems with the concept of a 'Euro-bomb'. To be credible it would have to be genuinely independent of the United States in terms of servicing, repairs, spares, and support from America's satellite-based targeting systems. This is certainly not the case with either the British Polaris or the intended Trident system which can credibly operate in future only on the basis of continuing American goodwill. Then there is the critical issue of how the other European NATO states are to be associated with a 'European' weapons system and potential decisions about its use. Any suggestion, for instance, of a West German 'finger on the nuclear trigger' could have a potentially catastrophic effect on Soviet attitudes towards arms control and future disengagement from Eastern Europe. But would even the British and French advocates of such a system really be willing to share decisions on its deployment or possible use with non-nuclear European states? And would the other European states be willing to finance it unless they did have a finger of their own on the button?

There is already a significant degree of bilateral defence co-operation between Bonn and Paris, even though France still remains outside NATO's integrated military command. Not only are there regular joint manoeuvres of both countries' forces but there has been speculation that the French might be willing to extend the range of their Hades and other missiles to 'cover' the Federal Republic. This might assume significance in the event of the withdrawal of the cruise and Pershing missiles. However, one of the present West German government's leading strategists, Kurt Biedenkopf, has openly disparaged talk of Anglo-French nuclear co-operation or of a European nuclear force. In the final analysis, even the conservative Bonn government may well put relations with Moscow and Eastern Europe before any putative advantages of being part of a Euro-bomb consortium.[29] On the French side there is interest in the financial contribution which West Germany could make to help France sustain its nuclear 'force de frappe' without the required level of expenditure undermining its defence budget in the way that the planned Trident system is already threatening the spending ambitions of the British navy and airforce. The whole question divides right-wing and more liberal members of the West German coalition. But there is no sign of Bonn being willing to play the role of paymaster to a basically Anglo-French nuclear force. All in all, an 'independent' European nuclear strategy seems a non-starter, although there were reports in the early months of 1987 of increased Anglo-French consultation about possible joint nuclear projects such as the provision of French short-range 'Cruise' nuclear missiles on British Tornado aircraft.

At the heart of the European reform project is the strengthening of the Common Market and the institutions of the EEC. While this has the formal support of all the present twelve member states, it is only slowly and uncertainly translated into effective action, particularly when the twelve face decisions on specific interests. Given the *de facto* block on majority voting on many issues in the Council of Ministers, the EEC camel train still tends to move at the pace of its slowest and most reluctant member.

The present European Commission, with the enthusiastic backing of the British and West German governments in particular, has striven hard to 'complete' the creation of a genuine 'common' market by 1992. But considerable barriers to such a fully integrated market do remain, many of them ostensibly technical or national bureaucratic controls which, in reality, are maintained to protect national industries or services threatened by competition from other EEC countries.

By the end of 1986, when the British had completed a term of Community Presidency, many policy directives aimed at removing such barriers or harmonizing national industrial and technological standards remained unenacted by the Council of Ministers. Progress on removing barriers to important services such as air transport (through the elimination of artificial price supports by some national airline authorities) or insurance remains painfully slow.[30] But removing internal market barriers can at best make only a very limited contribution to genuine economic integration. It would still leave all but a fraction of economic output determined on a purely 'national' basis. Resistance by the national states to anything approaching co-ordinated (let alone integrated) monetary, fiscal, or demand management policies remains deeply embedded. And the present imbalance in the pattern of Community budget expenditure in favour of a wasteful agricultural policy means that EEC spending on other potentially unifying common industrial, technological, or social policies remains marginal.[31]

This is fully recognized by the more committed European reformists. They hope that the so-called European Single Act, the amendment to the EEC Constitution strengthening decision-making, will be followed by a greater degree of supranationalism in policy-making and execution. National Parliaments remain suspicious but there is a growing consensus about the need for action to break the decision-making paralysis in the EEC. President Mitterrand in France and Prime Minister Papandreou in Greece are among the few leaders who urge more radical measures to bridge the gulf in social and economic standards which divides the rich and poor member states.[32] In the years ahead, however, it is probable that demands for common standards in welfare and social provisions will become louder and more assertive. The contrast between progress in creating single standards for capital and massive discrepancies in national welfare provision will come to be seen as intolerable.

The main political responsibility for the snail-like progress of the Community does not lie with the Commission, although it would help if member states saw the appointment of members of the Commission as a much more important political decision than they do at present. The Commission might, in theory, try to challenge the obstructionism of the member states by appealing over their heads to European public opinion. But this would require a veritable transformation in the political character of the Commission, so that it regained more political coherence, self-confidence, and willingness to mobilize a constituency among the people of Europe for its objectives. The Commission had some of these characteristics in the very different world of the 1950s. But in the post-Atlantic, de-industrializing Europe of today a similar capacity for leadership is most unlikely to be found among the dry bureaucrats who make up the modern Commission. To be fair, the French socialist President of the Commission, M. Jacques Delors, appointed in 1975, did make considerable efforts to raise the political profile of the Commission during his mandate, but to the ill-concealed irritation of some national governments.

The main obstacle to faster progress to union today is the Council of Ministers. The Council and its subsidiary agencies are the principal conduit through which the narrowest national interest makes itself felt. There is very little space for broader strategic concerns in the day-to-day wrestling with competing national interests which tend to be resolved on the 'lowest common denominator' approach to consensus. The malaise in Community decision-making is made worse by the lack of clear political priorities within the hierarchy of the different councils. The result is that relatively 'junior' ministerial meetings—for instance of farm ministers—can obstruct or even derail broader reform objectives set at a higher political level.

In theory the Council of Foreign Ministers has overriding authority, being subject only to the meetings of the European Council, the summit of EEC leaders. In theory the Foreign Ministers should be able to agree on political priorities within which the lesser councils dealing with specific policies would be obliged to negotiate. The result, therefore, should be that disagreements between ministers at a 'lower' level are not allowed to frustrate the goals set for wider political reasons. In practice it is not like that. Foreign ministers do not enjoy that kind of political authority over recalcitrant councils composed of their cabinet colleagues.

For their part, the heads of state and government meet too infrequently and the agendas of the summits do not lend themselves readily to exhaustive discussions of detailed EEC policy matters. Without a radical change in political attitudes in member states, it is difficult to see how the paralysis will be broken. One possible reform might be the appointment of ministers in national capitals who had special authority for all matters relating to the EEC, but would this be accepted by other ministers who might feel their status and authority threatened?

The creation of a more genuinely 'European' consciousness will require a change in popular attitudes. But a precondition of that is a thoroughgoing repoliticization of what Europe is about. The people of Europe should be presented with a range of choices about the kind of society they want. But for that to be meaningful, responsibility for key 'bread and butter' issues would have to be transferred from the national to the European level. Why not, for a start, transfer decisions over common social services, the environment, and a significant proportion of overall public expenditure? The result of such a repoliticization would certainly be controversy and division, but that is the stuff of real politics. Better a Community wracked by ideological conflict than one transfixed by apathy and indifference.

Another key priority must be to reverse the accelerating decline of European industry and competitiveness against the United States and the Pacific Rim economies. But efforts to encourage collaborative technology development, not to mention mergers between European multinational companies, have so far achieved only very limited success. As long as the EEC is part of a relatively open capitalist international trading and investment order, it will often make narrow commercial sense for many European companies to link up with American or Japanese corporations rather than with each other. In the longer run, though, such collaboration with non-EEC companies does risk being on terms which will eventually reduce whole sectors of European industry to technological subordination as they become mere fabricators and assemblers of foreign-designed products.

If present policies of subsidy and encouragement for specifically European corporate restructuring fail, the EEC will come under pressure to adopt a more full-blooded 'Fortress Europe' policy involving overt protection, to help European manufacturers resist subordination. Most European reformists shy away from such an approach. It would not only violate post-war assumptions about the primacy of international free trade, but would also pose the question of how far and in what way Europe's economy might have to be regulated on completely non-capitalist, non-market criteria. Rather than open the Pandora's Box of foreign-trade curbs and a more interventionist role for the public sector in rebuilding European industry, the reformists hope that Europe will be able to find sufficient areas of international comparative advantage to compensate for the seemingly irreversible loss of older industrial sectors. Unfortunately there is little evidence to support such optimism, which goes a long way to account for why the long-term forecasts for European unemployment remain so bleak.[33]

Both the Atlantic and the European reformists share a conviction that the international economic situation must eventually enter a new period of long-term growth, high employment, and technological innovation. So eventually it may. The question is whether what is left of the Atlanticist consensus can survive the interim strains which may last many years.

Western governments continue to put their trust in conventional economic strategies, whether Keynesian or monetarist. Unless their optimism is justified soon, the decline of the Atlantic order may not be accompanied by greater unity but could conceivably lead through internal conflict to a creeping Balkanization of Europe as each national capital attempts to fend for itself in a worsening crisis. In these circumstances the choice could be either a leap forward to a fuller economic union or progressive disintegration.

Given precisely the failure of the attempts to generate a free-market approach to secure Europe's industrial future, some politicians might yet be drawn to a form of European 'Gaullism'. In reaction to monetarism and *laissez-faire*, Euro-Gaullism would advocate a mixture of economic 'dirigisme' together with a more hawkish independent European foreign and defence policy. Some experts already believe that, to survive, the EMS may have to be supported in future by a more interventionist economic strategy on an EEC-wide basis.

It might seem like a contradiction in terms to speak of European Gaullism, since Gaullism in France is associated with a virulent form of nationalism and hostility to the supranational EEC. As a 'Europeanist' philosophy neo-Gaullism does not as yet have any clearly defined profile, though it is prefigured in the protectionist and interventionist industrial traditions of the EEC. In that sense, the more the EEC (possibly with the rest of Western Europe) evolves towards an economic 'Fortress Europe' and adopts an autonomous 'European' security policy, the more it will be opting for a form of neo-Gaullism.

Unlike the former French President from whom they draw their inspiration, some French national Gaullists have now concluded that French influence demands a stronger, more self-sufficient Europe. The neo-Gaullists see a diminishing contradiction between the national state and the Europe they envisage. They advocate far greater European political and security as well as economic independence from the United States while maintaining resolutely conservative and even militantly Cold War attitudes towards the Soviet Union and the Warsaw Pact.

Such a Euro-Gaullist approach still co-exists uneasily with traditional and still potent nationalism. Attempts are being made, however, to encourage a clearer and more assertive European cultural identity. But European cultural foundations and festivals, educational exchanges, and other attempts to stimulate a greater European cultural identity, while important, cannot and should not substitute for the rich and varied patchwork of national cultures which comprises the Europe of today.

The Eurovision Song Contest, and even proposals from the European Commission positively to discourage American influence on European television, have little purchase on the popular European psyche.[34] Even among those Europeans most opposed to US policy, there is very little support for a narrow European cultural chauvinism, while a blind cultural anti-Americanism has little appeal, above all for the young.

The question for aspirant European Gaullists is at what point a strong European state, greater planning, and economic nationalism would conflict with, not underpin, the capitalist free-enterprise system. The situation of modern Europe is very different to the France of the latter years of the Fourth Republic. It is very difficult to envisage a long-lasting marriage of economic planning and right-wing politics in the Europe of today.

The EEC is, of course, light years away from the strong state of the Gaullist ideal. Indeed, to the extent that Gaullism and nationalism have strength, they are rooted in political practices, whatever their intent, which find themselves opposed to European supranationalism. But will any of the mainstream political tendencies be able to legitimize a new Europeanism without violating other crucial aspects of their own political philosophies? It is difficult, for instance, to see how Western Europe's right-of-centre parties could embrace European non-alignment in international affairs or EEC-wide economic and industrial policies which relegated the now dominant role of the free market in favour of new public-sector agencies of investment, planning, and job creation. Although Atlanticism and free-market capitalism are failing Europe, it is almost impossible to see the mainstream centre-right parties readily rejecting them.

It is possible, however, that an attempt to push through a market-based strategy of restructuring European industry against an international background of deepening 'stagflation' and trade conflict would assume a very reactionary form indeed. A new economic recession could lead some right-wing parties to a more radical offensive on social spending, welfare policies, and civil and trade-union rights. The argument might be made by such parties that only by subordinating everything to the requirements of reindustrialization and international competitiveness could 'Western' society in Europe ensure its salvation. This would represent a qualitatively harsher species of monetarism than even that seen in the 1980s. It is unlikely to become a serious threat before organized labour in Europe has sustained much greater defeats than were inflicted during the 1970s and early 1980s.

A European neo-Gaullism drawing on reservoirs of racism, jingoism, and authoritarianism might, in such a gloomy situation, have a degree of appeal to the middle classes. However, it would not be an easy matter for the European Right to impose its will to that degree. The European far Right, which of course is organized outside the Gaullist tradition at present, might only be given such an opportunity if the Left failed to grasp the political opportunities now opening up through development within Europe, or, more likely, if the Left, in government, proved consistently and disastrously unequal to the challenge of arresting Europe's economic decline.

It should not be thought that any of the political categories described above neatly correspond to any of the main European political 'families'. Atlanticists and Europeanists are to be found in all the principal political parties. Species of national and even European Gaullism are to be seen on the Left as well as on the Right. These are differences which cut across the normal political alignments and do not necessarily reflect the Left–Right divide. Some Gaullist and quasi-Gaullist ideas, for example on protectionism, find an echo in the French Communist Party and in the Danish and British Labour parties. The bulk of the European Social Democratic parties fall into the camp of European reformism as, most enthusiastically, does the Italian Communist Party. A mild 'Euro-reformism' has become the official stance of virtually all the parties in the Confederation of European Socialist Parties (including most recently the British Labour Party), with the hesitant exception of the Greeks. Dwindling minorities of traditional unreconstructed Atlanticists are still to be found in most European political parties, notably in Britain, West Germany, and the Benelux states.

The fourth school of thought which has emerged in recent years, the Socialist United States of Europe, does not as yet command significant support in any of the leading Social Democratic or Communist parties in Europe, although some of its key ideas are supported by Left minorities in these parties and, more significantly, in smaller, more radical formations, notably the left-wing German Greens.

The idea of a Socialist United States of Europe is not, as we have seen, a new one. It was espoused by many Socialists before the First World War and by the early Communist movement before Stalin, but since then it has been echoed only by marginalized radical and revolutionary Socialist tendencies. It has enjoyed something of a renascence in recent years, partly because of the common crisis into which all the Social Democratic parties have been thrown by the economic slump and the swing to the Right in European politics during the past decade. Sections of the Left, disillusioned with the performance of 'Socialist' governments in Britain, France, and elsewhere in the 1970s and 1980s, have begun to examine the limits to what can be done in a single country and to assess the potential scope of supranational European strategies.[35] In the first instance, much of the discussion at the base of the official trade unions and among Left Socialists has been about the need for elementary defensive strategies at the European level. These have tended to centre on the issues of mass unemployment, industrial decline, and the attack by right-wing governments on national social and welfare services. But they have also come to embrace the important questions raised by the peace movement around disarmament as well as on the demands of the radicalized 'new social movements' of women and migrant and immigrant communities. Trade unionists have begun to take seriously cross-frontier organizations in large, often American-led, multinational companies such as Ford, General Motors, and Kodak but also in some large European corporations such as Philips of Eindhoven. Shop-floor representatives as well as trade-union officials have attempted to hammer out a common line on resistance to job losses, the transfer of technologies from Europe to the United States, and the harmonizing of the best practices in pay, safety, and working conditions.[36] The trade union movement seeks actively to influence policy-making at the European level, both directly and through, for instance, the Social and Economic Committee, on policy proposals of interest to people at work. The European Trade Union Confederation attempted, for example, to persuade the Council of Ministers to adopt a Commission proposal giving workers a statutory right to information about the affairs of their companies.

Following the swing to the Right in European politics in the 1980s, trade-union influence declined dramatically. It remains an open question whether there will be a counter-trend in the years ahead, and also whether, and to what extent, this may be dependent on an improvement in the European economic situation. The sudden upsurge of trade-union militancy in France at the turn of 1986–7 may prove an exception to the general trend in Europe. But if this kind of delayed-action rank-and-file workers' revolt spreads to other EEC countries, the impact on the political environment could be dramatic.

Many on the European Left understandably regard the EEC institutions with the gravest suspicion. Ironically, because of a 'timelag' effect, the Commission and the European Court have in general been less affected by the prevailing political swing to the radical Right than most of the national governments in the member states. The Commission has even made modest attempts to persuade the national governments to adopt more enlightened policies on women's rights, equal opportunities, and other matters. Commission directives and European Court of Justice rulings on a variety of equal-opportunities issues, such as equality of pension entitlements, have caused embarrassment to some of the more conservative national EEC governments. And the European Court of Human Rights in Strasbourg, an institution linked to the wider twenty-two-nation Council of Europe, is increasingly seen as an important court of appeal to uphold civil liberties when they are under threat or are circumscribed in particular member states.

Big business is also increasingly well organized at a European level, where it lobbies the Council, the Commission, and the European Parliament to influence policy decisions on a vast range of issues. In the battle over the so-called 'Vredeling' directive on company information disclosure, the business lobbyists succeeded in mobilizing enough right-wing governments in the Council effectively to kill it.[37] In addition, specific industries and industrial sectors find it increasingly necessary to make their voice heard in Brussels.

At the official level, the trade unions and Left political parties have concentrated on broader macro-economic questions such as concerted recovery from recession and unemployment.[38] But in recent years the few Socialist parties, such as the French, Greek, Portuguese and Spanish Socialist parties who formed governments, have been more or less rapidly driven off course by the international crisis. They have invariably ended up adopting austerity policies little different to those pursued by Conservative, Christian Democrat, or Liberal governments.

Left-wing economists have been studying the kinds of measures and changes in institutions which will be necessary to secure a concerted economic revival. Most recognize the need for stronger supranational institutions to implement recovery policies, including both new agencies to secure public ownership in European multinationals and changes in the EMS to guarantee that it serves rather than undermines recovery strategies.[39]

More radical ideas are being canvassed by the increasingly influential West German Green Party and by 'New Left' trends in other Western European countries, which start from the perspective of a radically different type of European economy. The feminist and ecological movements have had an obvious influence as have initiatives such as those of the British Lucas Aerospace trade unionists. The Lucas workers fought in the 1970s to persuade their employers to convert the defence-oriented company to the production of socially useful products including advanced high-technology aids for the disabled and novel forms of public transport including a 'road/rail bus'. Although the campaign failed, it had an influence on the thinking of a younger generation of trade unionists in Europe confronted with the problems of arms conversion and, more generally, of the need to mobilize wider community support for workers fighting plant closures and redundancies in declining industries. Among other ideas on this new agenda for radical economic and political change are production for social need, in addition to (and in certain areas in place of) production for the market and for profit; novel forms of social ownership, including workers' co-operatives and popular democratic planning by community organizations; and industrial democracy within enterprises. Increased attention is also being given to the importance and (at present) the gross social undervaluation of so-called 'domestic work' and the caring services hitherto carried out unpaid almost exclusively by women.

There is a new interest in the politics of production and not just in the politics of distribution. Much of the focus for this new socialist production strategy is 'micro'—that is, a concern with the purposes, priorities, technologies, and social-control systems operating within production. But there is increasing debate on how initiatives and alternatives taken at the level of the enterprise or economic sectors can be linked to a national and international 'macro' economic alternative strategy.

Although the New Left strategy is deeply suspicious of the state, as currently constructed, and sympathetic though it is to both regionalist and European-level initiatives, there remain key economic functions which only the state can fulfil and the debate continues as to how the national state itself should be reconstructed in a more democratic and socially responsive fashion.[40] These questions are posed in a particularly critical fashion when it comes to broader macro-economic issues such as control over currency and capital movements, the planning of foreign trade, and control of banks, finance houses, and investment institutions. The correct balance between a 'statist' and a 'decentralist' emphasis remains a current controversy in European New Left movements and will have to be resolved before these ideas can be turned into political programmes capable of winning the mass support necessary for achieving state power.

On the one hand, the new Left in Europe could place demands of an 'enabling' nature on the State. These might include policies of social reform and civil liberties. On the other hand, new ideas are being debated for alternative local, national, and international structures which are responsive to popular democratic control.

Support for a radical reappraisal of economic strategy along these lines has come from a number of left-wing regional and big-city authorities in recent years, notably by the now abolished Labour-controlled Greater London Council.[41] Indeed, decentralization, support for stronger regionally based public-sector development and job-creation agencies, and an attempt to reconcile the priorities of economic growth with the human-centred needs articulated by the feminist, peace, anti-nuclear, and ecological movements are all features of the 'new European Socialism'.

Issues such as the conversion of industries in the arms-producing sector to alternative, socially useful goods and services are also being taken up at a European level. European radicals also stress the critical character of the demands for reduced working hours. Indeed, the West German Metal Workers' Union has taken a leading role in campaigning and striking for the thirty-five-hour week, including the concept of 'liberated time', in which workers can produce for the wider needs of the community.[42]

Allied to this is a critical approach not only to the use but to the very content of new technology. The new European Left is associated with schemes, some of which have had financial backing from the EEC, to develop new forms of 'human-centred' technology. The object is to restore the balance between human skill and computer-based automation systems. The schemes are now attracting notice from international firms alarmed at the collapse of industrial skills which have been a casualty of ill-considered automation in industry.[43] They form part of a re-evaluation of work and its objectives and also of a renewed emphasis on democracy in the work place, which is under active discussion in the European Left and trade-union movement.

The European peace movement has also stimulated a wide-ranging debate not only about alternative defence policies but about wider issues of European foreign policy. The European New Left is not only anti-nuclear but increasingly hostile to European subordination to the imperatives of the Cold War and the division of Europe into military blocs. This debate is now focused on the most appropriate strategy for the liquidation of the Cold War blocs and for European non-alignment.

Support for withdrawal from NATO is strongest among sections of the British and West German Left. This is why both the US and the European NATO governments regard the future election of Left- or Green-influenced Labour or SPD governments with such apprehension. But while increasingly drawn to the objective of European non-alignment, the New Left is also critical of the Soviet economic and political system. The West German Greens, in particular, as well as broader umbrella organizations such as European Nuclear Disarmament, have established close working links with 'unofficial' peace and dissident groups in Eastern Europe, a development which has greatly displeased some Soviet and official Eastern European authorities. The position of the West German Greens, echoed by other New Left European Socialists, is that the cause of peace is inseparable from that of liberty.[44] It is the major dividing line between the New Left and supporters of the Eastern European regimes.

Some in the peace movement canvass the idea of reforming NATO through a denuclearizing strategy or even seeking US withdrawal from the Alliance.[45] This approach has influenced at least some of the leaders of the Western European Socialist parties, although no one has explicitly stated what, in practice, a NATO minus the Americans would really add up to. Increasing reference is made in this debate to possible future German and even European reunification. Certainly the younger generation of German radicals in the Green/Alternative movement feel no need to apologize for their German identity. However, support for German unification is highly controversial and is opposed by those who have rejected historical German nationalism and militarism.

The mere mention of German reunification remains a sensitive issue outside Germany as well. But it might assume a different aspect if new intra-German links formed part of a Central European disarmament and superpower disengagement agreement as discussed earlier. The European New Left is meanwhile developing radical alternatives to conventional military strategies. These draw to some extent on the traditions of civilian-based systems of self-defence in countries like Switzerland, including volunteer defence systems organized in the community and work places. Some have canvassed the notion of a new security alliance, open to all European nations, independent of NATO and the Warsaw Pact, partly building on the success of the movement for European nuclear-free zones in Scandinavia and the Balkans.[46] All of these ideas are very much in their infancy. The influence of the European New Left remains marginal. But interest in and support for radical alternatives will grow if the conventional political parties continue to prove incapable of resolving Europe's internal crisis or ending its subordinate relationship to the United States.

The immediate prospects for a new European Left are over-shadowed by the gloomy prospects for the mainstream Social Democratic and Communist parties in Western Europe. The West German SPD was defeated in the general election of January 1987 and the British Labour Party lost its third successive general election in June 1987. The French Socialist and Communist parties are only now recovering from very serious reverses at the hands of the Right. Elsewhere in Northern Europe most Social Democratic parties appear to be stagnating or in long-term decline. In Southern Europe the crises which have hit the Greek and Spanish Socialist governments have yet to show up in terms of the standing of these parties but they appear to be losing support to both their Right and their Left.

In contrast, some of the smaller Left parties have done quite well. The radical West German Green Party increased its share of the poll to nearly 9 per cent in the general election, and further gains were made in Lander regional elections in the months which followed. The Danish Left People's Socialist Party recorded up to 16 per cent in opinion polls, while in other Scandinavian countries, as well as in Greece, Spain, and, less certainly, the Benelux states, smaller 'green' and radical Socialist parties also reflected some increase in support.

It is by no means clear what the impact of a third successive election defeat for the Labour Party in Britain will have on the radical Left. However, even before the election there was increasing debate about the advantages which a future move to a proportional representation election system—as is advocated by the Liberal and Social Democratic Alliance—could have for any new independent Socialist party. Alternatively, it might be possible for a further period of internal dissension in the Labour Party to lead to the emergence of a new Left Socialist party involving further defections from the Labour Right wing to the British SDP. Conversely, some more radical-minded Liberals might be attracted, along with ecologists, peace activists, feminists, and ethnic minority groups, to form a radical alliance with a 'reborn' Socialist Labour Party.

One bond which unites many of these tendencies and groups (including the dissident 'Renewal' group within the French Communist Party and sections of the Italian Left) is a strong commitment to a clear European strategy. But contacts between these political forces is at a very early stage and there is nothing yet resembling a worked-out and agreed strategy for European economic, political, and social change.

A major obstacle confronting all variants of a post-Atlanticist European strategy is the continuing potency of the nation state and the almost exclusively national focus of political debate and action within the EEC. The world of the 1950s cannot, thankfully, be resurrected. But in the world of the 1990s the limits of economic and political nationalism will become even more critical. A new Europeanism as an intrinsic part of a new internationalism is needed to respond to economic and social conditions very different to those of thirty years ago.

Politicians on the so-called Left as well as on the Right tend, under pressure, to think and act in purely national rather than in 'European' terms. To some extent this simply reflects the strength of the lobbies and pressure groups which operate at a national level. But in the final analysis it reveals that 'Europe' as an operational political concept still means little or nothing to ordinary people. This is why, if it is to survive, Europe must become the 'citizens' Europe', the 'workers' Europe', the Europe of all those social constituencies currently excluded from or marginalized by existing power structures.

Many centrist and conservative politicians are sceptical, in private if not always in public, as to whether the institutions of the EEC, as they currently exist, really can respond to the challenges facing Europe. They still believe that only national governments, acting collectively, have the capacity for effective action. This leads some European reformers to urge an à la carte Europe in which new, flexible forms of intergovernmental co-operation could develop and focus on concrete collaborative tasks rather than what they see as the Utopian project of European union. But any weakening of the EEC institutions will almost certainly lead to a reinforcement, not a weakening, of the most negative and constricting features of the nation state. The result could be less, not more, effective joint European action.

Many on the Left deny the possibility that any Socialist reconstruction of society can be effected through the EEC institutions and a 'capitalist' Rome Treaty framework. It is one thing, they argue, to participate in bodies like the European Parliament, but ultimately the working people of Europe will have to build their own organs of power and government to achieve full economic and social democracy.[47] However, there is increasing recognition that it would be folly not to use the existing institutions to achieve such reforms as can be won and also as a public springboard to campaign for more radical change.

It is an extraordinary fact that while most people accept that in the Common Market the same rules governing trade, for example, or the movement in capital should apply in Bremen as apply in Birmingham, few stop to ask why there should not be common (or at least comparable) social benefit entitlements in Coventry as in Copenhagen or the same unemployment pay in Hull as in Hilversum. European Socialist parties have not succeeded in popularizing the demand for the highest common level of benefit or social rights across the Community. The idea of European unity will not come of age until the demand for common standards and rights becomes a burning issue in most member states. Its attractions should be most obvious to the labour movement in countries such as Britain, whose social welfare and other social standards have fallen so far behind the average, let alone the best, practice elsewhere in the EEC.

There is no point in pretending that the Treaty of Rome does not represent a serious potential inhibition on a range of policies which a radical Socialist government, left alone to tackle the problems of mass unemployment and deindustrialization, would be forced to take. The Treaty, and in a more qualified way the EEC decision-making institutions, at heart reflect the values, priorities, and prejudices of a capitalist, predominantly free-market economic system. Exaggerating these obstacles or making their existence an excuse for a retreat into nationalist isolationism has too often been an option of first resort by the British Left. But that is not to harbour illusions about the compatibility of the Rome Treaty with the kind of national restrictions on trade, capital movements, or free-market forces which individual Left governments would almost certainly have to impose if they could not persuade a majority of EEC governments to agree to them.

National action to bring about urgently needed economic or social change cannot wait on the uncertain timetable of wider political changes within the EEC. That said, there can be no justification for any Left government, however beleaguered, not making a pro-European strategy a major priority. Even the most self-confident Socialist government would be immensely strengthened by the sympathy and solidarity of the organized Labour and Socialist movement elsewhere in Europe. That support could be crucial in preventing the EEC institutions being utilized by the Right to isolate and impose sanctions on an errant radical government. Conversely, it would be a thousand times more difficult for a Left government to mobilize that support if it presented its policies in terms of national sovereignty or 'national interest'—or, worse still, in anti-European terms.

It would also be possible for a national Left government to cast its policies—for instance in using public purchasing powers or industrial subsidies in pursuit of employment objectives—in terms of wider social goals which apply in other countries. There is no reason, for example, why criteria for public purchasing policy should not embrace criteria such as the advancement of equal rights for women or other disadvantaged groups or greater cohesion between richer and poorer region or social communities.

The preparation for power should therefore begin long before polling day. The time is long overdue for the EEC Left parties while still in opposition to co-ordinate their national legislative and reform programmes. More than that, they should be laying the basis, even in opposition, for the joint planning of trade and investment across frontiers in Europe, which could provide the bedrock of their economic strategies in power. This would create the most favourable external environment for the expansion of national output and for social reform.

There are very real problems posed for radicals in the transition from the politics of the national state to the politics of a new European community. It will mean marching on both feet: that is, using the levers of power of the national state while at the same time seeking to build a broader movement for change in Europe as a whole. Among the difficult issues which the European labour movement must hammer out are the best forms of supranational trade planning and allocations of investment and new institutions to carry out these functions.

There are important longer-term questions on the relationship between democratic decision-making power at the level of a particular work place, at the level of industrial sectors, and at the regional, national, and European levels. It would be Utopian in the extreme to try to draw up a blueprint for such a system. Far better to draw on the experiences of trade unionists and local communities struggling on a daily basis in support for alternative, socially responsible development plans. Ultimately a genuine European economic democracy, where production is for social need and not merely for private profit, will need a new Treaty enshrining the values of the new democratic decision-making institutions.

This book has argued that the extent to which Europeans are going to be forced to reassess the way they live, work, and organize their societies is intimately linked to the unravelling of the Atlanticist system and the deeper forces transforming the international economy. Such an unravelling seems increasingly probable. But it is by no means yet inevitable. Changes might occur within the United States, or indeed the Soviet Union, which would transform the international environment in which Europe is forced to reassess its future. Europeans do not want conflict for its own sake with America. Both Atlanticists and European reformists want to preserve close ties and a friendly, if altered, relationship with the United States. The European Left also wants and needs closer ties with its allies in the American peace and labour movements. That is why no simplistic equation can be made between European opposition to US imperialism and a facile and reactionary anti-Americanism. But the European New Left will also have to reject any attempt to cultivate a new species of 'Euro-nationalism'. This can have no place on the agenda of any genuine internationalist project to confront global war, hunger, oppression, and social injustice.

There is a danger that the Europe which emerges in a regionalizing world system may reflect all the worst aspects of the old nationalist insularity. Such a Europe would be part of the international problem; not part of the solution. A xenophobic and militarist Europe would make the world an even more unstable and dangerous place to live in. On the other hand, a Europe which broke free from the chariot wheels of nuclear militarism and helped demonstrate new ways to master economic, political, and social problems could make an immense contribution to world freedom and peace.

Notes

Chapter 1: Outlines of a Crisis

1. In 1987 the EEC and the United States announced a series of trade sanctions to be implemented against each other (*Guardian*, 2 Jan. 1987).
2. The US supreme military commander of NATO, General Bernard Rogers, quoted in the *Guardian* 6 November 1986. He said he did 'not expect [US forces] to remain in their present strength forever'. He added there was a danger that withdrawal might take place 'overnight'. Speaking on Independent Television's Channel 4 special inquiry into the state of the NATO alliance on 29 September 1986, the US Secretary of Defence, Mr Caspar Weinberger, warned that 'current Labour Party defence policies' would 'increase [US] isolationism and strengthen demands for the withdrawal of American forces from Western Europe'. Speaking after a meeting of NATO defence ministers on 5 December 1986, General Rogers said that British Labour Party unilateral disarmament policies could lead to the 'break-up of the NATO alliance' and the 'withdrawal of 350,000 US troops'.
3. A poll commissioned for the US Information Agency and reported in the *Guardian* of 24 November 1986 found that 43 per cent of West Germans blamed President Reagan for the failure of the Reykjavik summit and only 6 per cent blamed Mr Gorbachev. Only in France, among the major European NATO states, was opinion more evenly divided on this issue.
4. *Guardian*, 11 Sept. 1986.
5. *The Mail on Sunday*, 24 Mar. 1985.
6. During the negotiations over US Lend Lease to Britain in February 1942, Winston Churchill bitterly resisted US pressure to dismantle 'imperial' preference' in trade between Britain and her colonies. He cabled President Roosevelt and warned: 'I found the cabinet at its second meeting on this subject even more resolved against trading the principle of imperial preference as consideration for lend/lease.' The final formula was a fudged compromise which left neither side fully satisfied.
7. *The Making of an Atlantic Ruling Class* (London: Verso Books, 1984).

8. Writing in the *Guardian* on 1 December 1986 Enoch Powell attacked the use made by America of its 'imperial hegemony'. He condemned America for trying to impose 'a united Ireland' and for successfully browbeating Britain into joining the EEC.

9. The issue of the relative share of responsibility of the United States and the Soviet Union for the renewal of East–West tensions and what has been described as 'the new Cold War' is still being energetically debated in organizations such as European Nuclear Disarmament, an umbrella body which co-ordinates West European peace movements with unofficial peace groups and dissidents in Eastern Europe.

10. See US poll, cited above.

11. Even the NATO Secretary-General, Lord Carrington, the former Conservative Foreign Secretary, told a NATO meeting in Istanbul that these policies would put NATO 'under the most severe strain' (*Independent*, 14 Nov. 1986).

12. Lord Weinstock, managing director of GEC, said: 'It will be extremely undesirable for the electronics industry of this country for Westland to come under the control of an American company. When companies come under the control of American firms they become industrial eunuchs and totally dependent upon their United States parents' (*Daily Telegraph*, 16 Dec. 1985). Speaking of the threat to Westland, Lord Gregson, President of the Defence Manufacturers Association, said: 'As the home helicopter technology base eroded, markets in Europe and elsewhere would be denied to Britain and weak European industries would topple one by one to the Americans' (*Guardian*, 9 Jan. 1986).

13. See Agence Europe, Brussels, p. 18 (19/5/81), p. 5 (17/12/81), p. 13 (23/12/81), p. 12 (30/4/82), p. 8 (6/5/82), for internal debate on discrimination and procurement policy for telecommunications.

14. Australia and New Zealand led a formidable GATT grouping who objected vigorously to EEC, and to a lesser extent US, farm-trade policies at the 1986 preparatory GATT conference in Uruguay.

15. See D. P. Geller, *The Imperious Economy* (London: Harvard University Press, 1982); and L. Anell, *Recession, the Western Economies and the Changing World Order* (London: Francis Pinter, 1981), p. 53.

16. A speech delivered by Henry Kissinger in 1977 first warned that America might not in the future necessarily be willing to respond with its strategic nuclear force to a limited Soviet military war in Europe. This led to a campaign about the danger of the 'uncoup-

ling' of the US strategic nuclear deterrent from the European 'theatre'. This in turn led to a campaign, headed by the then West German Chancellor, Helmut Schmidt, to win for NATO the 1979 Twin Track decision to deploy cruise and Pershing II intermediate-range nuclear missiles, ostensibly in response to the threat from Soviet intermediate-range missiles, but in reality as part of a political move to underline the US commitment to Europe.

17. See L. G. Franks, *The European Multinationals* (London: Harper, 1976), and F. E. Elliott and P. W. Woods, *The International Transfer of Technology and European Integration* (Research in International Business and Finance, vol. 2, 1981).

18. For a general account of the establishment, operation, and problems of Cocom, see G. Adler-Karlsson, *Western Economic Warfare* (Stockholm, 1968), and T. A. Wolf, *US–East/West Trade; Economic Warfare/Economic Welfare* (Lexington, Mass: Lexington Books, 1973).

19. See R. Morgan, 'The Federal Republic of Germany', in C. and K. J. Twitchett (eds.), *Building Europe—Britain's Partners in the EEC* (London: Europa Publications, 1981).

20. On 1 January 1987 the Japanese government announced that it was breaching the long-standing limit restricting Japanese arms expenditure to less than 1 per cent of national output.

21. See S. Holland (ed.), *Out of Crisis—a project for European recovery* (London: Spokesman Books, 1983).

22. See European Research Associates report for the European Commission on corporate links in the European telecommunications industry, Brussels 1986. See also R. Vernon (ed.), *Big Business and the State* (London: Macmillan, 1974).

23. The EEC governments have, for example, consistently associated themselves with the efforts of the Contadora group of Latin American states seeking a negotiated settlement of the fighting in Nicaragua, to the ill-disguised anger of the US administration which actively backs the right-wing Contra rebels against the Nicaraguan government.

24. This followed a letter to the WEU member governments from Mr Richard Burt, US Under-Secretary of State for European Affairs in 1983 (quoted in Independent Television's Channel 4 special inquiry, cited above).

25. See the letter from the former British Ambassador to the United States, Lord Gladwyn, in the *Independent*, 4 November 1986.

26. By the end of 1986 European firms had received SDI contracts worth less than $100 million.

27. After the breakdown of the Reykjavik summit in October 1986

there was a major disagreement between the US administration and its European NATO allies over interpretations of the scope under the 1972 ABM Treaty for America to carry out the kind of research and testing of SDI it wished to undertake.

28. The US Assistant Secretary of Defense, Richard Perle, is one administration official who has been cited by US journalists as an advocate of a sharply reduced priority for the Atlantic Alliance within US foreign and defence policy.

29. British submarine-based nuclear missiles are targeted in Omaha, Nebraska, 'in accordance with Alliance policy and strategic concepts under plans made by SACEUR (the supreme commander of NATO)'. The idea that the British and French independent nuclear forces might be the basis of a future European nuclear force was advanced in 1986 by the leaders of Britain's Liberal/Social Democratic Alliance. The idea has an older lineage, however, going back to proposals for Franco-British nuclear co-operation made by Lord Thorneycroft, when Mr Peter Thorneycroft, in 1961.

30. This idea formed part of a proposal by the European Commission to strengthen European television in 1986 and make it less dependent on imported (mainly American) television material. It has been widely criticized by European television companies who pointed out that US-made products such as 'soap operas' are invariably cheaper and more popular than their European equivalents. Plans to encourage a stronger European television identity also suffered a setback in 1986 with the collapse of the Europa Satellite network which had been backed by a number of national television networks.

Chapter 2: The American Empire

1. Memorandum E.B19, Oct. 1940, Council on Foreign Relations, War–Peace Studies, NorthWestern Library, Illinois.

2. Lawrence H. Shoup and William Minter, *Imperial Brains Trust* (New York: Monthly Review Press, 1977).

3. Debate in Arthur H. Vandenberg, *The Private Papers of Senator Vandenberg* (London: Lowe and Byrdine, 1952).

4. Shoup and Minter, op. cit.

5. Kees van der Pijl, *The Making of an Atlantic Ruling Class* (London: Verso, 1986).

6. Vandenberg, op. cit.

7. Dean Acheson, *Present at the Creation* (London: Hamish Hamilton, 1969). For a good account of Kennan's views see P. Braith-

waite, *NATO nuclear war and the Soviet Threat* (Nottingham: Spokesman Pamphlets, 1985).

8. A. Bullock, *Ernest Bevin, Foreign Secretary* (London, 1983).

9. Max Beloff, *The United States and the unity of Europe* (London: Faber and Faber, 1963).

10. Acheson, op. cit.

11. 'The Secret Cold War: the CIA and American Foreign Policy in Europe', *The Historical Journal*, vol. 25, no. 3, 1982.

12. *The Labour Party and the CIA* (London: Radical Research Services, 1966).

13. Bevin, op. cit.

14. US House of Representatives, Congressional Record, 80th Congress, 2nd Session, March 1948.

15. 'Policy Planning Staff Concerning Western European Union and Related Problems' (PPS 27, FRUS, Mar. 1948).

16. A detailed account of this decision is given in D. A. Rosenberg, 'The Politics of Overkill', *International Affairs* (Summer 1983).

17. Fred Halliday, *The Making of the Second Cold War* (London: Verso, 1983).

18. Hearings of US Senate Committee on Foreign Relations, April/May 1949, cited in Gabriel Kolko, *The Politics of War* (Random House, 1983).

19. D. A. Rosenberg, 'The Politics of Overkill', *International Affairs* (Summer 1983), p. 13.

20. Robert Scheer, *With enough Shovels?* (London: Secker, 1983).

21. G. Adler-Karlsson, *Western Economic Warfare* (Stockholm: Almquist & Wiksell, 1968).

22. B. Blechman and S. Kaplan, *Force without War* (Washington: Brookings, 1978).

23. Adler-Karlsson, op. cit. This argues that from the start America said the Europeans disagreed about what constituted sensitive 'strategic' exports and the latter only reluctantly accepted the very wide US definition.

24. *Independent*, 29 Dec. 1986.

25. *Financial Times*, 6 Nov. 1986.

26. Assessment by the International Institute for Strategic Studies (London, Nov. 1986).

27. Article in *Armed Services*, published with the Royal United Services Institute for Defence Studies, cited in the *Independent* (5 Dec. 1986).

28. Mike Davis, *Prisoners of the American Dream* (London: Verso, 1986).

29. Halliday, op. cit.

30. Raymond Gartoff, 'The NATO decision on Theatre Nuclear Forces', *Political Science Quarterly* (Summer 1983), p. 198.
31. Cited in J. Connell, *The New Maginot Line* (London: Secker and Warburg, 1986).
32. Davis, op. cit.
33. The President referred to the Soviet Union as 'the Evil Empire' in a speech to the National Association of Evangelists on 8 March 1983.
34. Halliday, op. cit.
35. *Observer*, 12 Oct. 1986.
36. *New Statesman*, 3 Oct. 1986.
37. Writing in *The Mail on Sunday* on 24 March 1985, Mr Richard Perle launched a sharp attack on the reservations about the American Star Wars project expressed earlier that week by the British Foreign Secretary, Sir Geoffrey Howe. Perle said Howe's speech showed that 'length is no substitute for depth'.
38. *The Economist*, 6 Dec. 1986.
39. By the end of 1986 contracts awarded to European companies under the SDI project had totalled a modest $100 million, a fraction of the hopes originally entertained by the West European governments who had reluctantly signalled their acquiescence in SDI earlier that year.
40. *Financial Times*, 13 Dec. 1986.
41. In his Boston speech during that visit to the United States, Mr Kinnock said: 'In the Labour Party we stand for strong national defence and for a strong contribution to NATO which is the fundament of our security.'
42. *Independent*, 29 Dec. 1986.
43. *Daily Telegraph*, 5 Feb. 1985.
44. Speaking at the British Labour Party conference in Blackpool in October 1986, Mr Kinnock underlined the fact that Britain also provided the United States with a number of highly important additional military facilities such as the Fylingdales early warning radar system in North Yorkshire. He appeared to hint that, should America take sanctions against a British Labour government for seeking the closure of US nuclear bases in the United Kingdom, the provision of these facilities might have to be reconsidered.

Chapter 3: Atlantic Strife

1. W. Hanrieder, 'The United States and Western Europe', in William Diebold Jr., ed., *The United States and Western Europe* (Cambridge, Mass.: Winthrop Publishing, 1974).
2. André Gunder Frank, *The European Challenge* (Nottingham: Spokesman Books, 1983).

3. Michael Smith, *Western Europe and the United States* (London: George Allen and Unwin, 1984).
4. 'The Revolution in Atlantic Relations', in Hanrieder, op. cit.
5. J. Chace and E. Ravenal, eds., *Atlantis lost* (New York University Press, 1976).
6. K. Kaiser and H. P. Schwarz, eds., *America and Western Europe* (Lexington, Mass.: D. C. Books, 1977).
7. E. Mandel, *Europe versus America?* (London: NLB Books, 1968).
8. J. Petras and R. Rhodes, 'The Reconsolidation of US Hegemony', *New Left Review*, no. 97 (May/June 1976).
9. Cited in the *Observer*, 25 July 1982.
10. M. Kidron, *Western Capitalism* (London: Weidenfeld and Nicolson, 1968).
11. J.-J. Servan-Schreiber, *The American Challenge* (London: Hamish Hamilton, 1968).
12. Petras and Rhodes, op. cit.
13. Giovanni Magnifico, *European Monetary Integration* (London: Macmillan, 1973).
14. H. Schmidt, *The Balance of Power* (London: William Kimber, 1970).
15. Kaiser and Schwarz, op. cit.
16. D. Calleo in Chace and Ravenal, op. cit.
17. Kaiser and Schwarz, op. cit.
18. Gunder Frank, op. cit.
19. *New York Times*, 9 Apr. 1974.
20. For a detailed discussion of the background see J. Frieden, 'The Trilateral Commission: Economics and Politics in the 1970s', *Monthly Review*, vol. 29, no. 7 (Dec. 1977).
21. R. Parboni, 'The Currency of Hegemony', *New Left Review*, no. 158 (July/Aug. 1986).
22. G. Urban, 'Conversations with Zbigniew Brzezinski', *Encounter* (May 1981).
23. Smith, op. cit., pp. 109–10.
24. *Financial Times*, 28 Oct. 1986. The article cites the case of US–Japanese negotiations on trade in semi-conductors, leading to an agreement which is expected to result in the undercutting of European producers.
25. Report by European Research Associates, Brussels.
26. *Guardian*, 12 Dec. 1986.
27. *The Economist*, 29 Nov. 1986.
28. Ibid.
29. Gunder Frank, op. cit.
30. *Financial Times*, 2 June 1982.

31. *Wall Street Journal*, 19 Sept. 1986.
32. *The Economist*, 30 Aug. 1986.
33. The best account of the international repercussions of the CAP, particularly on African producers, is to be found in 'Food—EEC Greed Versus African Need', *Agenor*, no. 96 (Apr./May 1986).
34. *Guardian* and *Financial Times*, both on 16 Dec. 1986.
35. *Guardian*, 15 Dec. 1986.
36. *The Economist*, 29 Nov. 1986.
37. *Guardian*, 10 Dec. 1986.
38. The annual report of the GATT, Geneva, published Oct. 1986.
39. *The Economist*, 6 Dec. 1986.
40. *International Herald Tribune*, 23 June 1982.
41. Gunder Frank, op. cit.
42. Ibid.
43. *Guardian*, 8 Dec. 1986.
44. Roger Morgan, 'Britain's partners in Europe' in C. and K. J. Twitchett, eds., *Building Europe* (London: Europa Publications, 1981).

Chapter 4: Britain—The Reluctant European

1. S. Strange, 'Sterling and British Foreign Policy: a Political View', *International Affairs*, vol. 47, no. 2 (Apr. 1971).
2. *The Times*, 15 Jan. 1963. It is clear that de Gaulle did not actually use these words but expressed agreement with them as used by a French journalist.
3. J. Monnet, *Memoirs* (London: Collins, 1978).
4. Ibid.
5. K. van der Pijl, *The Making of an Atlantic Ruling Class* (London: Verso, 1986).
6. A. Bullock, *Ernest Bevin—Foreign Secretary* (London, 1983).
7. Monnet, op. cit.
8. C. Tugendhat, *Making Sense of Europe* (London: Viking, 1986).
9. B. Pimlott, *Hugh Dalton* (London: Jonathan Cape, 1985).
10. Ibid.
11. Ibid.
12. L. S. Amery was speaking to the Conservative Party Conference, Earls Court, London, in October 1949.
13. House of Commons debate, 19 Aug. 1950.
14. Michael Newman, *Socialism and European Unity* (London: Junction Books, 1983).
15. Cited by J. Saville in *Ernest Bevin and the Cold War* (Socialist Register, London, 1984).
16. Newman, op. cit.

17. Ibid., pp. 129–30.
18. Ibid., p. 130.
19. Ibid., pp. 130–2.
20. Speaking at a Press Conference, 2 October 1986 (quoted in A. Eden, *Full Circle* (London: Cassell, 1960)).
21. F. Boyd, *British Politics in Transition 1945—1963* (Pall Mall Press, 1964).
22. Defence Committee Paper No. DO(48)59 of 10 Sept. 1948 in Public Record File AIR 20/8122 (cited in Andy Thomas and Ben Lowe, *How Britain was Sold* (London: Housmans, 1984).
23. *The Times*, 21 Aug. 1964.
24. 'Higher Command in War', report by the Joint Planning Staff (quoted in Thomas and Lowe, op. cit.).
25. Newman, op. cit.
26. M. Jenkins, *Bevanism—Labour's High Tide* (Nottingham: Spokesman, 1979).
27. In an address to Colombia University, 11 January 1952.
28. *Financial Times*, 15 June 1966.
29. *Guardian*, 15 June 1966.
30. S. Strange, op. cit.
31. A. Sampson, *The Anatomy of Britain* (London: Hodder, 1962).
32. R. Lieber, *Britain and the European Community* (Oxford University Press, 1964) and *British Politics and European Unity* (University of California, 1970).
33. *The Times*, 21 Aug. 1964.
34. D. Evans, *Destiny or Delusion* (London: Gollancz, 1971).
35. Ibid.
36. Newman, op. cit.
37. *Guardian*, 29 May 1961.
38. H. Overbeek, 'Finance Capital and the Crisis in Britain', *Capital and Class*, No. 11 (Summer 1980).
39. *Guardian*, 19 Nov. 1969.
40. Ibid., 17 Feb. 1970.
41. Attributed to the White House economic policy adviser, Francis Bator, quoted in ibid., 17 Mar. 1970.
42. *The Times*, 14 Nov. 1972.
43. Meeting at the end of December 1986, EEC agriculture ministers took significant action to cut production of some key surplus foodstuffs, notably milk and beef, in the first stage of a major overhaul of the CAP designed to reduce the 'food mountains' and avert a major budgetary crisis. Important though the measures undoubtedly are, few observers judged they could have a major impact either on surpluses or on the EEC budget in the next year or two.

Chapter 5: Dawn in the East

1. A particularly compelling account of this period is contained in Isaac Deutscher's three-volume biography of Leon Trotsky, notably vol. 2, *The Prophet Unarmed* (Oxford University Press, 1959) and in D. Hallas, *The Comintern* (London: Bookmarks, 1985).
2. For a coherent account of this complex and much disputed period see C. Harman, *Bureaucracy and Revolution in Eastern Europe* (London: Pluto, 1974).
3. Hallas, op. cit.
4. According to the American publication *Foreign Relations*, Stalin told Churchill he had 'no intention of criticising British activities . . . in Greece but merely would like to know what was going on'. Cited in H. Thomas, *Armed Truce* (London: Hamish Hamilton, 1986).
5. See Harman, op. cit.
6. *The Economist*, 17 Oct. 1944.
7. *New York Times*, 21 Sept. 1944.
8. *Era Noua* (Bucharest, 8 Nov. 1944), cited in Harman, op. cit.
9. P. E. Zinner, *Revolution in Hungary* (New York, 1962).
10. Thomas, op. cit.
11. Ibid.
12. J. Wzylenaski, *Communist Economic Strategy: the Role of East Central Europe* (Washington, 1959), pp. 68–77.
13. T. Cliff, *Russia, a Marxist Analysis* (London: S.R. Publications, 1963).
14. Ibid.
15. As early as 1937 Maurice Thorez, leader of the French Communist Party, told the party congress that the interests of all France's colonial people were in a 'free, trusting, and paternal' union which was 'the mission of France all over the world'.
16. 'National Unity' statement of the executive committee of the Communist Party of Great Britain, reported in *World News and Views*, vol. 25, no. 12 (24 Mar. 1945), p. 89.
17. For a comprehensive discussion of some of these issues see Robert C. Tucker, ed., *Stalinism: essays in political interpretation* (New York: W. Norton, 1977).
18. P. E. Zinner, *Communist tactics and strategy in Czechoslovakia* (London: Pall Mall Press, 1963).
19. See A. Gunder Frank, *The European Challenge* (Nottingham: Spokesman Books, 1983).
20. Ibid.
21. Ibid.
22. Ibid.

23. As late as 1986 Soviet officials admitted that their Comecon clients were paying above the world price for Soviet oil supplies (*Guardian*, 19 Feb. 1986).
24. Gunder Frank, op. cit.
25. An excellent account is given by a leading participant, Heinz Brandt (*The Review*, Brussels, Oct. 1959).
26. Covered in Robert Havemann, *An Alienated Man* (London: Davis-Poynter, 1973).
27. Harman, op. cit.
28. Good accounts of the Hungarian revolution are contained in P. Fryer, *Hungarian Tragedy*, (London: New Park Publications). See also M. Lasky, *Hungarian Revolution* (London: Secker and Warburg, 1957).
29. Fryer, op. cit.
30. The first two direct elections to the Strasbourg Assembly in 1979 and 1985 produced very low turn-outs even in countries with usually high national voting turn-out. In some UK Euro constituencies the turn-out was under 12 per cent.
31. J. Kuron and K. Modzelewski, *An Open Letter to the Party* (English edn., London, 1965).
32. *Independent*, 4 Nov. 1986.
33. *The Voice of Solidarity*, 8 Apr. 1986.
34. *END Journal*, Jan. 1987.
35. Cited in *The Bulletin of the East European Solidarity Campaign* (London, July 1986).
36. See *END Journal* (London, Nov. 1986).
37. Ibid. See also *Labour Focus on Eastern Europe*, vol. 8, no. 2 (May 1986).
38. Cited in *Against the Current*, vols. 4 and 5 (Detroit, Sept. 1986).
39. *END Journal*, no. 25 (Jan. 1987).
40. See interview with J. Kuron in *Socialist Alternatives* (Oxford, Dec. 1986).
41. Jan./Feb. issue of *Deutschland Archiv*, journal of the West German SPD.
42. *END Journal*, ibid.
43. *Daily Telegraph*, 16 Dec. 1985.
44. *Financial Times*, 9 Mar. 1984.
45. *Financial Times*, 22 Nov. 1986.
46. *Guardian*, 28 Dec. 1986.
47. Gunder Frank, op. cit.
48. The *Guardian* reported on 23 February 1985 a US administration study which admitted that Soviet defence-spending had 'been growing at two per cent per year since 1976, a slower rate than

earlier believed and a much slower rate than overall US defence outlays, according to a CIA report'.

49. *Independent*, 3 Nov. 1986.

50. *Financial Times*, 3 Apr. 1982.

51. *International Socialism Quarterly*, no. 10 (London: Autumn 1962).

52. On 23 January 1987 the American Secretary of Defense, Mr Caspar Weinberger, announced that the United States was in a position to deploy Star Wars by the early 1990s, much earlier than previously expected. The announcement was interpreted as an attempt to pressurize the Soviet Union into a compromise over SDI research in return for US agreement to delay deployment.

53. *New German Critique* (New York, Winter 1986).

Chapter 6: European Disunion

1. While Cyprus and Malta have made no attempt to convert clauses in their association agreements with the EEC into actual bids for accession, the government in Ankara has repeatedly served notice that Turkey wants to join the Community sometime in the 1990s. Partly because of Turkey's economic backwardness, partly because of its ambiguous geopolitical situation, straddling Europe and Asia, partly because of strong Greek opposition, and partly because of Turkey's bad civil liberties reputation, the EEC has strongly discouraged the overtures from the Ankara government.

2. This has already led to friction between the EEC Commission and the Swiss authorities, notably over the Hoffman La Roche case when the Swiss company used Swiss law in alleged retribution against a former executive who had leaked confidential information to the Commission about Hoffman La Roche practices which violated EEC regulations.

3. Since then the EEC has negotiated a reciprocal fishing agreement with Norway which safeguards its national fishing interests.

4. There is a measure of co-ordination of voting positions within the UN and other international agencies.

5. The Swedes have been particularly active in encouraging the greatest Western European participation in the EUREKA programme.

6. J. Monnet, *Memoirs* (London: Collins, 1979).

7. R. E. M. Irving, *The Christian Democratic Parties of Western Europe* (London: George Allen and Unwin, 1979).

8. K. van der Pijl, *The Making of an Atlantic Ruling Class* (London: Verso, 1984).

9. W. Hallstein, *The European Community* (Düsseldorf: Econ Verlag, 1979).

10. R. Vernon, *Big Business and the State* (London: Macmillan, 1971).

11. G. Franko, *The European Multi-Nationals* (London: Harper, 1976).
12. Hallstein, op. cit.
13. J. Paxton, *A Dictionary of the European Community* (London: Macmillan, 1984).
14. 'The Infernal Food Machine', *Agenor* 85 (Brussels, 1981).
15. Hallstein, op. cit.
16. Paxton, op. cit.
17. C. Pentland, *International Theory and Economic Integration* (London: Faber and Faber, 1973); and P. Taylor, *The Limits of European Integration* (London: Croom Helm, 1983).
18. R. Morgan, in C. and K. J. Twitchett, eds., *Building Europe: Britain's Partners in the EEC* (London: Europa Publications, 1981).
19. C. de Gaulle, *Memoirs of Hope* (London: Weidenfeld and Nicolson, 1971).
20. C. Tugendhat, *Making Sense of Europe* (London: Viking, 1986).
21. *The Times*, 15 Sept. 1986.
22. *Sunday Times*, 26 Nov. 1978.
23. Tugendhat, op. cit.
24. Ibid.
25. Ibid.
26. The mystery writer was subsequently revealed to be Ralf Dahrendorf, at that time the junior West German Commissioner. He resigned shortly after to take up academic life in Britain.
27. D. Combes, *The Future of the European Parliament* (London: Policy Studies Institute, 1978).
28. Ann Robinson, ed., *The Image of the European Parliament* (London: Policy Studies Institute, 1986).
29. One government minister who attempted to persuade the Council of Ministers to agree to open their legislative sessions to the media during the late 1970s was the then British Energy Secretary, Mr Tony Benn. He received no support from other ministers in his own or other EEC governments.
30. Tugendhat, op. cit.
31. See, for example, an extensive analysis I did for the *Guardian*, 28 Mar. 1976.
32. *Sunday Times*, 26 Nov. 1978.
33. P. Camiller, 'Madrid's NATO Socialist', *New Left Review*, no. 156 (London, Mar./Apr. 1976).
34. See a very perceptive study by Dr Wolfgang Hager in Margaret Sharp, ed., *Europe and the New Technologies* (London: Francis Pinter, 1978).
35. 'The Current State of Western High Technology', paper presented

by Giles Merritt to a conference on High Technology, Western Security, and Economic Growth in Brussels, Feb. 1986.

36. Ibid.

37. John Robinson, *Business Strategy to 1990* (Brussels: European Research Associates, 1986).

38. *Financial Times*, 1 July 1978. 'EUREKA' deals with advanced technologies such as robotics, lasers, and information-based sciences. 'ESPRIT' also encourages informatic and computerized manufacturing systems. 'RACE' concentrates on telecommunications and 'FAST' on bio-technologies.

39. Discussed in E. P. Thompson, ed., *Star Wars*, an outstanding analysis of the SDI project (London: Penguin, 1985).

40. During 1985 and 1986 these interests blocked attempts to deregulate both internal European airfares and a move to liberalize the establishment of insurance companies in the EEC.

41. European Research Associates, cited in n. 38 above.

42. Tugendhat, op. cit., p. 205.

43. *Financial Times*, 28 Mar. 1985.

44. European Research Associates, cited in n. 38 above.

45. *Guardian*, 17 June 1985.

46. Independent Television's Channel Four inquiry into the state of NATO, 29 Sept. 1986.

Chapter 7: After Atlanticism—Agenda for a New Europe

1. An increasing number of public figures are now convinced that a major crisis between the EEC and the United States is inevitable. The EEC trade Commissioner, Willy de Clercq, spoke in November 1986, of a 'major political crisis looming across the Atlantic'. Earlier the distinguished US academic writer, W. W. Rostow, writing in the *New York Times* (26 Jan. 1982), had come to similar conclusions.

2. *Wall Street Journal*, 15 Dec. 1981, cited in J. Connell, *The New Maginot Line* (London: Secker and Warburg, 1986).

3. Senator Sam Nunn, a potential Democratic candidate in the US Presidential election due in 1988, ibid., p. 246.

4. *Financial Times*, 22 Dec. 1986.

5. OECD, annual report on the United States economy, Paris, Dec. 1986.

6. *Guardian*, 27 Dec. 1986.

7. Talks to resolve some of these problems between the EEC and Japan made what was described as 'little progress' in the closing weeks of 1986. On 15 December 1986 the *Financial Times* wrote: 'Relations between the European Community and Japan seem

destined to continue on an adversarial course despite the latest review at the highest level of mutual grievances.' Since then the EEC has threatened to introduce across the board import controls on Japanese imports in retaliation for what it has deemed inadequate progress by the Japanese authorities in opening up the Japanese markets to European exports.

8. The OECD annual economic report on Japan (Paris, Dec. 1986) forecast a continuing sluggish rate of growth and warned: 'The large gains in Japan's terms of trade resulting from the yen's strong appreciation and the halving of oil prices are not translating as they should into higher domestic spending.'

9. The Gramm–Rudman Bill requires the US administration progressively to eliminate the federal budget deficit over a period of years to 1992. It calls for a deficit of $108 billion in 1987, a target which most experts believe is most improbable. See the *Guardian*, 5 Jan. 1987.

10. At the start of 1987 the so-called 'Plaza Agreement' between the major Western industrialized nations to concert the exchange rates of their currencies had brought very little stability to the international foreign exchanges. A limited stability between the US dollar and the Japanese yen highlighted the volatility in movements between the dollar and EMS currencies. Further depreciation in the value of the dollar was predicted by most informed commentators even though this was likely to hasten the advent of higher international interest rates and a new international economic recession.

11. By the end of 1986 there were hopes that Britain would finally bring sterling into the fixed exchange-rate regime at the heart of the EMS.

12. The threatened agricultural trade war between the United States and the EEC was leading by the end of 1986 to deadlock in the wider GATT negotiations on world-trade liberalization.

13. Typical of this hostile American reaction to what are seen as 'predatory' European takeover bids was the abortive bid by the Anglo-French entrepreneur, Sir James Goldsmith, for the Goodyear tyre company of Akron, Ohio, in 1986. It was withdrawn after meeting stiff opposition from the trade unions and the local community who feared job losses as a result of the takeover.

14. The British Conservative government was incensed at the suggestion, implicit in the Reykjavik negotiations, that the United States might ban all strategic weapons including the Trident submarine which Britain wants to buy to replace its ageing Polaris force. The same issue re-emerged following discussions between the United

States and the Soviet Union on European· intermediate nuclear missiles in Moscow in April 1987.

15. Following a visit by a reportedly angry Mrs Thatcher to President Reagan after the Reykjavik summit, America agreed to amend its negotiating position in future talks with the Soviet Union. As a result America is only formally committed to a halving of strategic nuclear forces—thus assuring Britain of US-supplied Trident nuclear submarines. The US Secretary of State, Mr George Schultz, has also talked of the possibility of an agreement on intermediate nuclear weapons in Europe short of the 'zero/zero' option agreed in outline in Reykjavik, which left some US missiles in Europe.

16. In December 1986 the NATO Council discussed a Soviet proposal to transfer the narrower talks on conventional arms and forces reductions in Central Europe from the framework of the Vienna-based conference on Mutual and Balanced Force Reductions (MBFR) involving only NATO and the Warsaw Pact to the wider Conference on Security and Co-operation in Europe (CSCE) established at Helsinki in 1975.

17. Earl Ravenal, writing in the US *Foreign Affairs*, cited in Connell, op. cit.

18. *Independent*, 16 Jan. 1987.

19. Ibid. 30 Dec. 1986.

20. See the Labour Party statement of defence policy, *Modern Britain in a Modern World* (Dec. 1986).

21. *Guardian*, 24 Apr. 1986, and *Financial Times*, 5 Sept. 1986.

22. Independent Television's Channel 4 inquiry into the State of NATO, 24 Sept. 1986.

23. Ibid.

24. *Daily Telegraph*, 7 July 1986.

25. See 1986 annual report by the World Bank (Washington, Oct. 1986).

26. The most outspoken statements of the case for a Federal Europe, from a non-socialist standpoint, can be read in the publications of the Federal Trust in London and the 'Crocodile Group', set up at the principal initiative of the former Italian Commissioner and member of the Communist group in the European Parliament, the late Altiero Spinnelli, and consisting of members of the European Parliament who are committed to full federal union.

27. By the end of the 1980s a number of other groups of countries were renewing efforts to organize themselves as an economic bloc. The largely Middle East OPEC oil states strengthened their production and price cartel during December 1986, pushing the world oil price

back up to $18 a barrel. Talks were under way about strengthening the Latin American 'Andean Pact' common market while the countries of the Association of South East Asian Nations (ASEAN) were planning greater internal economic integration.

28. *Guardian*, 10 Dec. 1986.

29. After initial interest in the idea of Franco-British nuclear co-operation, it had an uncertain future at the start of 1987 in view of scepticism about its military and political practicability in both countries and in other Western European states, notably West Germany.

30. When the British government handed over responsibility for the Presidency of the EEC to Belgium in January 1987, it claimed to have done 'better than expected' in removing some of the Community's internal trade barriers. However, its period of EEC Presidency ended as the agriculture trade crisis escalated dramatically with a decision in Washington to impose surcharges on EEC imports worth some $400 million a year, in retaliation at the loss of US grain markets when Portugal and Spain joined the Community in 1985, unless America was offered acceptable compensation.

31. The EEC entered 1987 amidst a major new budget crisis. It had a threatened deficit of some $4 billion thanks to the escalating costs of CAP surpluses. However, a meeting of EEC farm ministers in Brussels in December 1986 took a number of tough measures to curb output of dairy and beef surpluses.

32. This was the sense of the speech made by President Mitterrand to the Royal Institute of International Affairs in London, cited in the *Independent*, 16 Jan. 1987.

33. The annual report of the OECD (Paris, Dec. 1986) predicted that unemployment in Western Europe would remain at around 31 million for the foreseeable future.

34. The EEC Commission prepared a report urging member states to restrict the proportion of airtime European television networks allow for 'non-Community'—i.e. mainly American—productions. The move aroused considerable opposition among broadcasting organizations.

35. K. Coates, ed., *Joint Action for Jobs* (Nottingham: New Socialist/ Spokesman, 1986).

36. See reports on the Kodak and Ford projects published by the GLC, London.

37. See *European Business Strategy to 1990* (Brussels: European Research Associates, 1986) and 'Hush Don't Tell the Workers' (*Agenor* 90, Brussels, May 1983).

38. S. Holland, ed., *Out of Crisis: A project for European Recovery* (Nottingham: Spokesman University Paperback, 1985).
39. T. Ward and F. Cripps, 'Why do we need a European solution?' in *Joint Action for Jobs* and *Steps Towards European Political Integration* (Cambridge: Department of Applied Economics, 1985).
40. See 'Empowering the Powerless', policy statement by the Socialist Society (9 Poland Street, London WC1).
41. 'The London Industrial Strategy' (London: GLC Economic Policy Group, 1985).
42. Study by Dr Michael Cooley for the International Metal Workers Federation, Geneva, Switzerland.
43. Examples of this approach are the London Technology Networks, funded by the GLC and its job-creation agency, the Greater London Enterprise Board. A major human-centred computerized manufacturing system, involving software giving a greater role to skilled workers in the operation of new technology-based machine tools and other systems, is being developed by the Networks in collaboration with trade unions and academic and industrial bodies in Denmark and West Germany and is being largely funded under the EEC ESPRIT programme.
44. See END Manifesto outlining a new strategy for peace and freedom in Europe agreed by a range of Western European peace groups and Eastern European 'dissidents' in 1983.
45. *New Statesman*, 15 Dec. 1985.
46. P. Tatchell, *Democratic Defence a non Nuclear Alternative* (London: GMP Publications, 1986).
47. E. Mandel, *Europe versus America* (London: New Left Books, 1968).

Index

Acheson, Dean, 34–5, 82
Adenauer, Konrad, 83–4, 136
Afghanistan, 14, 58, 67
Albania, 116, 119
America, see Latin America; USA
American Federation of Labor, 36
Amery, Leo, 87
Anti-Ballistic Missile Agreement (1972), 47, 53, 55, 125, 162
ANZUS Pact, 58, 170
Arab–Israeli conflict, 22, 47
arms control, 2, 17–18, 23–6, 28, 53–4, 124, 127–9, 153, 162–3
Association of South-East Asian Nations, 18
Atlantic Alliance, see Atlanticism; NATO
Atlantic reformism, 164–5
Atlanticism: collapse and aftermath of, 20–9; demise of, 1–20, 156–92; Japan and, 18–19; Soviet Union and, see Soviet Union; USA and, see USA
Attlee, Clement, 34, 90, 94
Austria, 134

Baker, James, 77
Balkanization, 2, 13, 155
Belgium, 25, 36, 38, 49
Benn, Tony, 101
Berlin Crisis, 37–9, 90, 113
Berlin Wall, 44
Bevan, Aneurin, 92–3, 99
Bevin, Ernest, 36, 84–5, 87
Biedenkopf, Kurt, 174
Brandt, Willy, 66
Brazil, 66
Bretton Woods Agreement (1944), 11, 31, 62, 135, 142
Britain, see UK
Brosio, Manlio, 42
Brown, Harold, 50

Brzezinski, Zbigniew, 47, 57, 67, 159, 166
budget deficit (US), 9–10, 57, 61, 71–3, 171; Gramm–Rudman Bill, 160
Bulgaria, 109, 119

Canada, 15, 27, 31, 51
CAP, see Common Agricultural Policy
Caribbean, 31
Carter, Jimmy, 10, 22, 40, 48–9, 51, 66–9, 70, 76; and President Reagan, 67–8
CBI, 138
Ceauşescu, President (Romania), 16, 116, 124
CENTO, 44, 47
Central Intelligence Agency (CIA), see CIA
Chapultepec Act (1945), 32
Charter 77, 40, 119, 122
Chiang Kai-shek, 37, 108
Chile, 52
China, 19, 36–7, 47, 64, 108
Christian Democrats, 5, 26, 69, 83–4, 105, 130, 136–7, 173
Churchill, Winston, 32–4, 39, 87, 90, 93, 112
CIA, 35–6
CND (Campaign for Nuclear Disarmament), 48
COCOM, 14, 42–3, 50, 78
Cold War, 1–2, 4, 16, 18, 28, 35, 37, 39, 40–2, 49, 67, 83, 89–93, 100, 103, 111–12, 114, 117, 124, 126–7, 133, 141, 157, 159, 186; phases in, 40–2; see also détente
COMECON, 15–16, 20, 40, 79, 114–16, 127, 133
Committee of Permanent Representatives, see COREPER

Common Agricultural Policy (CAP), 69–70, 76, 101, 103–4, 139–40, 144, 146–8, 155
Common Market, *see* EEC
Commonwealth, 83, 85, 87–9, 91, 94, 97–8; 100–2, 147
Communism: China, 108; emergence in Europe, post-war, 107–19; 'Euro', 38; French, 188-9; Greek, 109; Italian, *see* PCI; US attitude, post-war, 34–8; *see also* Soviet Union
'containment' doctrine, 33–4
COREPER, 146
Council for Mutual Economic Co-operation, *see* COMECON
Council of Europe, 83, 87, 89, 91, 97, 183
Council of Ministers, post-Atlantic, 176–7
Crossman, Richard, 92, 101
Cuba, 15, 44
Czechoslovakia, 17, 37, 40, 44, 92, 110, 113, 115, 119, 121–2

Dalton, Hugh, 86, 88, 91, 99
debt crisis, 15
de Gaulle, President (France), 5, 16, 43, 62, 82–3, 93, 96–7, 101–2, 124, 140–1; 'European Gaullism', 164, 173, 179–81
Delores, Jacques, 176
Democratic Party (USA), 13, 29, 51, 75, 158–60, 166
Denmark, 23, 26, 27, 39, 55, 134, 142, 145, 154, 167, 181, 188
détente, 12, 40, 43, 47–9, 53, 63–4, 67, 115, 124, 127, 141, 159; *see also* Cold War
dollar (US), 60–3, 73, 77, 143, 160
Du Cann, Edward, 100–1
Dubcek, President (Czechoslovakia), 119
Dulles, John Foster, 41, 89

East Germany, 16, 17, 78–9, 110, 114, 117–21, 124, 130–1; and German unification, 187

Eastern bloc, and Soviet Union, 15–18, 35, 37, 39–40, 46, 48, 58, 63, 66–7, 78–9, 90, 92, 108–16, 118, 120–6, 130–1, 134, 187
ecology movements, 2, 106, 119, 121, 136, 186, 188
Economic Recovery Programme, 35, 37
ECSC, 84–6, 89, 97, 137–8
ECU, 148
Eden, Sir Anthony, 87, 93–4, 112
EEC, 8–9, 11, 13–16, 20–2, 29, 60–1, 66, 68, 70–1, 73, 75–9, 82–3, 85–6, 91, 94, 96–106, 115, 131, 133–52, 158, 161, 174–5, 177–8, 180, 189–90; Luxembourg Compromise, 140
EFTA, 15, 20, 22, 97, 101, 133–5
Egypt, 47, 68, 78
Eisenhower, President (USA), 6, 89
El Salvador, 69
EMS, 11, 15, 21, 104, 134, 148, 161, 179, 184
END, 121, 123
Erhardt, Ludwig, 63
ESPRIT, 21, 150
EUREKA, 21–2, 135, 150–1
Europe, Western: and American 'imperialism', 30–58; defence policies, 1–18; disunion, 132–55; economic policies, 8; Eastern Europe and, 18; emergence of Communism, post-war, 107–19; European Federation, 85–7; Socialist United States of, 181–3; UK attitude, 82–106; USA and, 1–18
European Coal and Steel Community (ECSC), *see* ECSC
European Court of Human Rights, 183
European Currency Unit, *see* ECU
European Defence Community, 84, 94, 137
European Economic Community, *see* EEC
European Free Trade Association, *see* EFTA
European Gaullism, 164, 173, 179–81
European unification, 17–18, 21, 123, 127–8, 136, 138, 140, 190
European Monetary System, *see* EMS

European Nuclear Disarmament, *see* END
European Parliament, 144–5

FAST, 150
FBI, 101
Federation of British Industries, *see* FBI
feminism, 2, 106, 136, 185, 188
Finland, 107, 133–4
First Cold War, *see* Cold War
Ford, Gerald, 10, 48
France, 5, 11, 16, 21, 23, 25–8, 33, 36, 38, 42–5, 50–1, 69, 74, 82–3, 85–6, 96, 102, 105, 111–12, 124, 130, 132, 137–40, 143, 146, 149–51, 153, 163, 165, 173–4, 179, 180–4, 188; Communists, 111–12; Indo-China and, 36; nuclear missiles, 25–6
free trade, 32, 35, 75, 77, 135–6, 172, 178
FRG, *see* West Germany
Friedman, Milton, 71

Gaitskell, Hugh, 99–100
Gaspari, Alcide de, 86, 136
GDR, *see* East Germany
General Agreement on Tariffs and Trade (GATT), 11–12, 75, 77, 152, 160–1, 172
Genscher, Hans-Dietrich, 130
Germany, *see* East Germany; West Germany
Giscard d'Estaing, Valéry, 11
'Glasnost', 17
gold–dollar link, 60–3
Gorbachev, Mikhail, 17, 24, 54, 115, 124–5, 128, 162
Gramm–Rudman Bill, 160
Great Britain, *see* UK
'Great Society' programme (USA), 9
Greece, 5, 21, 23, 27, 33, 50, 55, 74, 105, 109, 148–9, 151, 154, 175–6, 181, 188; Civil War, 33
Green movements, 2, 17, 27, 36, 55, 131, 154, 182, 184, 186–8
Group of Soviet Forces in Germany (GSFG), 46
Gunder Frank, André, 59
Gyllenhammar, Pehr, 150

Halliday, Fred, 40, 49
Hallstein, Walter, 138–41
Healey, Denis, 88–9
Heath, Edward, 100, 102–3
Hegedus, Andras, 122
Helsinki Conference, 134
Helsinki Human Rights Declaration (1975), 134–5
Heseltine, Michael, 8
Holland, 25–7, 36, 38, 55; and Indonesia, 36
Honnecker, Erich, 124
Howe, Sir Geoffrey, 53
Hull, Cordell, 31
human-rights groups, 119, 122–3, 125, 183
Hungary, 7, 16–17, 40, 44, 110, 114, 115–17, 118–19, 121–4, 127

Iceland, 113
IMF, 12, 32, 172–3
imperialism: American, 30–58; British, 30, 43, 91, 96
internationalism, monetary, 10
India, 19, 36
Indo-China, 36, 43, 47, 51, 112
Indonesia, 36
inflation, 10, 15, 61, 63, 65
International Monetary Fund, *see* IMF
Iran, 33, 42, 49, 51, 56, 67, 75, 164
'Irangate', 128
Iran–Iraq Gulf War, 164
Iraq, 47
Ireland, 39, 133, 142, 154
Israel, 6, 22, 49–50, 65, 68, 164
Italy, 7, 20, 25, 27, 33, 36, 39, 51, 82–3, 111–12, 136, 138–9, 151, 181, 188; Communism in, *see* PCI

Japan, 3, 6, 8, 11, 13–14, 18–19, 21, 22, 51, 61, 63, 66–78, 80, 98, 108, 141, 149–50, 152, 155, 159–60, 171, 178; and China, 19
Jaruzelski, Wojciech, 120
Jay, Douglas, 101
Jenkins, Roy, 99–100
Johnson, Lyndon, 9, 61

Kadar, Janos, 124
Kaldor, Nicholas, 99

Keep Left group, 91–2
Kennan, George, 33
Kennedy, John F., 7, 61, 96
Keynesianism, 66–7, 74, 178
Khomeini, Ayatollah, 67, 164
Kinnock, Neil, 56, 169, 198
Kissinger, Henry, 12, 25, 52, 59–60, 64, 65, 68, 169
Kohl, Helmut, 105
KOR (Committee for the Defence of Workers), 119
Korean War, 12, 37, 41, 43–4, 72, 84, 91, 93–4
Kuron, Jacek, 119–21

Labour Party (UK), 8, 21, 27, 34, 55–6, 58, 84, 86–8, 91, 97–9, 101, 104–6, 154–5, 168, 181, 188; *see also* Socialism, and United States of Europe
Latin America, 3, 15, 22, 31; and Chapultepec Act (1945), 32
Lend-Lease, 6, 11, 32
Leninism, 108
Liberals, 5, 26, 31–2, 188
Libya, 4, 7, 14, 169
Luxembourg, 38
'Luxembourg Compromise', 140

McCarthy, Joseph, 37, 40
MacLeod, Ian, 95
Macmillan, Harold, 91, 95–6, 98, 101, 147
Malaya, 36
Marcos, President, 69
Marshall Aid, 11, 33–5, 37, 85, 112; and Soviet Union, 35, 79; West Germany, 37
Mexico, 66
Middle East, 3, 4, 14, 19, 22, 49–50, 66–8, 78, 105
Middle East Wars: 1967, 65; 1973, 10, 65
Mikardo, Ian, 93
Mitterrand, François, 175
Molotov, Vyacheslav, 109
monetarism, 8–12, 23, 71–4, 135, 149, 178
Mongolia, 15
Monnet, Jean, 3–6, 136
Morgan, Roger, 79

Mulley, Fred, 50
multinationals, 9, 11, 21–2, 48, 62, 78, 137–8, 150

Nagy, Imre, 118
NATO, 1, 4, 7–8, 12, 14, 16, 23–9, 38–9, 41–2, 44–51, 53–7, 60, 64, 67, 69, 70, 78, 80, 90, 91, 93–4, 97, 103, 120, 123–5, 127–9, 131, 133–4, 151–8, 162–71, 173–4, 186–7; costs of, 57, 166–7; 'European', 170; 'flexible response', 50; founding of, 38; intermediate nuclear forces (INF), 51; Rapid Deployment Force (RDF), 49, 166; 'Twin Track' decision (1979), 25
neutron bomb, 50–1
New Left, *see* Socialism, and United States of Europe
New Zealand, 57–8, 170
Newly Industrialized Countries, *see* NICs
Nicaragua, 7, 56, 69, 121
NICs, 13
NIMROD, 165
Nixon, Richard, 10, 32, 40, 47–8, 60, 63–5, 70, 143; economic policy, 60
Nordic Council, 134
North Atlantic Treaty Organization, *see* NATO
Norway, 27, 39, 133
nuclear-free zones, 27, 120, 129, 171, 187
nuclear missiles, 2, 4, 8, 12, 18–19, 23–9, 39, 42, 44–5, 50–6, 90–1, 162–3; balance of power, 45–6; costs (for UK), 168; cruise, 50–1; 'European theatre', 50; Soviet Union, 115
Nunn, Sam, 158, 166

OECD, 12, 159, 172
OEEC, 85
oil prices, 19, 65, 75, 143; *see also* OPEC
OPEC, 10, 19, 49, 65, 78
opinion polls, 4, 7
Organization for Economic Co-operation and Development, *see* OECD

Organization of Petroleum Exporting Countries, *see* OPEC
Ostpolitik, 16, 17, 47–8, 123, 130, 141

'Pacific Rim' countries, 13, 18, 71, 156–7, 160, 177
Palestinians, 7, 22, 49–50, 65, 68
Palme, Olaf, 66
Papandreou, Andreas, 149, 175
Paris Agreements, 44
Partito Comunista Italiano (Italian Communist Party), *see* PCI
'Pax Americana', 30
PCI, 7, 27, 38, 136, 188–9
'Peace and Freedom', 121
peace movements, 7, 28, 48, 53, 106, 119, 121–4, 136, 185, 186–8; *see also* CND
Perle, Richard, 5, 41, 169, 198
Permanent Arms Economy, 72
Philippines, 69
PLO, *see* Palestinians
Plowden, Lord, 84
Poland, 7, 14, 16–17, 31, 33, 110, 112, 114, 117–22; martial law in, 14; *see also* Solidarity
Portugal, 21, 39, 70, 134, 158, 161, 184
Post Hostilities Planning Staff, 31
Powell, Enoch, 6
Prague Musicians' Union, 122
'Prague Spring', the, 7, 44, 115, 119
protectionism, 13, 29

Qadaffi, President (Libya), 4, 14

RACE, 150
Rakosi, Matyas, 118
Rapallo Pact (1922), 130
Reagan, Ronald, 4–5, 9–10, 13, 22, 24, 40, 51, 59, 66, 128, 157, 159–60; military spending, 52; and President Carter, 67–8; Soviet Union, 'Evil Empire', 41–2, 52
Reaganism, 9–10, 22, 24, 40–1, 49–52, 54, 56, 59, 66, 67–75, 128, 157–60, 164, 166
Realpolitik, 107
referendum (UK), 102
reformism: Atlantic, 164–72; European, 172–3, 178

Republican Party (USA), 29, 157–8
Reykjavik Summit (1986), 24–8, 53–4, 122, 125, 128, 154, 162, 167
Rogers, General, 4, 45
Romania, 16, 109–10, 116, 118–19, 124
Roosevelt, Franklin D., 32, 71, 112, 137
Royal Services Institute for Defence Studies, 46

SALT, 47, 49, 53, 55, 63–4, 66–7
sanctions, 14, 63
Schmidt, Helmut, 10–11, 50
Schuman, Robert, 83–4, 89, 136
SDI ('Star Wars'), *see* Strategic Defense Initiative
SDP (UK), 188
SEATO, 44, 47
Second Cold War, *see* Cold War
Second World War, *see* World War II
semi-conductors, 75–6, 149
Servan-Schreiber, Jean-Jacques, 62
Seven Days' War, *see* Middle East Wars (1967)
Shultz, George, 54
Single European Act (1985), 21, 145, 175
'Snake', 142–3
Social Democrats, 2, 5, 7–8, 17, 27, 137–8, 173, 182, 188
Socialism, and United States of Europe, 181–92
'Socialist United States of Europe', 181–3
Solidarity (Poland), 7, 40, 119, 122
Solidarnosc, *see* Solidarity (Poland)
South Africa, 154
South America, *see* Latin America
South Korea, 18, 159
Soviet Union, 1–3, 5, 7, 11, 13–14, 15–18, 31, 63–4, 107–31, 162–3, 166, 168, 170, 174, 187, 192; and American withdrawal from Europe, 58; buffer states and, 37; and Cold War, *see* Cold War; as 'Evil Empire', 41–2, 52; and Marshall Aid, 35, 79; and nuclear missiles, 115; and 'Oscillatory Antagonism', 40; Siberian gas pipeline, 14; and US relations, immediately

Soviet Union (*cont.*)
  post-war, 33–5; *see also* Communism; Stalinism
Spain, 5, 20–1, 23, 27, 45, 55, 70, 105, 134, 149, 158, 161, 184, 188
SPD (West Germany), 8, 27, 55, 123, 130, 168–9, 186, 188
'special relationship' (UK/USA), 82, 96
'stagflation', 10, 15, 180
Stalinism, 7, 32–3, 38, 41, 88, 90, 92, 107–10, 111–13, 114–15; economic policy, 114
Stans, Maurice, 103
'Star Wars', *see* Strategic Defense Initiative (SDI)
steel, 75
Steel, Ronald, 70
Stockholm Peace Research Institute, 45
Strategic Arms Limitation Treaty, *see* SALT
Strategic Defense Initiative (SDI), 3, 5, 7, 18, 24, 28, 52–4, 63, 72, 125–6, 128–9, 151–6, 162–3, 169
Suez Crisis, 6, 44, 89–91, 94–5
Sweden, 39, 133
Switzerland, 133–4
Syria, 14, 154

technology, European and US, 8–9, 11, 15, 21, 62, 72, 135, 149, 152
terrorism, 14
textiles, 75
Thatcher, Margaret, 8, 69, 104
Third World, 10, 19, 22, 37, 46, 64, 66, 69, 73–4, 76, 78, 172; debt, 73–4
Tindemans, Leo, 143
Tito, President (Yugoslavia), 37, 40, 113–14
trade, international, 10, 13–15, 74–80
trade unions, 2, 21, 36, 106, 161, 182, 186; *see also* Socialism, and United States of Europe
trade war, 14–15, 29, 63, 71, 73, 75, 76–8, 81, 148
Trilateral Commission, 66
Truman Doctrine, 34
Truman, Harry S., 34–5, 39, 83, 90, 94, 112

Turkey, 33, 52
'Twin Track' decision, 25, 68

UK: attitude to Europe, 82–106; economy, 8; imperialism, 30, 43; industrial decline, 98; nuclear missiles, 25–6; and US relations, 4, 82, 96
unemployment, 2, 10, 15, 51, 74, 160
United Nations, 11–12, 32, 39, 91
USA, 114, 115: anti-Americanism, 6; anti-colonialism, 36–7; budget deficit, *see* budget deficit (US); defence budget, 52, 57; economy, 3, 8, 9–10, 13, 57, 59–81; EEC summits, 148; 'egocentrist' attitude, 10; European defence and, 1–29; European relations, post-war, 1–29; 'imperialism', 30–58; left-wing Europeans and, 7, 20–1, 27, 181–92; right-wing Europeans and, 5–7, 20–1; Soviet Union and, *see* Soviet Union; Soviet Union, immediately post-war, 33–5; 'special relationship' (with UK), 82, 96; trade, 13–15; troops in Europe, 57; Vietnam War, 7, 44, 47–8, 61–3; Watergate scandal, 48; and Western European Union, 23; and Westland affair, 8; withdrawal from Europe, 58
USSR, *see* Soviet Union

Vandenberg, Senator, 32
van der Pijl, Kees, 6, 31
Venice Declaration (1980), 68
Vietnam War, 44, 47–8, 61–3
'Vredeling', 183

Walker, Peter, 94
Warsaw Pact, 15–16, 28, 44–6, 54–5, 120, 123–4, 128, 163, 179, 187
Watkins, James, 53
Weimar Republic, 30
Weinberger, Caspar, 169
Werner, Pierre, 142
West Germany, 8, 10, 17–18, 20–1, 25, 26–7, 29, 38–9, 45, 47–8, 51, 55, 63, 69, 73, 78–9, 82–4, 87, 94–6, 102, 105, 112–13, 117, 120, 129–32, 139–44, 146–8, 151, 154–5, 159,